The **Princeton** Review®

Cracking the

WITHDRAWN

CBEST®

3rd Edition

Rick Sliter
and the Staff of The Princeton Review

PrincetonReview.com

| Penguin
Random
House |

The Princeton Review
555 W. 18th Street
New York, NY 10011
E-mail: editorialsupport@review.com

Published in the United States by Penguin Random House LLC, New York, and in Canada by Random House of Canada, a division of Penguin Random House Ltd., Toronto.

ISBN: 978-1-101-88193-4
eBook ISBN: 978-1-101-88238-2
ISSN: 2378-587X

Editor: Selena Coppock
Production Editor: Emily Epstein White
Production Artist: Deborah A. Silvestrini

Printed in the United States of America on partially recycled paper.

10 9 8 7 6 5

3rd Edition

Editorial

Rob Franek, Senior VP, Publisher
Casey Cornelius, VP Content Development
Mary Beth Garrick, Director of Production
Selena Coppock, Managing Editor
Meave Shelton, Senior Editor
Colleen Day, Editor
Sarah Litt, Editor
Aaron Riccio, Editor
Orion McBean, Editorial Assistant

Random House Publishing Team

Tom Russell, Publisher
Alison Stoltzfus, Publishing Manager
Melinda Ackell, Associate Managing Editor
Ellen Reed, Production Manager
Kristin Lindner, Production Supervisor
Andrea Lau, Designer

Dedication

This book is dedicated to all the teachers in my family—Fred, Judy, and Julie, and to Kathleen, from whom I learn and share with every day.

Acknowledgments

The Staff of The Princeton Review would like to add a special thank you to Heidi Holton and Sionainn Marcoux for their fantastic work on the 3rd edition of this book.

Contents

Register Your

1   Go to **PrincetonReview.com/cracking**

2   You'll see a welcome page where you can register your book using the following ISBN: 9781101881934.

3   After placing this free order, you'll either be asked to log in or to answer a few simple questions in order to set up a new Princeton Review account.

4   Finally, click on the "Student Tools" tab located at the top of the screen. It may take an hour or two for your registration to go through, but after that, you're good to go.

Note: If you are experiencing book problems (potential content errors), please contact EditorialSupport@review.com with the full title of the book, its ISBN number (located above), and the page number of the error.

Experiencing technical issues? Please e-mail TPRStudentTech@review.com with the following information:

- your full name
- e-mail address used to register the book
- full book title and ISBN
- your computer OS (Mac or PC) and Internet browser (Firefox, Safari, Chrome, etc.)
- description of technical issue

Book Online!

Once you've registered, you can...

- Get more practice with a full-length practice CBEST

- Access detailed answers and explanations to help you identify areas of strength and weakness and tailor your test preparation accordingly

- Check to see if there have been any corrections or updates to this edition

Look For These Icons Throughout The Book

 Proven Techniques

 Applied Strategies

 Study Break

 More Great Books

The Princeton Review®
Your Goals. Our Expertise.™

Part I
Orientation

Chapter 1
Introduction

WHAT IS THE CBEST?

The California Basic Educational Skills Test, or CBEST, is a four-hour exam divided into three different sections—a multiple-choice Reading Section, a multiple-choice Mathematics Section, and a Writing Section, which contains two essays. Currently, the CBEST is offered in two formats: the computer-based test and the paper-based test. The specific breakdown of the test is as follows:

Reading Section

According to the authors of the CBEST, the Reading Section "assesses basic skills and concepts that are important in performing the job of an educator." While this may sound intimidating, the reading questions are presented in a straightforward, multiple-choice format. The Reading Section is presented first, and contains 50 multiple-choice questions. The questions are broken down into two main categories:

From the Horse's Mouth
Check the California Education Credentialing Examinations homepage for more information and updates about the CBEST:
www.ctcexams.nesinc.com

1. Critical Analysis and Evaluation   40%
2. Comprehension and Research Skills   60%

All reading questions will be based on information presented in written passages, tables, and graphs. Passages range from 100 to 200 words in length. Often, more than one multiple-choice question will be based on the same passage.

No outside knowledge will be required to answer these multiple-choice questions. All correct answers can be found by interpreting the information presented in the passage, table, or graph.

Mathematics Section

The Mathematics Section contains 50 multiple-choice questions. These questions cover three major skill areas:

1. Estimation, Measurement, and Statistical Principles   30%
2. Computation and Problem Solving   35%
3. Numerical and Graphic Relationships   35%

What level of math is covered? To survive the CBEST Mathematics Section, you'll need to brush up on the basics—arithmetic, measurements, introductory algebra, and introductory geometry. Note that there is, sadly, no calculator permitted on the exam. Don't worry, there will be no calculus, advanced statistics, or trigonometry on the CBEST.

Writing Section

This section will include two writing topics that assess your ability to write effectively. You will be asked to write one essay from each of the following areas:

1. Analysis of a Situation or Statement
2. A Personal Experience

Readers who use a specific set of criteria to evaluate each essay will score your essays. (We'll explain this in more detail in Part IV.)

WHERE DOES THE CBEST COME FROM?

The CBEST is written by National Evaluation Systems, Inc. Unlike other companies that write a multitude of standardized exams, NES focuses primarily on this one exam. The CBEST was created, in the words of the authors, "to meet requirements of laws relating to credentialing and employment."

WHO NEEDS TO TAKE THE CBEST?

The CBEST is only used in California and Oregon. In California, you must take the CBEST if you are applying for a first teaching credential, if you are applying for an emergency permit, or if you have not taught in a public school for approximately four years prior to employment. In Oregon, you must take the CBEST for licensure as a teacher, personnel specialist, or administrator.

There are ways in which teachers in both states may be exempt from taking the CBEST. If you are uncertain as to whether you need the CBEST, read the CBEST registration bulletin, or contact either the California Commission on Teacher Credentialing or the Oregon Teacher Standards and Practices Commission.

WHEN IS THE CBEST ADMINISTERED?

The computer-based CBEST is offered year-round, by appointment at Pearson testing centers. Appointments are available Monday through Saturday, on a first-come, first-served basis. You should register for your exam well in advance, as seating is limited.

The paper-based CBEST is offered six times during the year. Currently, you can take the paper-based CBEST in the following months: September, November, January, March, May, and July. To register for the CBEST, visit the CBEST website at **www.ctcexams.nesinc.com**. Note that if you are taking the paper-based CBEST, the registration deadline will be approximately 1 month before the exam.

SHOULD I TAKE THE COMPUTER-BASED CBEST?

The decision to take the computer-based or paper-best CBEST is up to you. The structure and content of the exam will not vary between the two formats. You should choose the test format that is more comfortable or convenient for you.

The computer-based CBEST has an added fee. One benefit of the computer-based CBEST is that you will know your preliminary results (except the Writing section) immediately after finishing the exam. Official score reports are mailed in approximately two weeks.

If you take the paper-based CBEST, official score reports are mailed in approximately 3 weeks.

WHERE CAN I LOOK AT A CBEST EXAM?

We've included two full-length practice CBEST exams in the back of this book, complete with explanations and sample essays for each test. These tests have been designed to look exactly like the real thing, so you won't see anything you don't recognize on the day of the actual exam. In addition to our practice tests, the CTC website (**www.ctcexams.nesinc.com**) has a full-length practice CBEST, available in computer-based test format or printable PDF.

HOW IS THE CBEST SCORED?

The scoring of the CBEST is somewhat complicated. We'll take the scoring of each section one at a time.

Reading Section

The Reading Section contains 50 multiple-choice questions. You will receive one raw score point for each correct answer. You will not lose any points for incorrect answers. This raw score of 0 to 50 is then converted into a scaled score, ranging from 20 to 80. To pass the Reading Section, you need a minimum scaled score of 41.

Mathematics Section

The Mathematics Section is scored in exactly the same way as the Reading Section. The Mathematics Section contains 50 multiple-choice questions. You will receive one raw score point for each correct answer. You will not lose any points for incorrect answers. This raw score of 0 to 50 is then converted into a scaled score, ranging from 20 to 80. To pass the Mathematics Section, you need a minimum scaled score of 41.

Writing Section

Two readers will evaluate each essay. These readers will assign each essay a value from 1 to 4 according to a specific set of criteria. Thus, a total of four readers will assign a score, yielding a Writing Section total that will range from a low of 4 to a high of 16. Again, this raw score will then be translated into a scaled score from 20 to 80. To pass the Writing Section, you need a minimum scaled score of 41.

ONE MORE WAY TO PASS!

If you have an overall total of 123 or higher, it is possible to pass the CBEST with a scaled score on one or two sections as low as 37. If you do not receive at least a 37, you will not pass that section, regardless of your combined CBEST score.

IS THERE ANY REASON TO TAKE THE CBEST AGAIN AFTER PASSING?

Not really. Whether you have a 123 or a 170, you pass. Credential programs will not use your overall score to determine entrance into any program (in fact, all that NES reports is that you have passed all three sections).

There is only one situation in which you may want to retake a section you have already passed. Let's say, for example, that you passed the Writing Section with a 42, the Reading Section with a 42, but did not pass the math section (you got a 38). Your overall total is 122, one point shy of the 123 total needed to pass all sections. You could take the Math Section again, and hope to improve that total. Or, you could take the Reading or Writing Sections again. If you improve those scores, your overall total will pass 123, and you will pass all sections of the CBEST, even with a math score of 38.

This situation is pretty rare. In general, once you pass the CBEST, you're done. Congratulations.

WHAT HAPPENS IF YOU DON'T PASS EVERY SECTION?

If you scored below 37 on one section, or between 38 and 40 on a section with an overall total under 123, you will need to retake only the sections you didn't pass the first time. When you retake the CBEST, you will be given all four hours to complete the sections you need to redo (even if you only need to take one section).

Applied Strategies
Look for these through-
out the book

HOW THIS BOOK IS ORGANIZED

In the chapters that follow, you will get a step-by-step review of the fundamentals that are crucial to the CBEST. We will break down each of the three sections, and provide both content review and strategies for the types of questions contained in each section. Finally, you'll have an opportunity to practice for the CBEST with the two full-length tests we've included at the end of this book.

Because test-taking techniques and strategies that apply to all sections of the CBEST are so important, we've started the book with them. Chapter 2 contains the basic strategies for the CBEST. Be sure to apply these techniques to all parts of the exam.

YOUR STUDY PLAN

This book is intended to give you a fairly accelerated review for the CBEST. It's best to complete about one sub-section per day in order to adequately learn and absorb the material. Don't rush so much that you can't adequately take it all in, but likewise, don't go so long between sections that you forget everything you've learned!

Here is a suggested study schedule, which you can modify to fit your needs:

Week 1	Read and work through Part I: Orientation chapters
Week 2	Take Practice Test 1 in the book to see where your strongest and weakest sections. Carefully read through the answers and explanations.
Week 3	Read and work through Part II: Cracking the Reading Section chapters and complete the Reading Section Drills. Carefully read through the Reading Drill Answers and Explanations.
Week 4	Take Practice Test 2 in the book. Carefully read through the answers and explanations.
Week 5	Read and work through Part III: Cracking the Mathematics Section chapters and work all practice problems.
Week 6	Read and work through Part IV: Cracking the Writing Section.
Week 7	Take Practice Test 3 online. Carefully read through the answers and explanations (also found online).
Week 8	Take the real CBEST

For additional practice, visit **www.ctcexams.nesinc.com** to take the official practice CBEST.

WHAT'S MISSING IN THIS BOOK

In this book, we will not review the following: vocabulary words, calculus, trigonometry, idiomatic phrases, antonyms, world history, derivatives, analogies, and linear programming. Why? Because none of these topics are covered on the CBEST.

It might sound obvious, but we are only going to prepare you for what you'll likely see on the CBEST exam. We're not going to waste your time by including a large, detailed generic review of math and English. Instead, we're going to help you focus specifically on what you need to know to pass the CBEST.

WHAT IS THE PRINCETON REVIEW?

The Princeton Review offers the nation's best in test preparation. We have offices in more than fifty cities across the country, and many outside the U.S. as well. The Princeton Review offers classroom and online courses, private and small group tutoring, and test preparation books, flashcards, and materials for myriad test types.

The Princeton Review's strategies and techniques are unique, and most of all, successful. We've written this book after carefully studying the CBEST, analyzing the patterns of the exam, and testing our techniques to make sure we're providing you with the most effective and efficient way to take this test.

More Great Books
The Princeton Review publishes an assortment of test preparation and educational books, including
WordSmart
WordSmart 2
MathSmart

And Finally . . .

We applaud your efforts to become a teacher. The CBEST should be a minor hurdle in your desire to teach. For most CBEST takers, it has been years since you have had to take a standardized exam. Don't get frustrated if you don't remember everything at once. It takes some time for these skills to come back. Stay focused, practice, and before you know it, you'll be giving tests, instead of taking them.

Chapter 2
Test-Taking Strategies

Before we get started, we need to set some ground rules for taking the CBEST. It is crucial that you use these strategies and techniques throughout the test. We'll refer back to these throughout the book to make sure you are incorporating them into your practice. First, we will discuss how to take the test and how much time to spend on each question. Then, we will focus on the multiple-choice questions and how to take advantage of their structure.

TIME—YOU'RE IN CONTROL

In Chapter 1, we broke out the format and structure of the CBEST. You may have noticed that we left out the timing of each section. Good news! You have four hours to complete your work on the CBEST, and you may do so in any way you please. There are no time restrictions on any one section of the exam, so you will decide exactly how to map out your strategy for taking this test.

How should you use these four hours? Well, since all test-takers have different strengths and weaknesses, there is no ideal strategy for all students. We recommend that you take Practice Test 1 with the following strategy:

> 1 hour, 10 minutes for the Reading Section
> 1 hour, 20 minutes for the Mathematics Section
> 1 hour, 20 minutes for the Writing Section

You will determine how much time to spend on each section (there are no section time requirements on the CBEST).

This strategy will give you a ten-minute cushion at the end of the test in case you get behind, want to check your work, or just want to take a few minutes relaxing between each section.

Of course, you may want to adjust our recommended timing to better fit your strengths and weaknesses. If you find that this timing is not ideal after taking Practice Test 1, add ten minutes to the section that gave you the most trouble (and subtract ten minutes from the section you finished with the most time remaining). Continue to adjust your timing after Practice Test 2, so on the actual test day you will have a timing strategy that works for you.

If you are retaking the CBEST, you will still be given the entire four hours to work on the exam, even if you only need to complete one section. If you would like, spend as much time as necessary working on that one section. You *can* spend all four hours on the exam.

WHERE TO START?

You are in control of how much time you spend on each section, and you are also in control of the order in which you complete the sections. While you may complete the sections in any order you choose, we recommend that you start with the section you find the most difficult, and finish with the simplest. Leaving your least favorite section until the end of the test day will leave you tired, unfocused, and generally cranky at the end of the exam.

AN EMPTY SCANTRON SHEET IS NOT A GOOD SCANTRON SHEET

There is no guessing penalty on the CBEST! Your score is only determined by the number of questions that you answer correctly. You will not lose points for incorrect answers. Therefore, when you take the CBEST, there is one thing that you must do before you turn in your test:

> **You must answer every single question on the CBEST!**

There are 50 questions in the mathematics section, and 50 questions in the Reading Section. Before you turn in your test, make sure that you have selected an answer for all 100 questions on the CBEST.

So, now you know that you must select an answer on every question. Great. Now, let's talk about how to be an intelligent guesser.

PROCESS OF ELIMINATION (POE)

Try the following question:

> What is the capital of Malawi?

Unsure? Do you know even where Malawi is located? If not, don't panic. Geography and world capitals are not topics tested on the CBEST. If you had to answer this question without any answer choices, you'd probably be in trouble.

Of course, on the CBEST, you will have some answer choices to choose from. Rather than close your eyes and select an answer choice at random, take a look at the answer choices—you might find some information that can help you. Try the following example:

Proven Techniques

1. What is the capital of Malawi?

   A. Paris

   B. Lilongwe

   C. New York

   D. London

   E. Moscow

Use Process of Elimination (POE) to get rid of impossible answer choices.

Here's How to Crack It

Now do you know? Can you identify an answer choice that is not the correct answer? Sure! You can probably eliminate (A), (C), (D), and (E). While you probably didn't know that Lilongwe was the capital of Malawi, you could tell that (B) was the correct answer by eliminating incorrect answer choices. This procedure is called Process of Elimination, or POE for short.

Process of Elimination will help you become a more accurate guesser. Often it is easier to spot incorrect answer choices than the correct answer. If this happens to you, be sure to cross out any answer choice that you know is incorrect. Then, if you need to make a guess, select an answer from your remaining choices.

It is unlikely that POE will help you eliminate all incorrect answer choices as we did in the previous sample problem. However, every time you get rid of one answer choice, the odds of correctly answering that question increase significantly. Rather than a 20 percent chance of guessing a correct answer, you will often find yourself guessing with a 33 percent or 50 percent chance of getting a question correct.

Let's try one more example:

———————————◯———————————

2. Store X recently had a sale promoting a 20 percent discount on all items. If Teresa bought a dress priced originally at $64, what did she pay for the dress during the sale?

    A. $12.80

    B. $32.00

    C. $51.20

    D. $76.20

    E. $128.00

Here's How to Crack It

Later in this book, we'll review exactly how to answer percent questions. For now, let's just think about the question. Teresa is buying a dress on sale. If the dress was originally $64, then the price she paid for it would be less than $64. Thus, you should be able to eliminate answer choices (D) and (E). You may have also noticed that answer choices (A) and (B) were much, much lower than the original price, and eliminated those too. (C) is the correct answer. At worst, if you needed to make a guess on this question, you would have a one in three chance. Again, using POE can help you get more points on the CBEST.

———————————◯———————————

Process of Elimination is an important concept that we'll be referring to throughout this book, including in the explanations provided for the practice tests. There are some specific POE strategies for the reading and mathematics sections that will be presented in the chapters ahead. It is important that you practice using POE. Getting rid of incorrect answers is a powerful tool on the CBEST.

THE BEST ANSWER

CBEST questions are not about selecting the "right" answer, but the "best" answer. An answer choice that looks bad can actually be the credited response, as long as all the other choices are even worse. An answer choice that looks good can be wrong if another choice is even better.

CBEST questions, even ones that require you to "read between the lines," are NOT a matter of opinion. CBEST must have one single justifiable answer for each question; otherwise, they'd face a flood of lawsuits and challenged scores.

Your job is to find the best answer.

Best Answer and POE Go Hand in Hand

There are a variety of reasons why you may choose a particular answer to a particular question. If you had to justify your answer to a question, you might respond in any one of a few different ways, depending on the question and how you tackled it.

Different reasons to choose an answer can be summed up as follows:

- I think that this answer makes the most sense
- I eliminated the remaining answers
- I derived the answer on my own

While any one of those justifications may be valid, it's important that you take a careful, thoughtful approach to each question.

One way to feel more confident about your responses is to use not just one, but two different ways to justify an answer. Here are some example scenarios:

- You looked at the answer choices and determined that "A" seems to make the most sense. Great! Now, look at the remaining choices again, and think about the reasons that might allow you to eliminate some of them.
- You looked at the answer choices and you feel good about eliminating "A," "B," "C," and "D." Neat! It must be "E," then, right? Well, perhaps, but it's better to give choice "E" some careful consideration on its own.
- You completed a math problem on scratch paper, and derived an answer. The answer matches one of your choices. Super! Now, you might try a basic trick like estimation, and see if you still agree with your answer. You can catch silly mistakes this way!
- You looked at a Reading question, and as you read it, you realized that you knew what the best answer should say. One of the choices matches your predicted answer. Lovely! Now, carefully consider each choice and make sure that you're choosing the best one.

Try to approach each problem in a couple of different ways.

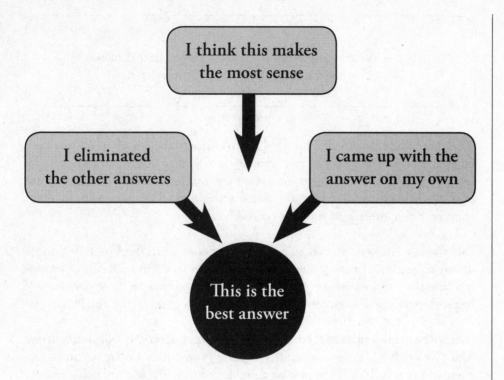

I think this makes
the most sense

I eliminated
the other answers

I came up with the
answer on my own

This is the
best answer

I'll Just Go From Question 1 to Question 50, Right?

There are some tests that contain an order of difficulty within each section. On these tests, the first question is generally very easy, and the questions become progressively more difficult. On the CBEST, however, there is no order of difficulty on the two multiple-choice sections of the exam. Questions will vary in difficulty throughout the mathematics and Reading Sections in no particular order. So, doing the test straight through, from question 1 to question 50, may not always be your best strategy.

Uhhhh, I Know This One. Just One More Minute!!

Have you ever been given a question that stumped you, but were sure you could do? Have you ever said "Just one more minute. I know I can figure this out!" Well, we all have. Unfortunately, one more minute usually means five more minutes, and often, we don't end up with the right answer at all.

Don't let one question ruin your day. No single question is that important. You've got 50 questions per section to tackle, and allowing just one of them to throw off your timing would really set you back. Here is a general rule for the reading and mathematics sections:

Do not let one question ruin your test day. If you are struggling on a particular question, leave it and move on.

> **If you haven't figured out the correct answer in 90 seconds, skip the question and come back to it later.**

We're not telling you to give up. If you can't answer the question, make a note on your scratch paper, so you can come back to it later. After you complete the section, go back to the questions that you were unable to solve. Remember to use POE on these questions. Make sure you have selected an answer choice for every question before turning in your answer sheet.

This strategy is often referred to as the two-pass system. The first time you go through a section, try every question. If a question seems too difficult or stumps you, move on. Once you've completed the section, go back to those questions. If you still aren't sure how to solve the problem, make a guess after using POE.

Often when you return to a problem later, the right approach will simply strike you. (We've all left a test and said "Oh yeah! Now I know what the answer to question five was.") So if you pass on a problem during the test, try going back to it later, and giving it another try.

YOU ARE IN CONTROL

We know the CBEST can be an intimidating exam. We know the importance of passing this test. As with many such tests, we know that sometimes it feels as if the CBEST is totally out of your control.

However, the opposite is true. You are in control. While you can't decide what kind of pencil you must bring to the exam, or where to sit during the test, you can decide how you take the CBEST. Let's review what we've discussed in this chapter. First, you can use the four-hour testing period in any way you see fit. Spend more time on your weakest sections. Second, you can take the sections in any order you choose. Want to start with mathematics? Great. Want to write an essay before doing the Reading Section? No problem. Third, you get to take advantage of the multiple-choice format of the Mathematics and Reading Sections. With no guessing penalty, and tools like Process of Elimination, you can add points to your score, without even knowing the correct answer.

By the end of this book, you'll be prepared to handle any question on the CBEST!

Finally, you control the exact order of questions within each section. If question 12 is really stumping you, move on to question 13, and save question 12 for later.

So, you really are in control of the CBEST. And as you work through the next few sections, you'll gain more confidence in your knowledge of the material tested.

Part II
Cracking the
Reading Section

The Reading Section of the CBEST consists of 50 multiple-choice questions based on information presented in a variety of passages, tables, and graphs. Passage topics are drawn from a variety of sources, and are designed to simulate high school and college-level materials, student textbooks, teachers' guides, and written materials on psychology or student behavior. These passage topics will vary in difficulty, and are drawn from a number of different fields, such as social sciences, humanities, health, and consumer affairs.

You will be able to answer all reading questions without having any specialized knowledge about the subject matter (in fact, bringing in outside knowledge will often lead you to an incorrect answer). So, if the topic covers material that you are completely unfamiliar with, don't panic. All the information you need will be presented in the passage.

Passages will vary in length and difficulty. Some passages will be as short as one or two sentences. Other "short" passages will consist of about 100 words. The "long" passages you will see will consist of approximately 200 words. In general, longer passages will be accompanied by more multiple-choice questions. The number of questions based on each passage will vary greatly. Some passages will only have one question, while other passages could have up to five questions.

In this chapter, we will cover general strategies that you should apply to all questions presented in the Reading Section. Chapters 3 and 4 will provide you with specific strategies for handling the types of questions you might be asked. First, let's dissect the types of questions that may be asked on the CBEST Reading Section.

CRITICAL ANALYSIS AND EVALUATIONS

Approximately 40 percent of the questions on the Reading Section will come from this skill area. Here are some of the things that a critical analysis question will ask you to do:

Sample question: "With which of the following statements would the author most likely agree?"

- Identify the author's tone, attitude, opinion, or viewpoint expressed in the passage.
- Find the techniques used by an author to make his or her point.
- Identify the assumptions an author makes to support his or her claim.
- Recognize the type of audience that the author is trying to address.
- Find examples, details, or facts that support an author's claim.
- Predict the outcome of an event based on the information presented in a written passage.
- Choose statements that will strengthen or weaken the claims made by the author in a reading selection.
- Distinguish between facts and opinions within a reading passage.
- Compare/contrast ideas or information presented in different sections of a reading selection.

- Identify inconsistencies or differences in points of view.
- Determine whether facts or ideas are relevant to an argument.
- Challenge the statements and opinions presented in the passage.

All of these types of questions will be discussed in detail in Chapter 3.

COMPREHENSION AND RESEARCH SKILLS

Approximately 60 percent of the questions on the Reading Section will come from this skill area. Here are some of the things that comprehension questions will ask you to do:

- Recognize the order of a passage (this may include outlining a passage, separating general ideas from specific ideas in a passage, and determining the sequence of events or steps in a reading selection).
- Identify the main idea of a passage.
- Summarize or paraphrase a reading selection.
- Identify the conclusion of a passage.
- Determine the meaning of underlined words in the context of the passage.
- Identify words and phrases that serve as transitions between ideas in a passage.
- Make an inference based on the information provided.
- Identify facts and details presented in a reading section.

Sample question: "What is the best conclusion to the passage above?"

In addition to these comprehension-based questions, you will need to solve questions that are based on information presented in table or graphic form. For these questions, you will be asked to:

- Locate the place in a book, chapter, article, or index where a specific kind of information can be found.
- Identify how a written passage is organized.
- Find conclusions that are supported by the information presented in a table or graph.
- Use the table of contents, section headings, index, and similar sections of a book to locate information.

Sample question: "How is the index below organized?"

Chapter 4 will cover all possible question types involving comprehension and research skills.

READING INSTRUCTIONS

Before we begin with the general strategies you'll need to take the CBEST, let's take a look at the instructions presented by the test writers. Here are the directions that will appear at the start of each Reading Section:

> Each question in the Reading Section of the test is a multiple-choice question with five answer choices. Read each question carefully and choose ONE best answer. Record each answer on the answer sheet provided.

Take the time to familiarize yourself with these directions, so you won't have to waste time reading them on the day you take the test.

The Treasure Hunt

If we told you that we had hidden $50,000 somewhere in your hometown and then handed you an envelope filled with clues, would you search every inch of your hometown before you opened the envelope and looked at the clues? Of course not! You'd look at the clues first and then decide on a plan of action. You'd use them to select some places where the treasure might be, and eliminate places where the treasure could not possibly be hidden. Well, the same is true with the Reading Section of the CBEST. Every reading passage contains some hidden treasure (points toward your overall CBEST score). Your job is to find that treasure. Where are the clues? Some of the clues are located in the passage; most are located in the questions and the answer choices. Our job over the next three chapters will be to help you identify these clues for every possible CBEST question.

CRACKING THE READING SECTION

So what exactly do these instructions mean? While these instructions tell you what you need to do on the Reading Section, they certainly don't tell you how to do the section. The rest of this chapter will tell you what you need to know. Let's talk about the three elements of a Reading Section: the passage, the questions, and the answer choices.

The Passage

Believe it or not, the passage is the least important piece of the Reading Section. The questions will determine what parts of the passage you will need to use. If you actually tried to comprehend the reading passages on the CBEST—by carefully reading and analyzing every word until you understood all components of the passage—you'd find that you wouldn't have much time remaining for any of the other sections of the CBEST! Remember that your goal on the CBEST is to earn as many points as possible. We will show you how to accomplish this without having to read the entire passage for all question types. Some questions will only require that you use one or two sentences out of a 200-word passage. The types of questions you are asked will determine how much time you spend on the passage.

It is often unnecessary to read the entire passage before attempting to answer the questions.

The Questions

When attacking a reading passage, the first thing you should read is the question (or questions) that follows the passage. Each question type will give you clues as to the specific information you need to find within the passage. Some questions give you an obvious direction as to where you need to go within the passage:

- "Which of the following is the best meaning of the word <u>solution</u> as it is used in the passage?"
- "Which words should be inserted into the blanks on line 6 of the passage?"
- "According to the information presented in the passage, the inventor of volleyball created the sport in order to..."

All of these questions ask for specific information to be taken out of a passage. These questions provide you with a guide for finding the needed information. Where would you go to find the answer to the first sample question? First, you should locate the word "solution," and then read enough of the passage above and below the word to make sure you understand its context. Based on the question, you can reduce the amount of reading you need to do in order to find the correct answer.

We call the above types of questions "specific"—these questions focus only on a specific piece of information in the passage. We'll talk about specific questions in much more detail in the chapters ahead.

"Specific" questions ask you to find detailed information within a passage.

Other questions are not that specific. Instead, they will ask that you identify general information about the passage as a whole:

- "Which of the following would be the most appropriate title for this passage?"
- "Which of the following inferences may be drawn from the information presented in the passage?"
- "Which of the following best summarizes the main points of the passage?"

Do you think you'll need to know every detail about a passage in order to answer these questions? Absolutely not. You will need to have a general idea of what the passage states, how it is written, what techniques are used, etc. There are a number of techniques to solve the many different types of general questions, which we will discuss in the chapters ahead.

In summary, the types of questions you are given will determine the type of information you need to find within the passage. The questions are your treasure map—use them to help you narrow your search for the correct answer. We will show you how to distinguish question types from one another, and give you a specific list of things to find for each question type.

The Answer Choices

Have you ever read a question, then looked at the answer choices and thought that all of the answer choices could be correct? Many students feel that the most difficult part of the Reading Section is distinguishing among answer choices that sound the same. In the general introduction we emphasized the importance of Process of Elimination, or POE. On the Reading Section, POE plays a vital role in helping you narrow down the number of possible answer choices. Below we will talk about six things to look for that will help you eliminate answer choices:

1. Understanding the Author
2. Controversial Answer Choices
3. Strong Language
4. Scope
5. Common Sense
6. Stick to the Passage

Understanding the Author

An author will not be overly critical of professionals (teachers, administrators).

One key to doing well on questions of tone, attitude and style is understanding the CBEST authors' very predictable feelings about certain types of people. CBEST authors are deeply respectful of school administrators, educators, doctors, lawyers, scientists, etc. (essentially, anyone with a college degree). It is very unlikely that you will have a passage about an uncaring educator, a sloppy doctor, or a ruthless lawyer. This will help you to eliminate certain negative answer choices. Here is an example:

---

1. The author views the speech from the superintendent with:

    A. angered skepticism

    B. complete confusion

    C. resigned approval

    D. reluctant criticism

    E. sneering disrespect

Here's How to Crack It

Without even reading the passage, we know that the CBEST writers believe that a superintendent, like all educators, is a responsible professional. A superintendent ought to be admired. Therefore, you will not be presented with a passage that is negative toward someone that the CBEST authors like. If we look at the answer choices, we can see that (A), (B), and (E) are extremely negative. These answer choices leave no doubt that the author is against what the superintendent has to say. We can eliminate these three answer choices. This will be true of any professional. The author's attitude will be one of praise, admiration, approval, appreciation, or respect. It will never be one of disdain, apathy, puzzlement, confusion, disrespect, or cynicism.

On the rare occasion that a passage is somewhat critical of a group of professionals, the criticism will be mild at most. Choice (D) is an example of this ("reluctant criticism" isn't positive, but it certainly isn't aggressive).

Controversial Answer Choices

CBEST authors go to great lengths to avoid correct answers that would make anyone upset. (Most people are upset enough about having to take the CBEST!) The last thing the authors would want is to publish a test that gives students credit for selecting controversial or bizarre answers. On your test, you may encounter a reading passage about an ethnic group, an environmental issue, or a touchy political issue. You will want to be sure you eliminate all answer choices that seem negative toward one of these kinds of topics. Here is an example:

> Avoid any answer choice that may be controversial.

---

2. The author views the actions taken by the environmental group with:

   A. apathy

   B. naivete

   C. hopelessness

   D. admiration

   E. anger

Here's How to Crack It

The correct answer, (D), should be fairly obvious. CBEST authors will not include a passage where the writer has a negative view on environmental issues. The CBEST authors want to avoid any answers that say something negative or controversial. In the example above, the only possible answer is admiration. Apathy, naivete, hopelessness, and anger all convey a negative opinion of the environmental plan.

Strong Language

CBEST authors want to make sure that the correct answer to a question is not open to interpretation. Imagine the number of questions or complaints that would be fielded by the CBEST office if even a small percentage of test takers challenged some of the correct answer choices. In order to avoid this, CBEST authors will use correct answers that are almost impossible to argue against. Consider the following two answer choices:

> A. Plant biology is absolutely the most vital component of the sixth-grade science curriculum.

> B. Plant biology is an important part of the sixth-grade science curriculum.

Of these two answer choices, which one would be the easier to challenge? Statement (A) of course! Who is to say what the most important science topic is? How does one evaluate the importance of each topic to the overall curriculum? It's easy to think of a number of ways that one could challenge Statement (A). Statement (B), on the other hand, is much more vague and general, and is therefore very difficult to challenge.

In general, the more detailed and specific a statement is, the easier it is for someone to raise objections to it. The more vague and general a statement is, the harder it is for someone to challenge it. Because of these facts, we can learn a few things about correct answer choices:

> Answer choices that say something *must be true* are usually incorrect.
>
> Answer choices with *extreme language* are usually incorrect.

What is extreme language? We're not talking about R-rated movie language here, we're talking about words that are so categorical that they make it very easy to challenge an answer choice. Here are some examples of extreme words:

Must	Always	Impossible	Never	Cannot
All	Only	Totally	Every	Each

Be careful when you see these words in the answer choices. Ask yourself, "could someone make an objection to this statement?" If so, eliminate the answer choice. Let's take an example of another question, with some of the answer choices already eliminated.

Use POE to eliminate answer choices with extreme language.

---

3. With which of the following statements would the author of the passage probably agree?

   A. There is no useful purpose in studying the works of Freud.

   B. A more complete understanding of recent theories may be achieved through the study of the works of Freud.

   C. <eliminated>

   D. <eliminated>

   E. It is impossible to gain more understanding of recent theories by studying authors of the past.

Here's How to Crack It

Do any of the statements involve extreme language? Answer choices (A) and (E) do. Choice (A) argues that there is no useful purpose to studying Freud. This statement is expressed in absolute terms. If someone were to find anything useful in Freud's works, the statement would be incorrect. The author of the passage would not make such a bold statement. Answer choice (E) is even more ridiculous. It goes far beyond what the text of the passage will support by making the sweeping statement that nothing can be learned in the present by studying the past. Not even once in a while? Obviously, there are some exceptions to this statement. Choice (B), however, is much more vague. Notice the use of the word "may." With the word "may," all we need is one example to prove this statement correct.

Cracking the Reading Section | 27

We talked about the need to avoid answer choices that used extreme language. Here are some words that are much more wishy-washy, and are therefore much more difficult to argue with:

May	Could Be True	Some	Most
Sometimes	Might	Probably	Suggests

Answer choices containing these words are often correct. When you spot these words, be sure to spend some time evaluating the statements in which they appear.

Scope

A CBEST passage, which is no more than 200 words, will have to be narrow in focus.

The passages that you will be working with are not that long. Sure, some of them will be a few paragraphs, and up to 200 words long, but at least you won't have to read a thesis! With the limited number of words, it becomes difficult for an author to accomplish a number of things within the passage. In other words: the focus, or scope, of the passage is very narrow. Imagine writing a fifty-page paper about the experiences you've had in education. What would it involve? What mechanisms would you use to support your paper? Would you use examples, anecdotes, and stories to enhance your claim? As you think about what would go into this paper, imagine if it had to be reduced to a twenty-page paper. What would you cut out? How would you narrow your focus? Again, what if you had to write a paper in just 200 words? You certainly wouldn't be able to address all the experiences you've had in education. At best, you would select one specific example, and use it to make a very specific point.

A dangerous answer choice on the CBEST is the one that tries to do too much. In other words, the answer choice is out of scope.

Here is an example:

---

4. The primary purpose of the passage is to:

    A.   Present an overview of the Great Depression.

    B.   Document the use of taxation as a means to control the economy.

    C.   Acknowledge all the social effects on Americans during the Great Depression.

    D.   Examine one way taxation helped to slow the effects of the Great Depression on the middle class.

    E.   Compare and contrast differing viewpoints of the Great Depression.

Here's How to Crack It

Try to eliminate answer choices that describe something that could not possibly be accomplished in a couple of paragraphs. Use this in combination with extreme language to help you eliminate answer choices. Choice (A) is probably too ambitious. The Great Depression was a complex time, involving many social, political, and economic factors. While the word "overview" is certainly less specific than say, "complete account," it is still pretty impossible to do with the limited length of CBEST passages. Choice (B) is so vague that it seems to encompass a number of things. Taxation to control the economy—whose economy? During what time frame? This is a topic for several volumes of work, not a CBEST passage. Choice (C) uses extreme language, and is therefore out of scope. How could a 200-word passage describe *all* the social effects of the Great Depression? Choice (D) is perfect. It is possible to examine one way that taxation helped the middle class. As you can see, the scope of this answer choice is very narrow. That is exactly what we're looking for. Choice (E) is probably too lengthy. It would be quite a challenge to compare and contrast differing viewpoints. First, you'd have to identify the viewpoints, then compare them, and then contrast them. This is too much work for a CBEST passage. Using scope as a means to eliminate answer choices only takes a little common sense, which is our next technique.

Common Sense

Correct answers on the CBEST will never contradict an established fact. Therefore, common sense can enable you to eliminate answer choices that seem absurd or incorrect, without even reading the passage. Here is an example:

---

5. According to the passage, the first response of an individual to a shortage of atmospheric oxygen is:

    A.   a surge of activity in the bone marrow

    B.   an increase in respiratory intake

    C.   an increase in the number of respiratory passages

    D.   an increase in the growth rate of muscles

    E.   an increase in the blood cell count

Here's How to Crack It

You may be wondering why we're asking you to use common sense on a biology question. Well, even if you haven't had biology in years, take a look at the answer choices, and see which seem reasonable. The question asks what happens when someone is short of oxygen. Choice (A) says that bone marrow becomes more active. Actually, bone marrow has nothing to do with getting less oxygen. If you realize this, eliminate (A). Some of the answer choices may not only be unreasonable, but also downright silly. Take a look at (C)—an increase in the number of respiratory passages. Can people grow new respiratory passages in response to a lack of oxygen? Obviously, (C) is incorrect. So is (D)—do muscles suddenly grow when you are at a high altitude? Even if you know nothing about biology, you have a 50 percent chance of answering this question correctly. The answer must be either (B) or (E). In fact, the correct answer is (B)—an increase in the respiratory intake occurs with a shortage of oxygen.

To summarize, correct answer choices will make sense. Feel free to use factual information you know to be true to help you eliminate answer choices. But don't go too far, otherwise you'll fall into the trap the next technique discusses.

Stick to the Passage

What type of reading passage would you prefer to read—a passage on a topic you are familiar with, or a passage on a topic you know nothing about? Most would answer the former. We enjoy reading about topics we know. It is easy to relate the information to books we've read, personal experiences, and so forth. However, the danger of a familiar topic is that you may insert your own opinions, experiences, and facts about a topic into the information presented. The trap is that you may select or eliminate answer choices that are based upon what you know, rather than upon what is presented in the passage.

Everything you need to know has to be found somewhere in the passage. You should always rely on the information in the passage, not what you know about a topic, to answer the question. If you are familiar with a topic, make sure you can "prove" your answer choice. There must be support somewhere in the passage in order for an answer choice to be correct.

What about the passages that you know nothing about? Often, passages you know nothing about can be the easiest because you'll be so focused on the material presented.

Do not try to use outside knowledge to answer a reading question. All correct answers will be supported by information found in the passage.

APPROACH TO THE READING SECTION

As we've stated throughout this chapter, the questions are your key to the Reading Section. The question type will give you a specific method for solving the problem. You can aid your search by eliminating answer choices according to the rules we've discussed above. Now that we know how to approach a reading passage, is there an ideal order to approach the questions?

First, it is important to recognize that there is no set order of difficulty within the Reading Section. So, proceeding from question 1 to question 50 will help you keep your place, however, it won't provide any advantage for you in terms of order of difficulty. Here are a few things that you should focus on when practicing the Reading Section:

Is time a problem? If you find that the Reading Section takes a large amount of time, you may want to select the passages that are accompanied by the most questions. For example, start with the passages that have four or five questions following the text. This way, you'll maximize the number of questions you answer for the time it takes to dissect one passage. After you've finished these questions, move to passages that have three questions following the text, then two questions, and so on. Of course, if time is a significant problem, review the techniques included in this manual. You also may need to adjust your pacing for each section on the exam.

Do you prefer one question type to another? Unfortunately, one passage can include a number of different types of questions. This makes it difficult to search for specific question types without going back and forth between passages (something you do not want to do). Some students are very comfortable with the "research" questions—questions that involve charts, tables of contents, indexes, etc. If you are comfortable with these questions, make sure you give yourself a chance to do them.

In the chapters that follow, we'll be discussing many techniques for specific types of questions. It is important that you learn to distinguish these types of questions from one another, so that you can maximize your efficiency and effectiveness on the Reading Section.

Summary

o The Reading Section consists of 50 multiple-choice questions based on information provided in passages, graphs, charts, or research material.

o Approximately 40 percent of the reading questions are based on critical analysis and evaluation; approximately 60 percent of the reading questions are based on comprehension and research skills.

o It is not necessary to read the entire passage in order to find the information needed to answer a question. The type of question you are asked will dictate how you approach the passage.

o Reading passages can take many forms—a chart, a one-sentence passage, a passage of 100 words, or a passage of up to 200 words.

o Questions can be very specific or very general. You will learn techniques for how to approach each type of question.

o Process of Elimination is an important part of the Reading Section. The most common reasons to eliminate answer choices are:
   • Understanding the author's attitude toward his subject
   • Controversial answer choices
   • Strong language
   • Scope
   • Common sense
   • Stick to the information contained in the passage

Chapter 3
Critical Analysis
and Evaluation
Questions

Approximately 40 percent of the reading questions on the CBEST will test "critical analysis and evaluation." Throughout this chapter, we will identify the ways in which these questions can be asked. We'll also provide specific instructions for how to find the correct answer for these questions in a passage. Finally, we'll help you distinguish between the different types of questions in the Reading Section. Analysis and evaluation questions can be broken into three major areas:

- **Questions about the author.** We'll go through five different types of questions that ask about the author's attitude, assumptions, audience, evidence, opinions, and techniques.
- **Questions about facts within a passage.** Certain analysis questions will require you to distinguish between facts and opinions, and to identify the relevant facts of an argument.
- **Questions that ask for additional information for a passage.** We will learn how to select statements that will complete the meaning of a passage, weaken the argument made in a passage, or strengthen the argument made in a passage.

KNOW THE AUTHOR

If you take a look at the back of this CBEST book, you will find a section titled "About the Author." This section provides general biographical information about the author (in this case, me). What can you learn from this section of the book? You can learn more about who I am, what I do for a living, and why I am qualified to write a CBEST preparation book.

It would be very helpful if there were a quick summary about the author next to each passage in the Reading Section. That way, we could gain some insight into the author's expertise, motivation, opinion, and so forth. Since we won't be given this quick biography, we will need to examine the style, tone, and information presented in a passage to get a feel for who the author is.

How can you recognize questions that ask you for something about the author? Here are some sample question stems:

- Which of the following would be most consistent with the writer's purpose?
- This passage uses which of the following argumentative techniques?
- The primary message of the author is...?
- What is the attitude of the author toward...?
- The author is most likely speaking to what group?
- In what type of publication would the author's work be found?
- The author would most likely agree with which statement below?

We will use the passage below to discuss the different types of "author" questi
Sample passage 1:

> Recent dissatisfaction with the current tax code has inspired local Congressman David Moore to introduce legislation that will get rid of the "marriage tax." The "marriage tax" describes the higher taxes that a married couple currently pays compared to two single individuals. If a married couple and two single individuals together earn the same amount of money, the married couple could pay up to $1,400 more in federal taxes each year. While there are certain benefits in the tax for married couples, especially if one of the individuals does not work, most such couples find themselves disadvantaged due to their married status. Congressman Moore believes that the tax code should treat married couples the same as two single individuals. While some critics argue that the tax system is currently too complicated to simply equate married and single individuals, almost all agree that some revision of the "marriage tax" is necessary.

1. Which of the following best describes the author's attitude toward the proposed legislation put forth by Congressman Moore?

   A. Uncertain

   B. Supportive

   C. Opposed

   D. Elated

   E. Disdainful

Here's How to Crack It

Question 1 is an example of an "attitude" question. Often, you may be asked about the author's attitude, opinion, or viewpoint. In order to answer attitude questions correctly, we need to look for certain information in the passage as well as use one of our keys to eliminating answer choices—understanding the author. First, we need to go back to the passage to look for clues about the author's attitude. Start with the first sentence to gain an understanding of the topic at hand, and paraphrase the sentence. From the first sentence, we know that Congressman Moore is looking to get rid of the "marriage tax." After you have a general understanding of the main topic, look for sentences that distinguish the author's opinion from the subject matter. Take a look at the passage above and see if you can identify a sentence that presents the author's opinion. The fourth sentence gives us some clues as to the author's viewpoint: "While there are certain benefits in the tax for married couples, especially if one of the individuals does not work, most such couples find themselves disadvantaged due to their married status." The last part of the sentence indicates that the author is against the "marriage tax." If Congressman Moore is looking to get rid of the tax, the author is going to be in favor of his proposal. Now, let's look at the answer choices. Only two answer choices are positive—"supportive" and "elated." "Elated" is a bit too strong, and therefore not appropriate for this passage. Choices (C) and (E) are very negative, and negative choices are often incorrect answers to CBEST questions. Remember that CBEST authors will show respect to professionals. Therefore, (B) is the correct answer choice.

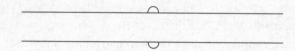

2. In what type of publication might this passage be found?

    A. A law journal

    B. An encyclopedia

    C. A local newspaper section

    D. A history textbook

    E. A book on the tax code

Here's How to Crack It

Some questions about the author will ask you to determine where the passage is most likely to be found. Your first key to these questions is to determine whether the passage is technical or general. A technical passage is written with the understanding that the reader possesses a high level of knowledge about the topic at hand. Scientific journals are a very common example of a publication that contains technical passages. In general, any passage that uses complicated language, without explaining or defining most terms, is a technical passage. A general passage involves more simple language, and is often more opinion based. A general passage will define any new concepts for the reader and will strive to do more than provide factual information. These passages can also be persuasive and opinionated.

How do you determine if a passage is technical or general? Scan the passage to take a look at the choice of words used. Is the text complicated? Does the author

Technical or general? Determine how the passage is written so you can identify in what publication the passage will most likely appear.

make assumptions about the reader's knowledge? Does the passage contain an author's viewpoint? Does the passage explain new terms or concepts?

You should be able to identify the passage above as a general passage. There are two ways to spot this. First, the passage explains new concepts in detail (the definition of "marriage tax" is one example). Second, the passage contains the author's argument that the marriage tax is bad (we saw this in our analysis of Question 1). Since this passage is intended for a general audience, we want to eliminate answer choices that mainly include technical pieces of writing. Choices (A) and (E) would require language much more complex than that used in the passage. Choice (B) can be eliminated—an encyclopedia will not include proposed legislation. Further, common sense helps us to eliminate (D)—a history textbook would not cover such recent information; a newly proposed piece of legislation probably wouldn't make its way into a history book. Therefore, (C) is correct. A newspaper could include this passage, possibly in an editorial section. The passage is directed toward a general audience.

Remember POE! Always think about what answer choices you can eliminate on all reading questions.

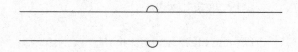

3. What technique does the author employ to demonstrate a problem with the "marriage tax"?

   A. a quotation

   B. a numerical example

   C. a sarcastic comment

   D. an anecdote

   E. a plea to the reader

Here's How to Crack It

Some questions will ask you what literary technique an author uses in order to make his or her point. These questions are easy, because all you need to do is go back to the passage in order to find the correct answer. Take a look at the answer choices first to get a feel for the types of things to look for in the passage. We can immediately eliminate (A), because there are no quotations contained in the passage at all. We can also see that (D) is incorrect; there are no anecdotes contained within the passage. Choice (E) is also incorrect; at no point in the passage does the author make a direct statement to the audience. Choice (C) is somewhat more difficult to evaluate, however, not only are there no sarcastic comments in the passage, but also a sarcastic comment could be an example of extreme language. Eliminate it. Choice (B) is correct, the author uses a numerical example (the dif-

Critical Analysis and Evaluation Questions | **39**

ference of $1,400 between the tax owed by the married couple and that owed by two single individuals) in order to demonstrate the effect of the "marriage tax."

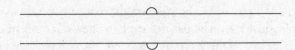

4. Which of the following statements would the author most likely agree with regarding the "marriage tax"?

A. The "marriage tax" is inevitable due to complex rules in the tax code.

B. The "marriage tax" unfairly punishes single men or women since there are tax benefits to being married.

C. Despite other benefits in the tax system, married individuals are unfairly treated by the "marriage tax."

D. Critics of the "marriage tax" will be unable to make any changes in the federal tax code.

E. A $1,400 adjustment in taxes is not significant enough to attempt changing the tax code.

On an "agree" question, find an answer choice that the author may include in his or her passage.

Here's How to Crack It

This type of question asks you to identify a statement that the author would agree with. Therefore, you need to find a statement that supports the main idea within the passage. Note that this type of question is not the same as a similar-looking type of question, called a strengthen/weaken question (which we'll come to later in the chapter). To solve these questions, try fitting each statement somewhere into the passage. Does it agree with information provided in the passage? Does it restate a sentence already found in the passage? If so, you've probably found the correct answer.

Let's begin by analyzing each answer choice. Choice (A) is incorrect. Notice how the CBEST authors will try to trap you by including words and phrases found in the passage. The passage does state that the tax code is complex; however, it does not say the "marriage tax" is therefore *inevitable*. Eliminate (A). Choice (B) states the opposite of what the author claims. The "marriage tax" negatively affects married individuals by taxing them more than single individuals—therefore, eliminate (B). Choice (D) voices the strong opinion that critics will not be able to change the system. This issue is not addressed by the passage; therefore, we cannot make any assumptions about the author's opinion on this issue. Eliminate (D). Choice (E) is also incorrect. The author, by presenting the proposed legislation, argues that the tax penalty gives us a reason to change the tax code. Choice (C) is correct. The numerical example shows how *married* individuals are treated unfairly in the tax system.

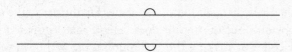

5. Which of the following assumptions can be made about the author's view of the current "marriage tax" and the tax system?

    A.   The author believes that changes in the tax system are possible through legislation.

    B.   The author believes that there should be no benefits in the tax code for married individuals.

    C.   The author believes that married individuals should be given favorable treatment in our tax system.

    D.   The author believes that Congressman Moore's legislation will pass.

    E.   The author believes that the "marriage tax" is the greatest problem with the current tax code.

Here's How to Crack It

First, we need to be clear about what an assumption is. An assumption is something that an author believes to be true. This belief is necessary in order for the author to establish his point. Assumptions are not stated in the passage; instead, they can be identified by interpreting the information presented in the passage. Therefore, the correct answer to an assumption question cannot be found in the passage; it must be derived from the passage. When you're asked an assumption question, look to eliminate answer choices that contradict the author's main point. Further, make sure that you are not choosing a statement that is presented in the passage. In general, assumption statements are obvious. Don't try to find a very detailed answer—assumptions can be very basic.

The correct answer to an "assumption" question will not be written in the passage.

Answer choice (B) is incorrect. We cannot assume that the author is against *any* benefits for married individuals. We know that the author is against the "marriage tax," but we don't know whether or not he believes in benefits for married couples. Choice (C) is also incorrect. Nothing can be drawn from the passage that would indicate that the author believes this. The passage gives us no clear answer about (D), and (E) is too extreme. We know the author is concerned about the "marriage tax" (why write an article if it wasn't important to the author?), but we can't assume that it is the *most* important issue. Finally, let's take a look at (A). It seems rather obvious, but the author does believe that legislation can be used to change the tax code. By making this assumption, the author moves from discussing Moore's proposal to the tax changes that could result from it. Choice (A) is correct.

JUST THE FACTS

On the CBEST, you will be asked to identify statements as either facts or opinions. Further, you will need to identify which facts are the most important to convey the overall meaning of a passage. What is the difference between a fact and an opinion? A fact is a true statement or a real occurrence. An opinion is a belief or conclusion that is held with confidence but cannot be proven. "Bill is wearing the color red" is a fact. "I don't like the color of Bill's sweater" is an opinion. You cannot challenge the fact that Bill is wearing red. But you could dispute whether or not you liked the color of Bill's sweater; this is a matter of taste, which is open to debate. Here is a passage with questions that involve distinguishing between facts and opinions:

> It is disappointing that more individuals are not aware of the effect of insulin on weight gain. Insulin is a critical hormone that allows individuals to absorb simple sugars (like glucose and fructose) from their food as it is digested. Most individuals produce the right amount of insulin. In fact, most individuals are not aware of the presence of insulin in the bloodstream. Recently, nutritionists have discovered that foods known as complex carbohydrates—potatoes, carrots, and pasta among them—break down into simple sugars. Other complex carbohydrates are highly refined foods, like white bread and white rice. Sometimes this breakdown into sugars occurs so rapidly that the sugars may trigger a strong insulin response. This can be problematic. A high level of insulin will inhibit the breakdown of fatty deposits. An accumulation of fatty deposits will lead to increased weight gain. Therefore, eating too many carbohydrates leads to too much insulin, which in turn promotes the accumulation of fat.

6. Which sentence best expresses an opinion of the author, not a fact?

    A.   It is disappointing that more individuals are not aware of the effect of insulin on weight gain.

    B.   Insulin is a critical hormone that allows individuals to absorb simple sugars (like glucose and fructose) from their food as it is digested.

    C.   Sometimes this breakdown into sugars occurs so rapidly that the sugars may trigger a strong insulin response.

    D.   A high level of insulin will inhibit the breakdown of fatty deposits.

    E.   An accumulation of fatty deposits will lead to increased weight gain.

Here's How to Crack It

This question type may be labeled "Find the opinion." The question asks us to consider the five statements and identify the one statement that is an opinion. When given this type of question you shouldn't have to go back to the passage at all! Simply evaluate each sentence, and determine whether the statement is opinion or fact. Try to find words in each statement that express an opinion. Look for words that express the author's feelings. If you find that only one statement is an opinion, you've got the correct answer. You may refer back to the passage if you have trouble determining if a statement is a fact or an opinion. Choice (A) contains a word that describes the author's feelings. The word "disappointing" is our clue that the statement is an opinion and not a fact. Is this statement universally true? No! While the author may be disappointed that people are not well educated about the effects of insulin on weight-gain, others may be ambivalent or unconcerned. Choice (A) is an opinion of the author. Choices (B), (C), (D), and (E) are all facts that could be verified. Choice (E) is a logical conclusion drawn from previous statements within the passage, so it is not an opinion and thus incorrect. The correct answer is choice (A).

Ask yourself if you can challenge the statement. If so, it is an opinion, not a fact.

7. Which of the following statements is least relevant to the main idea of the passage?

    A.   Other complex carbohydrates are highly refined foods, like white bread and white rice.

    B.   Sometimes, this breakdown into sugars occurs so rapidly that the sugars may trigger a strong insulin response.

    C.   A high level of insulin will inhibit the breakdown of fatty deposits.

    D.   An accumulation of fatty deposits will lead to increased weight gain.

    E.   Therefore, eating too many carbohydrates leads to too much insulin, which in turn promotes the accumulation of fat.

Here's How to Crack It

Which statement would you be able to eliminate from the passage, and still have the passage clearly convey its message? We want to locate a fact in the passage that, while adding to the depth of the passage, is unnecessary to convey the overall message. Often, these statements are descriptive. How should you approach these questions? First, ask yourself whether the statement reflects the main theme of the passage. If so, then see whether future statements are based upon that information. Locate the statement in the passage, and read a few lines above and below the statement.

In general, the first sentence and last sentence of each paragraph will be relevant. Topic sentences often come at the start of each paragraph, and the final thought, or conclusion, typically comes at the end of each passage.

Choice (A) provides examples of complex carbohydrates. If we eliminated this statement from the overall passage, would the main point still be made? Yes. Choice (A) certainly adds value to the passage by giving the reader a better understanding of complex carbohydrates, but it is not a crucial part of the passage. Choices (B), (C), (D), and (E) all explain vital steps in the description of how insulin can lead to weight gain. Without one of these statements, the reader would not have a clear understanding of the passage. Choice (A) is the least important statement in the passage and is therefore the correct answer.

MORE INFORMATION, PLEASE!

Sometimes, you will be asked to provide more information than that which appears in the passage. These questions can come in a few forms—they may ask you to complete the meaning of a passage, identify a statement that will strengthen the author's claim, or identify a statement that will weaken the author's claim. Occasionally, you will be asked to complete the meaning of a passage by inserting a phrase or statement into a blank. If you are given a fill-in-the-blank question, read a few lines above and a few lines below the blank to get a feel for the type of sentence that is needed.

Refer to the passage on insulin and weight gain for the following questions:

8. Which sentence, if inserted into the blank line, would best complete the passage?

   A. Clearly, insulin's effect on weight gain is more important than its influence in causing diabetes.

   B. Individuals concerned with their weight should concentrate on avoiding large amounts of complex carbohydrates.

   C. Meats and other proteins are not complex carbohydrates.

   D. The FDA needs to take action to make more individuals aware of the effects of insulin.

   E. Exercise is one way to decrease the amount of insulin in your system.

Here's How to Crack It

Since the blank comes at the end of the passage, you will need to select a sentence that provides a final comment on the topic. You may want to look for a conclusion in one of the answer choices (we'll cover conclusion statements in detail in the next chapter). If you read a few statements above the blank, you should be able to get a feel for the main point of the passage—we should be concerned about insulin, since a rise in insulin results in an inability to break down fatty deposits, and will therefore lead to weight gain. Let's analyze the answer choices to find a statement that adequately finishes the passage. Choice (A) is out of scope. Nowhere does the passage address the importance of insulin in causing diabetes; there is no comparison made between the two in the passage, so eliminate (A). Choice (B) will work; it ties the issue of weight gain back to complex carbohydrates. There is no reason to eliminate (B). Choice (C) does not summarize the main point of the passage. Choice (D) is also out of scope. If the passage were several pages long, this very well might be a topic the author would want to address. However, we're looking for the best sentence at the end of our brief passage, and (D) is out of scope. Choice (E) can be eliminated for the same reasons. The passage is concerned with describing why insulin is important, not how to reduce the amount of insulin in the body. Therefore, (B) is correct.

On a "weaken" question, find an answer choice that makes the author's conclusion less convincing.

9. Which of the following, if true, would weaken the author's argument?

    A.   Meats and other proteins are not complex carbohydrates.

    B.   Lack of exercise is the major reason doctors cite as the cause of obesity.

    C.   Complex carbohydrates help to fill up individuals quickly, reducing the amount of calories eaten per meal.

    D.   Certain foods, like whole grains and cereals, can counteract the tendency of other complex carbohydrates to raise insulin levels.

    E.   Most diet books stress intake of vegetables as the key to weight loss.

Here's How to Crack It

This question asks us to weaken the argument presented by the author. In order to do this, we first need to identify the argument. Skim the passage to get an understanding of the main theme presented by the author. We've already discussed the main point of this passage—a high amount of insulin leads to weight gain. Therefore, we should look for an answer choice that will dispute or contradict the author's claim. Choice (A) is useless. It provides no attack on the author's main point; it merely states a fact. Choice (B) is a bit tricky. If lack of exercise is the main reason for obesity, then is the author's claim weakened? Actually, no. The author does not claim that a large quantity of insulin is the primary reason for weight gain. The author simply states that it is one reason. Choice (C) is also appealing. However, in order to weaken the claim, the statement would need to state that carbohydrates do not lead to high levels of insulin. At first, (D) may seem out of scope. Who cares about whole grains and cereals? Well, if these foods counteract the effects of other complex carbohydrates, it may be possible to still eat these foods without worrying about weight gain. Look at one of the statements in the passage: ...*eating too many carbohydrates leads to too much insulin, which in turn promotes the accumulation of fat.* If statement (D) is true, the author's claim would be weakened, for (D) shows that carbohydrates might *not* lead to more insulin, and thus *not* lead to weight gain. Choice (E) is out of scope. The suggestions from diet books do not weaken the author's claim that carbohydrates lead to more insulin, which in turn leads to weight gain. Choice (D) is the correct answer. It directly weakens one of the statements put forth by the author.

———————————◯———————————

Conversely, if you are asked to identify a statement that strengthens the argument, choose the answer choice that adds the best support to a statement already in the passage. Common correct answer choices are those that provide statistical support for an author's claim.

Summary

o   Critical analysis and evaluation questions come in roughly three major topic areas: questions about the author, questions about the facts in a passage, and questions that ask you to add meaning to the passage.

o   Use Process of Elimination techniques, looking for things like scope and tone.

o   Determine whether the passage is technical or general when asked to identify the type of publication in which a passage may be found. Look at the complexity of the writing, and whether or not the author uses opinions to persuade the reader.

o   Try to fit each answer choice into the passage to determine which statement the author would agree with.

o   For "technique" questions, go back to the passage and look for the method the author uses to make a claim.

o   For "assumption" questions, do not select an answer choice that is found in the passage. Look for an obvious statement that an author uses to help build an argument.

o   Look for words that describe the author's feelings when identifying an opinion statement.

o   You do not need to go back to the passage to solve a "find the opinion" question. Evaluate each answer choice, and select the one that is not a fact.

o   In order to identify a fact as the "least relevant," try removing the statement from the passage, and see if the passage loses meaning or consistency.

o   If you are asked to complete a sentence in the passage, choose an answer choice that is consistent with the author's message.

o   If you are asked to weaken an author's claim, first find the main point. Then, find an answer choice that directly contradicts that main point.

Chapter 4
Reading Comprehension and Research Skills

Approximately 60 percent of the reading questions on the CBEST will test "comprehension and research skills." In this chapter, we will identify the ways in which these questions can be asked. We'll also provide specific instructions for how to find the correct answer for these questions in a passage. Finally, we'll help you distinguish question types from one another. Comprehension and research questions can be broken into four major areas:

- **What's the point?** Many questions will ask you to identify the main idea, central theme, or conclusion in a passage.
- **Identify the structure.** There are three different types of questions that require you to understand the structure and layout of a passage.
- **Specific questions.** Some questions will ask a very direct question based on a word, phrase, or quote within a passage. These specific questions require different strategies from most of the general questions we discussed in the previous chapter.
- **Research questions.** Through the use of indexes, charts, graphs, and tables of contents, you will be asked questions about the structure and placement of various items.

WHAT'S THE POINT? THE 2-T-2 TECHNIQUE

The 2-T-2 technique will help you understand the passage without having to read every sentence.

Many questions will ask you to identify the main idea. Some questions are very straightforward ("What is the main point of the passage?"), while other questions will ask you to rephrase the main idea by choosing a title for the passage, or by summarizing the passage. When you are given a main idea question, you may not have to read the entire passage. Instead, you should focus on the crucial parts of the passage—the first two sentences, all topic sentences, and the last two sentences. We call this the 2-T-2 technique (where "2-T-2"stands for the first two sentences, all topic sentences, and the last two sentences). The first two sentences will introduce you to the topic that is being discussed. If there is more than one paragraph, each topic sentence will give you a clue about each paragraph. Further, if there are any transitions in the passage, you will be able to recognize them by reading the topic sentences. The final two sentences will give you a feel for how the passage concludes. The following is a passage that we will use to discuss all possible types of "main idea" questions. As always, read the questions before going to the passage.

One type of fixed-income security is the municipal bond, which is issued by state and local governments. Interest income derived from municipal bonds is exempt from federal, state, and local income taxation. There are two types of municipal bonds. One type, called a general obligation bond, is fully backed by the issuer. The other type, called a revenue bond, is issued to finance particular projects. Revenue bonds are backed by the revenues from a project or from the organization responsible for the project. Typical issuers of revenue bonds are airports, hospitals, or port authorities. Revenue bonds are riskier in terms of default than general obligation bonds. One specific type of revenue bond is the industrial development bond, which is issued to finance commercial enterprises such as the construction of a factory that can be operated by a private firm.

The appeal of municipal bonds to investors is their tax-exempt status. Because investors need not pay federal taxes on the interest proceeds, they are willing to accept lower yields on these investments. This greatly helps state and local governments, which are able to save tremendous amounts of money. Sadly, many investors shy away from municipal bonds, discouraged by the low rate of return. However, if an investor were to study the after-tax returns on municipal bonds compared to other investments, he or she would see that municipal bonds have been one of the most profitable types of fixed-income security over the last 15 years, especially for investors in high tax brackets.

1. Which of the following best describes the main topic of the passage?

   A.   All about municipal bonds

   B.   The role of the industrial development bond

   C.   The tax benefits of municipal bonds

   D.   An analysis of general obligation versus revenue bonds

   E.   Investment choices for investors in high tax brackets

Tip! Scope will be a helpful POE tool on main idea questions.

Here's How to Crack It

Question 1 is an example of the most basic type of main idea question. This question could also be asked in the following ways:

- What is the main point in this passage?
- What does the author state in this passage?
- What is the central message conveyed by this passage?

All of these questions, and others similar to them, mean the same thing—What's the point?! We want to know why the author took the time to write the passage, and what information the author is trying to convey. As we mentioned above, you do not need to read the entire passage in order to get the main point. Let's read the passage, according to the formula mentioned above—the first two sentences, the topic sentences, and the last two sentences:

> One type of fixed-income security is the municipal bond, which is issued by state and local governments. Interest income derived from municipal bonds is exempt from federal, state, and local income taxation. ~~There are two types of municipal bonds. One type, called a general obligation bond, is fully backed by the issuer. The other type, called a revenue bond, is issued to finance particular projects. Revenue bonds are backed by the revenues from a project or from the organization responsible for the project. Typical issuers of revenue bonds are airports, hospitals, or port authorities. Revenue bonds are riskier in terms of default than general obligation bonds. One specific type of revenue bond is the industrial development bond, which is issued to finance commercial enterprises such as the construction of a factory that can be operated by a private firm.~~
>
> The appeal of municipal bonds to investors is their tax-exempt status. ~~Because investors need not pay federal taxes on the interest proceeds, they are willing to accept lower yields on these investments. This greatly helps state and local governments, who are able to save tremendous amounts of money.~~ Sadly, many investors shy away from municipal bonds, discouraged over the low rate of return. However, if an investor were to study the after-tax returns on municipal bonds compared to other investments, he or she would see that municipal bonds have been one of the most profitable types of fixed income security over the last 15 years, especially for investors in high tax brackets.

The first two sentences introduce us to the topic—municipal bonds. We know that they are issued by local governments and are exempt from some taxes. The topic sentence in the second paragraph expands on the subject of taxation. Finally, the last two sentences discuss how people often misinterpret the tax benefits and value of municipal bonds.

From the information we've learned by using 2-T-2, let's look at the answer choices. Choice (A) is extremely broad. Do you think that a 200-word passage can adequately describe everything about municipal bonds? Of course not. (Don't forget to use our scope technique to eliminate answer choices!) By the same rationale, (D) is too broad. Choices (B) and (E) describe topics that are contained within the passage. However, these topics show up too briefly in the passage to be the main focus of the passage. In general, beware of the CBEST authors using these partial answer choices as traps on main idea questions. Did (C) appeal to you? Both paragraphs of the passage discuss the tax implications of municipal bonds. Choice (C) is the correct answer.

―――――――――○―――――――――

Here are a few more questions related to the main idea, but with a twist:

―――――――――○―――――――――

2. Which of the following would be the best title for the passage above?

    A.   Municipal Bonds

    B.   Fixed-Income Securities

    C.   Tax-Exempt Investments

    D.   Tax Benefits of Municipal Bonds

    E.   Airport Use of Revenue Bonds

Applied Strategies
On a "title" question, ask yourself: Is the title narrow enough so that a CBEST passage could adequately address the topic?

Here's How to Crack It

We've already discussed how to find the main idea by selectively reading the text (using the 2-T-2 technique). In this question, we are asked to select a title for the passage. Approach this problem the exact same way we approached Question 1. Look for an answer choice that incorporates the main idea of the passage into the title. Use scope to eliminate titles that are too broad, and eliminate titles that only speak about a very small part of the passage. Choices (A), (B), and (C) are too broad, and should be eliminated. Be careful with (C), even though it includes the word "tax," which is part of the main idea, it does not discuss municipal bonds. Choice (E) is too narrow; even though an airport bond is mentioned in the passage, it is only a detail and not part of the central theme. Choice (D) adequately titles the passage. The passage primarily talks about the tax benefits of municipal bonds, therefore (D) is the correct answer.

―――――――――○―――――――――

3. Which of the following best summarizes the passage?

A. There are many different types of municipal bonds, such as general obligation, revenue, and industrial development bonds.

B. Investors shy away from municipal bonds because they do not look past the low yield.

C. Airports often raise funds for expansion by offering revenue bonds.

D. The tax-exempt feature of municipal bonds is one reason that investors and local governments choose them.

E. Municipal bonds are the best type of investments for individuals in a high-tax bracket.

Here's How to Crack It

Same idea, just another way to ask the question—what's the point?! When you are asked to summarize a passage, first use the 2-T-2 technique. Then, try to eliminate answer choices that are out of scope or that contradict the main idea of the passage. Further, eliminate answer choices that deal with too narrow a topic. Make sure that the answer choice you select does not add anything to the passage. A correct summary will simply restate the passage in a concise and organized fashion.

Choice (A) summarizes the first three sentences of the passage quite well. However, there is much more information in the passage than what is contained in the first three sentences, so (A) is incomplete. Choice (B) is also tempting (it paraphrases parts of the second paragraph), but it does not express the central point of the passage. Choices (C) and (E) are out of scope. Choice (C) is much too general for this passage. The main focus of the passage is not about airports. Choice (E) reiterates one of the last sentences in the passage, but again, does not provide an overall summary. Choice (D) is the best answer choice. As (D) suggests, the passage mainly describes different features of municipal bonds and their tax-exempt status. Choice (D) is the correct answer.

PASSAGE STRUCTURE

Several questions on the CBEST will require you to understand the organization and structure of a reading passage. There are three types of structure questions— passage arrangement, missing sentences, and useless information. We'll tackle all three types of questions using the passage below. For now, skip the passage and start with Question 4.

Three of the most common sources of energy are fossil fuels, nuclear power, and hydroelectric power. Each of these three methods of energy production has its advantages and disadvantages.

Fossil fuels are the most widely used energy source in the United States. The burning of oil and coal derivatives releases energy that is used to boil water. The released steam turns turbines and produces energy. Today, fossil fuels are relatively abundant, which makes this form of energy production inexpensive. However, one of the problems with fossil fuels is that burning oil and coal derivatives releases chemicals that are harmful to the environment.

Nuclear power harnesses the energy contained in atoms. An atom contains protons, neutrons, and electrons. The energy released is used to convert water to steam, which in turn drives turbines. This form of energy production has proven to be even less costly than fossil fuels, but there is no foolproof method for storing all of the dangerous by-products from nuclear power plants. There is a significant fear that nuclear waste may be released into the environment, and some accidents have already occurred (the Chernobyl incident is just one example).

Hydroelectric power is produced by using the force of water to turn turbines. This is the cleanest of the three methods of energy production. _____ _____. Further, rivers with hydroelectric plants are much more vulnerable to the effects of erosion.

4. Which of the following best describes the structure of the passage?

A. The passage starts with a central theme, gives three examples, and draws a conclusion.

B. The passage starts with a question, and then explains the answer to that question.

C. The passage introduces a topic, then gives a more detailed account of the topic.

D. The passage presents an argument, then a counter-argument, then refutes the counter-argument.

E. The passage starts with a statement, which is then analyzed by several different experts.

Tip! The 2-T-2 technique will help you identify the structure of the passage.

Here's How to Crack It

You can identify the structure of the passage by using the main idea technique presented in Chapter 3—read the first two sentences, all topic sentences, and the last two sentences. Let's take a look at the passage using this 2-T-2 technique:

Three of the most common sources of energy are fossil fuels, nuclear power, and hydroelectric power. Each of these three methods of energy production has its advantages and disadvantages.

Fossil fuels are the most widely used energy source in the United States. ~~The burning of oil and coal derivatives releases energy that is used to boil water. The released steam turns turbines and produces energy. Today, fossil fuels are relatively abundant, which makes this form of energy production inexpensive. However, one of the problems with fossil fuels is that burning oil and coal derivatives releases chemicals that are harmful to the environment.~~

Nuclear power harnesses the energy contained in atoms. ~~An atom contains protons, neutrons, and electrons. The energy released is used to convert water to steam, which in turn drives turbines. This form of energy production has proven to be even less costly than fossil fuels, but~~

there is no foolproof method for storing all of the danger-ous by-products from nuclear power plants. There is a significant fear that nuclear waste may be released into the environment, and some accidents have already occurred (the Chernobyl incident is just one example).

Hydroelectric power is produced by using the force of water to turn turbines. This is the cleanest of the three methods of energy production. _____ _____. Further, rivers with hydroelectric plants are much more vulnerable to the effects of erosion.

What has been discussed? In the first two sentences, the author describes the three most common sources of energy, and mentions that there are advantages and dis-advantages to each. Then, we get a topic sentence about each type of energy source. There is no real conclusion— the last two sentences discuss the disadvantages of hydroelectric power.

Use Process of Elimination to find the correct answer. You may want to glance back at the passage if you find more than one possible answer choice. In the exam-ple above, (A) and (B) can be eliminated immediately. There is no conclusion to the passage, nor did the passage begin with a conclusion. If you glance at the next three paragraphs, you will find that no experts are mentioned. The best answer is (C); the author introduces the topic of energy sources, and then describes the advantages and disadvantages of the three most common types of energy sources.

—————————————◯—————————————

Questions requiring this sort of information can be asked in somewhat different ways. See the example on the next page.

5. Which of the following best organizes the information presented in the passage?

    A.   I.   Hypothesis
           II. Conclusion

    B.   I.   Introduction
           II. Explanation

    C.   I.   Question
           II. Analysis

    D.   I.   Quotation
           II. Examples

    E.   I.   Theory
           II. Research
           III. Discussion

Here's How to Crack It

This question is very similar to the first sample question we discussed, only the format of the answer choices is different. Using the same techniques as above, we can quickly eliminate (A), (C), (D), and (E). Choice (B) clearly describes the organizational pattern of the passage.

STRUCTURE—SENTENCES

Some structure questions will deal specifically with individual sentences contained within a passage. You may be asked to identify a sentence that is irrelevant to the overall meaning of the passage, or you may be asked to insert a sentence into a passage in order to strengthen the passage. We'll do an example of each beginning on the next page.

6. Which of the following sentences in the third paragraph is least relevant to the main idea of the third paragraph?

A. Nuclear power harnesses the energy contained in atoms.

B. An atom contains a proton, neutron, and electron.

C. The energy released is used to convert water to steam, which in turn drives turbines.

D. This form of energy production has proven to be even less costly than fossil fuels, but there is no foolproof method for storing all of the dangerous by-products from nuclear power plants.

E. There is a significant fear that nuclear waste may be released into the environment, and some accidents have already occurred (the Chernobyl incident is just one example).

Here's How to Crack It

First, go directly to the paragraph. Read the topic sentence to get an idea of the information that will be discussed. (By the way: the first sentence will never be the correct answer. The topic sentence will always be relevant to the overall meaning of the paragraph, and to the passage as a whole.) In the example above, the topic sentence of the third paragraph introduces us to nuclear power. Now read the remaining sentences in the paragraph, and try to identify a sentence that stands out as awkward or unnecessary. If you still have answer choices remaining, then use the 2-T-2 technique, and choose the sentence that is least relevant to the overall meaning of the passage. In the example above, the paragraph describes how nuclear power works, and some advantages and disadvantages to this energy source. The second sentence is out of place. Describing the properties of an atom is unnecessary to the overall meaning of the paragraph. Choice (B) is the correct answer.

If you are having trouble eliminating a sentence, try reading the paragraph without a sentence. If the paragraph does not lose any overall meaning, you've found the correct answer.

7. Which sentence, if inserted into the blank line, would best fit the overall structure of the passage?

    A.   Politicians should require more cities to use hydroelectric power, since it is the cleanest method.

    B.   However, not all communities have access to rivers, making access to hydroelectric power rare.

    C.   Some experts argue that hydroelectric power is up to 50 percent cleaner than fossil fuels.

    D.   Cities should take whatever steps are necessary to convert to hydroelectric power.

    E.   The depth of the water in the river is not a factor in the ability to turn turbines.

Here's How to Crack It

First, go straight to the paragraph that contains the missing sentence. Eliminate as many answer choices as possible before going to the entire passage. Place each answer choice into the sentence. Determine if the sentence is relevant to the paragraph. Next, make sure the sentence "fits" into the paragraph. Does the paragraph flow? Does the tone of the author remain consistent? If not, eliminate the answer choice. In our question above, (A) and (C) are not consistent with the author's tone. The entire passage has been a straightforward explanation of the pros and cons of energy sources. Inserting an argumentative sentence wouldn't fit the paragraph.

Make sure to read the sentences before and after the missing sentence in order to determine its meaning. Notice how the last sentence starts with the word "further." This sentence explains a problem with hydroelectric power. Therefore, the blank sentence should also describe a problem with hydroelectric power. Choice (B) is the only choice that discusses a drawback to hydroelectric power. Choice (B) is the correct answer.

SPECIFIC QUESTIONS

Up to this point, we've focused on questions that dealt with the overall meaning of the passage. There are also questions on the CBEST that will ask us for very specific pieces of information. These "specific" questions are often easier for students than "general" questions, since the answers can often be found directly in the passage. Some questions will ask you to find a piece of information in the passage; other questions will ask you to find the meaning of a particular word or phrase. In order to learn about specific questions, we'll use the passage below (again, skip to the questions following the passage):

There has a been a great increase in the number of different anticancer drugs for women available in the United States in the past five years. However, the U.S. Food and Drug Administration has warned that certain of these drugs may be more harmful than they are beneficial.

Tamoxifen, the first of the designer estrogen-based drugs, has been used to treat breast cancer for more than twenty-five years. This derivative of estrogen acts to starve tumors that feed on estrogen. New research suggests that Tamoxifen can not only help reduce the effect of tumors once they appear, but the drug can also decrease the risk of developing tumors by up to 45 percent. While this evidence would seem to indicate that Tamoxifen could benefit all women, additional information shows that Tamoxifen comes with several risks. The research further explained that women who took Tamoxifen developed uterine cancer twice as often as those who did not. There are additional side effects. Others died from blood clots probably triggered by the medication. Further, the effect of Tamoxifen seems to decrease over time. Research shows that its effectiveness starts to decrease after five years, making the decision about when to start taking the drug difficult. Deciding whether women should take Tamoxifen has become so complicated that the National Cancer Institute (NCI) has developed a computer program to help women determine whether they should take the drug.

8. In addition to the risk of uterine cancer, what is a potential side effect of taking Tamoxifen?

    A.   increase in tumor development of up to 45 percent

    B.   starvation

    C.   blood clots

    D.   loss of energy

    E.   none of the above

Here's How to Crack It

This first question asks us to identify a specific piece of information in the passage—a danger in the use of Tamoxifen. In attacking these specific questions, try to identify keywords that you can search for in the passage. "Tamoxifen" is certainly a keyword, although it appears so often in the passage that it may not be of tremendous help to you. Another phrase is "side effects." Probably the best key to the question is the phrase "uterine cancer." The correct answer will probably be located near this phrase. Line 11 of the passage describes the risks of uterine cancer. Two lines further down, the passage mentions the risk of blood clots. Choice (C) is the correct answer.

Tip! Use keywords to help you locate the correct answer within a passage.

Here is an additional specific question about the previous passage:

———————◯———————

9. What is the National Cancer Institute's position on Tamoxifen?

    A.   The NCI states that no one should take the drug due to its risks.

    B.   The NCI believes that only women in the late stages of breast cancer should take the drug.

    C.   The NCI is concerned about giving women the proper tools to decide whether or not Tamoxifen is right for them.

    D.   The NCI supports any drug approved by the FDA.

    E.   The NCI argues that uterine cancer is harder to treat than breast cancer.

Here's How to Crack It

This specific question gives us a great keyword to work with—the National Cancer Institute. This keyword can be found near the end of the passage. When you spot a keyword, read approximately two lines above and two lines below the line on which the keyword appears, in order to get a feel for the context in which it is mentioned. In this case, we find that there are many pros and cons to taking Tamoxifen, and that the NCI has set up a computer program to help women understand the benefits and risks. Choice (C) best paraphrases the information in the passage.

Finally, you may be asked to recognize the meaning of a particular word or phrase within a passage. To find the correct answer to these "vocabulary in context" questions, first locate the word in question. Next, read a few lines above and a few lines below the word to understand its use in the passage. Finally, be careful. CBEST authors will often ask about words that can have multiple meanings. Be sure to select the meaning that best fits the word's use *in the passage*, not the definition you know best. The following is an example using the previous passage.

———————◯———————

Applied Strategies
Be sure to read a few lines above and a few lines below the vocabulary word you are searching for in order to understand the overall meaning.

10. Which of the following is the best meaning of the word "designer" as it is used in the first sentence of the second paragraph of the passage?

A. fashionable

B. trendy

C. pure

D. altered

E. planned

Here's How to Crack It

The word "designer" can be found at the beginning of the passage, so be sure to read a few lines below the line on which it appears. Let's take a look at the answer choices. Is the drug fashionable or trendy? This is probably not the author's intention when describing the drug. Choice (C) is contradicted by the word "derivative" a few lines below. "Designer" must not mean "pure." We're left with (D) and (E). "Planned" does not fit into the passage, leaving "altered" as the remaining answer choice. The drug Tamoxifen has been modified from the natural form of estrogen, making (D) the correct answer.

RESEARCH QUESTIONS

Research questions account for approximately 10 percent of all reading questions on the CBEST. These types of questions are probably the easiest ones on the Reading Section. Most students will treat all research questions as first-pass questions. While some of these questions can be tricky, all of the information can be found in a table, graph, or passage.

There are three basic types of questions that ask you about the structure of a passage. First, questions will ask you to identify and locate information. For these questions, tables of contents and indexes are most often used. You may also be asked to find information within a section heading, book, chapter, or article. Next, CBEST authors may ask you how a passage is organized. Finally, you may be asked questions about information found in a graph or table. These questions will ask you to either find information within a given table, or to identify conclusions, generalizations, or relationships from the information presented in the table.

The most common type of passage in a structure question is an index. We will use the index below to analyze some common types of structure questions.

Use the excerpt from an index to answer the questions that follow:

Video:

       Black, 286–287
       Input, 145–147
       Insert, 150
       Output, 168–169
       Switcher:
              Distribution, 348
              Production, 348–353, 396
       Tracks, 277

Videographer, 16

Videotape recorder (VTR), 131–132

Viewfinder, 24, 46–49

Voice-over (VO), 252, 262–263, 343

11. On which pages should one look to find information about a direct video input?

A.   286–287

B.   131–132

C.   46–49

D.   145–147

E.   262–263

Here's How to Crack it

This question is an example of the most common type of research question. The question asks us to identify and locate a specific piece of information. First, take a look at the item we are asked to locate (in the example above, we're looking for keywords "direct video input"). Next, glance down the index to see if any of the keywords match topics in the index. In the question above, there aren't any matches for direct, but we do have a location for video input, found on pages 145–147. These pages are listed as (D), which is the correct answer.

These same types of questions can also be asked using a table of contents. Use the table of contents to answer the questions that follow:

Preparing for a Wedding:	
Announcing the Engagement	2–20
Budget Planning	21–25
Finding a Location	26–35
Purchasing a Wedding Dress	36–49
Ceremony Decisions	50–92
Reception Planning	93–116
Cake	117–129
Decorations	130–134
Honeymoon and Beyond	135–161
Photography	162–175

12. On what pages would you look to find information on how to reserve a site for a wedding?

   A.   162–175

   B.   21–25

   C.   26–35

   D.   130–134

   E.   2–20

Here's How to Crack It

Using the techniques described above, first identify the keywords of the information we need to find—"reserve," "site," "wedding." Next, try to find a match for one of those words. "Wedding" appears everywhere, so that isn't a big help. However, "site" is another word for "location," and "reserving a site" is similar to "choosing a location." The correct answer is (C).

PASSAGE ORGANIZATION

CBEST authors will often ask about the manner in which a topic or table of contents is arranged. Here is an example using the previous table of contents:

---

13. Which of the following best describes the organizational pattern used in the table of contents?

    A.   alphabetical

    B.   chronological

    C.   by order of importance

    D.   by cost

    E.   by category

Here's How to Crack It

Process of Elimination is key to answering questions about the organizational structure of an index or table of contents. It is fairly obvious that the topics are not organized alphabetically—eliminate (A). Choices (C) and (D) are impossible to prove, and therefore can be eliminated. Choice (B) may seem correct, because there are some topics that do seem to follow in a logical order. However, there is a better answer choice. Choice (E) breaks each topic into a different category. The book deals with the different categories of things to be done when planning a wedding. Choice (E) is the correct answer.

GRAPHS AND CHARTS

The CBEST Reading Section may use graphs and charts to ask you structure questions. The only tricky thing about graphs and charts is that the authors may leave some information blank. In this case, try to complete the information (filling in missing figures, labeling graphs) before tackling the questions. Below is an example of a reading question using a line graph.

Use the graph below to answer the question that follows.

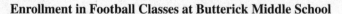

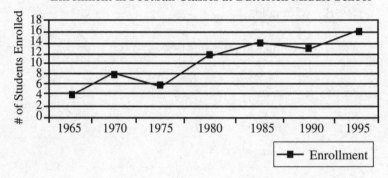

14. Between what five-year period was the increase in enrollment in football classes the greatest?

    A.   1965 to 1970

    B.   1970 to 1975

    C.   1975 to 1980

    D.   1980 to 1985

    E.   1985 to 1990

Here's How to Crack It

The question asks us to identify the time period that saw the greatest increase in enrollment. First, look at the graph, and try to identify answer choices that may be eliminated. There are decreases in enrollment between 1970 to 1975, and 1985 to 1990. Therefore, eliminate (B) and (E). Visually, you may be able to identify the correct answer. If not, find the difference between the time periods for the remaining answer choices. The correct answer is (C). There was an increase of six students during that time period.

Summary

o   When asked for the main idea, read the passage according to the 2-T-2 technique: the first two sentences, all topic sentences, and the last two sentences. Try to get a feel for the main point of the passage without having to read the entire passage.

o   Eliminate answer choices that are out of scope on main idea questions. Eliminate any title that gives a description that is too broad for the passage.

o   On specific questions, identify keywords to search for the correct answer. Read a few lines above and a few lines below in order to understand the point of the paragraph.

o   When asked to find the meaning of a vocabulary word or phrase, be sure to select the definition that is most relevant to the passage, not the most common definition.

o   Structure questions require you to understand how the passage is organized. To recognize the structure, read the passage using the 2-T-2 technique.

o   On questions that ask you to identify a page number in an index, use keywords and search the index to find one or more of your keywords. Then select the most appropriate index page based upon your remaining choices.

o   Fill in any missing information in graphs or charts in order to solve chart questions.

Chapter 5
Reading Section
Drills and Answers
and Explanations

Read the passage below and answer the question that follows.

Adverse possession is a legal principle by which a person may acquire valid title to a property owned by someone else, provided certain requirements are met. Typically, the law requires that the disseisor hold possession for an extended period of time, openly occupying the property in a hostile or non-permissive manner, and that the possession be continuous and exclusive.

1. To make this passage more clear to a general audience, the author could do which of the following?

   A. Define professional jargon, such as *disseisor*, in simpler terms.

   B. Explain other methods whereby a person can obtain property.

   C. Eliminate the description of the requirements for adverse possession.

   D. Cite the legal precedents for adverse possession.

   E. Note that the typical time requirement for adverse possession is seven years.

Read the passage below and answer the question that follows.

Law enforcement officers and traffic safety experts unanimously agree that texting while driving is always dangerous. Nevertheless, the number of people who admit to texting while driving increases every year.

2. Which of the following is suggested by the passage?

    A.   More people admit to texting while driving because it is more socially acceptable to do so.

    B.   Using a cellular phone while driving is only acceptable in emergency situations.

    C.   Texting while driving is illegal in every jurisdiction.

    D.   People who drive dangerously must have compelling reasons for doing so.

    E.   Those who text while driving may be ignoring the known risks involved.

Read this excerpt from a book index and then answer the question that follows.

3. On which pages would one be most likely to find information about popular disco artists of the 1970s?

  A.   217-18

  B.   226-29

  C.   232-35

  D.   245-50

  E.   257-59

Read the passage below and answer the question that follows.

Since the 1980s, education experts have increasingly acknowledged the importance of differentiated instruction geared toward different learning modalities. Research has shown that individual students respond differently to visual, auditory, and tactile input. Contemporary teachers have largely embraced this research, and attempt to incorporate different modalities into their lessons in order to better reach their students.

4. One of the main points in the passage is that

A. prior to the 1980s, no one acknowledged the importance of differentiated instruction.

B. lessons that do not incorporate different learning modalities will be largely ineffective.

C. education theories tend to vary frequently over time.

D. contemporary teachers have learned from studies that support the use of differentiated instruction.

E. education theories prior to the 1980s supported only one modality of teaching and learning.

Read the passage below and answer the four questions that follow.

Since the early 2000s, digital music consumption has dramatically increased, while physical album sales have decreased by more than 70%. The interest in digital music has largely been fueled by the appearance of peer-to-peer file sharing services in the early 2000s, which have since paved the way for immensely successful online retailers that sell music in digital formats. _____ services have allowed consumers to build their music collections one song at a time, instead of having to purchase full albums.

(1) Another effect of these digital music services is the growing popularity of independent artists. (2) Previously, the only way for artists to gain exposure was through physical album sales and radio play, which typically required the support of a successful record company. (3) Today, the digital music market allows consumers to discover artists that may not have the benefit of any record company resources. (4) Although physical music sales have declined, many music fans are still willing to pay top dollar to attend concert performances. (5) Some artists have gained millions of fans simply by uploading a self-produced video to the internet. (6) _____, we may see a trend toward digital music being offered for free, which would come with the benefit of increased audiences of loyal fans.

5. Which words, if inserted *in order* in the blank spaces in the first and second paragraphs, would provide the most clarity in the sequence of the author's ideas?

   A. Some; Before

   B. Other; Quickly

   C. Those; Afterward

   D. All; Later

   E. These; Soon

6. Which of the following best defines the term exposure, as it appears in the second paragraph of the passage?

   A. Vulnerability

   B. Publicity

   C. Lack of privacy

   D. Access to company resources

   E. Commercials

7. Upon reviewing the essay, the author noticed a sentence that should be omitted. Which of the following numbered sentences has the least relevance to the main idea of the passage?

   A. Sentence 1

   B. Sentence 2

   C. Sentence 3

   D. Sentence 4

   E. Sentence 5

8. From the passage, which of the following can be inferred about the music industry prior to the early 2000s?

   A. Independent artists did not have any significant presence in the music industry.

   B. Physical album sales were continually increasing.

   C. Digital music formats did not exist.

   D. The primary way to purchase music was to buy complete albums.

   E. Physical media formats had inferior sound quality compared to today's digital formats.

Read the passage below and answer the question that follows.

Independent practice, such as homework, is an important component of student learning. It allows students the opportunity to reinforce skills and knowledge without the guidance of the teacher.

9. Which of the following is implied by the passage?

A. Students will struggle to learn without the guidance of the teacher.

B. Teachers do not assign as much homework as they should.

C. Homework is most useful when it integrates multiple learning modalities.

D. Students should do at least some regular independent practice to reinforce their learning.

E. Homework is unnecessary if the teacher has provided sufficient guided instruction.

Read the passage below and answer the question that follows.

Credential candidates at Madison College must meet all of the following requirements during their internships.

- Early Childhood workshop (required during first or second semester)

- At least 500 total service hours in any primary grades (grades 1-3)

- At least 500 total service house in any intermediate grades (grades 4-6)

- Three courses in chosen emphasis (Physical Education, Fine Arts, or Science)

- Hold a valid State Substitute Certificate, **or**, passing scores on **both** the Teacher Competency Exam and the Subject Qualification Exam.

10. Which of the following academic plans would meet the requirements at Madison College?

   A.   Service hours (400 in grade 2, 100 in grade 3, 500 in grade 4); early childhood workshop in first semester; Fine Arts courses 412 and 415; Science course 310; passing scores on Teacher Competency Exam and Subject Qualification Exam

   B.   Service hours (300 in grade 1, 425 in grade 2, 400 in grade 4); early childhood workshop in second semester; Physical Education courses 301, 305, and 306; State Substitute Certificate

   C.   Service hours (550 in grade 1, 580 in grade 5); State Substitute Certificate; early childhood workshop in first semester; Fine Arts courses 305, 308, and 312

   D.   Service hours (250 in grade 2, 255 in grade 3, 500 in grade 6); early childhood workshop in third semester; Science courses 305, 310, and 407; passing scores on Teacher Competency Exam and Subject Qualification Exam

   E.   Service hours (800 in grade 2); early childhood workshop in second semester; Fine Arts courses 305, 309, and 315; Science course 409; passing score on Subject Qualification Exam.

Read the passage below and answer the questions that follow.

(1) President Theodore Roosevelt signed the Food and Drug Act in 1906. (2) The Act included restrictions on additives that are "filthy" or "injurious to health," and led to the creation of the Food and Drug Administration (FDA) in 1927. (3) However, after an incident of mass fatality involving a drug called Elixir Sulfanilamide, it was clear that additional regulatory authority was needed. (4) The newer Food, Drug, and Cosmetic Act was signed by President Franklin Roosevelt in 1938. (5) This law required safety reviews of all new drugs, and also banned the use of false claims in labeling.

11. In relation to the passage, Sentence 3 does which of the following?

A. It speculates that lives would have been saved if the 1938 act had been passed sooner.

B. It describes the first mass tragedy involving pharmaceuticals in the United States.

C. It implies that the Act signed in 1938 was mostly indistinguishable from the one signed in 1906.

D. It suggests a reason for the creation of the Food, Drug, and Cosmetic Act in 1938.

E. It supports the author's argument that expanded regulation is needed in the future.

12. Which of the following sentences, if inserted after Sentence 5, would best fit the tone and sequence of ideas in this passage?

A. Another regulatory agency formed in the 1900s was the Federal Highway Administration.

B. It was the first Act to explicitly grant authority to the FDA to oversee the safety of food, drugs, and cosmetics.

C. These regulations are really helpful for consumers nowadays.

D. The Food, Drug and Cosmetic act defined and regulated specific food coloring additives, such as "Yellow no. 5."

E. A cosmetic is a product intended to alter or improve a person's appearance.

13. This passage would be most likely to appear in which of the following?

    A.   A brief essay discussing regulations in US food and drug industries

    B.   A biography of President Theodore Roosevelt

    C.   A manual of food and drug legislation

    D.   A dissertation about the Food and Drug Act of 1906

    E.   An argument about the benefits of safety regulations

Use the chart below to answer the question that follows.

GlobalNet Solutions Inc.

Employee Survey Results

Job Status:

Full time: 74%

Part time: 26%

Gender of Employees:

Male: 57%

Female: 43%

Average employee income: $67,292

Highest individual employee income: $156,034

Employees by Department:

Executive: 154

Accounting: 1,238

Sales: 3,952

IT Support: 510

---

14. All of the following can be determined from the information shown in the chart EXCEPT:

A. Some employees earn less than $67,292 in income.

B. A greater percentage of employees work full time than work part time.

C. Full time employees earn higher income than part time employees.

D. The Executive department has the fewest employees of any department listed.

E. There are more male employees than female employees.

Read the passage below and answer the question that follows.

At Taft Middle School, students have access to the shared computer lab for 40 minutes per week. Teachers report that, during this time, they teach typing and word processing skills. In order to learn the more advanced skills that will be required of them in tomorrow's job market, our students need to spend more time with technology and a staff member who is capable of teaching these concepts. Clearly, an increase in the technology budget is well warranted.

15. Which of the following functions does the first sentence perform?

    A.   It is an expression of the author's opinion.

    B.   It highlights a contrast with the final sentence.

    C.   It includes an unnecessary detail that distracts from the author's purpose.

    D.   It sets the author's tone using vivid imagery.

    E.   It provides information to support the author's conclusion.

Read the following passage and answer the question that follows.

A calorie (also called kilocalorie or nutritional calorie) is the approximate amount of energy needed to raise the temperature of one gram of water by one degree Celsius.

16. The preceding excerpt would be LEAST likely to appear in which of the following?

    A. An introductory text on physical science

    B. A glossary of scientific terms

    C. A beginner's guide to nutrition

    D. A brief editorial discussing the causes and effects of obesity in the United States

    E. An encyclopedia

READING DRILLS ANSWERS AND EXPLANATIONS

1. **A** This would be the most effective way *to make this passage more clear to a general audience.* Since a general audience would typically not understand specific legal terminology such as *disseisor*, it would help to provide definitions for these terms. Choice (B) is not the correct answer. The addition of *other methods* could be relevant to this topic, but it would not improve the audience's understanding of the existing sentences. This change would not *make this passage more clear to a general audience.* Eliminate (B). Choice (C) is not the correct answer. Eliminating the discussion of requirements would serve to eliminate much of the specialized vocabulary in the passage, but it would not help a general audience to understand what adverse possession is. The description of requirements should be clarified or simplified, not eliminated. Eliminate (C). Choice (D) is not the correct answer. Legal precedents may be of interest to a profession in the legal or real estate industries, but this information would not serve to *make this passage more clear to a general audience.* Eliminate (D). Choice (E) is not the correct answer. The addition of this detail could be relevant to this topic, but it would not improve the audience's understanding of the existing sentences. This change would not *make this passage more clear to a general audience.* Eliminate (E).

2. **E** The statement that *law enforcement officers and safety experts unanimously agree* supports the idea that there are *known risks* to texting while driving. The fact that people are still texting while driving suggests that these people *may be ignoring* the risks. Note the use of "may be" in the answer, which means that the answer is not too extreme. Choice (A) is not the correct answer. The passage does not speculate as to whether or not it is *socially acceptable* to text while driving. Eliminate (A). Choice (B) is not the correct answer. The passage does not indicate that *emergency situations* are considered. Also note the more general situation of *using a cellular phone,* while the passage is specifically about *texting.* Eliminate (B). Choice (C) is not the correct answer. The passage does not reveal the legality of texting while driving. Note that *law enforcement officers* is irrelevant to this answer; their opinion does not necessarily mean that texting while driving is *illegal.* Eliminate (C). Choice (D) is not the correct answer. The passage does not speculate as to the *reasons* that people text while driving. Also note the use of the word *must*, which makes this answer extreme. Eliminate (D).

3. **C** The category of "Disco" is where one could find information about popular disco artists of the 1970s. The other categories list other types of music. Choices (A), (B), (D), and (E) refer to Pop music, Teen pop, Alternative, and Pop Rock, respectively. Since these genres are different from Disco, these choices should be eliminated.

4. **D** This answer is best supported by the final sentence, which states that contemporary teachers have *embraced this research, and attempt to incorporate different modalities into their lessons.* Choice (A) is not the correct answer. This answer uses extreme language. The passage does not state that *no one acknowledged the importance of differentiated instruction.* This language is much stronger than the language in the passage. Choice (B) is not the correct answer. This answer uses extreme language. The passage does not indicate that certain types of language will be *largely ineffective.* This

language is much stronger than the language in the passage. Choice (C) is not the correct answer. This answer uses extreme language. Although the passage indicates a change in education theory, this indicates only one change, and there is no indication that the theories *tend to vary frequently*. This language is much stronger than the language in the passage. Choice (E) is not the correct answer. Although the passage reveals a change toward acknowledging different learning modalities, there is no evidence that the former theories *supported only one modality*. This language is much stronger than the language in the passage.

5. **E**   The first blank refers directly to the *peer-to-peer file sharing services* and *online retailers* mentioned in the previous sentence. Look for a word that continues the thought. *These* works best. The second blank refers to a prediction: *we may see a trend toward digital music being offered for free.* Look for a word that applies to the future. *Soon* is the best choice, and *Later* may be somewhat acceptable; however, in considering both blanks, (E) is the best answer. Don't forget to use Process of Elimination on this question. Choice (A) is not the correct answer. *Some* might be adequate for the first blank. However, *before* is a reversal of what works in the second blank. The second blank needs to refer to the future, not the past. Eliminate (A). Choice (B) is not the correct answer. The word *other* would indicate a contrast. However, we want a word that indicates agreement with the previous sentence. For the second blank, *quickly* does not have the same meaning as *soon* in the context of the sentence. Eliminate (B). Choice (C) is not the correct answer. The difference between *those* and *these* is fairly subtle; in general, *these* indicates a "proximity" to the speaker or idea, whereas *those* indicates more distance. Since the referenced *services* are directly in the previous sentence, *these* is better. Additionally, the word *afterward* does not fit the meaning of the second blank, since the blank refers to a prediction for the future, while *afterward* should refer directly to an event in the preceding sentence. Eliminate (C). Choice (D) is not the correct answer. *All* is too extreme for the first blank. The passage does not refer to *all* music services; rather, the blank refers specifically to the digital music services mentioned in the preceding sentence. *Later* may be somewhat acceptable; however, in considering both blanks, this is not the best answer. Eliminate (D).

6. **B**   This answer is supported by the statement that exposure is gained through *physical album sales and record play,* which indicates that it may increase the author's success or popularity. Additionally, the following two sentences states that digital music *allows consumers to discover artists, and that some artists have gained millions of fans* through the use of digital media. The word *publicity* best defines *exposure* in the context of the passage. Choice (A) is not the correct answer. This is a trap answer based on an alternate definition of *exposure*. The passage indicates that exposure is gained through *physical album sales and record play,* which would indicate a positive outcome, rather than a negative outcome such as *vulnerability*. Eliminate (A). Choice (C) is not the correct answer. This is a trap answer based on an alternate definition of *exposure*. The passage indicates that exposure is gained through *physical album sales and record play,* which would indicate a positive outcome, rather than a negative outcome such as *lack of privacy*. Eliminate (C). Choice (D) is not the correct answer. This is a trap answer based on the recycled language *company resources*. The passage indicates that artists can gain popularity without company resources, as illustrated by the example

of artists gaining *millions of fans simply by uploading a self-produced video to the internet.* Eliminate (D). Choice (E) is not the correct answer. This is a trap answer based on a potential misreading of the passage. The passage does not refer to direct advertising such as *commercials*, but rather, the popularity gained through *physical album sales and radio play,* as well as *the digital music market.* The word *exposure* in this context most clearly refers to the artists' popularity or success. *Commercials* does not fit here. Eliminate (E).

7. **D** Since the passage is mainly concerned with the increasing popularity of digital music, mentioning concert performances would be irrelevant. This information does not have a meaningful connection to the rest of the passage, and should be omitted. Choice (A) is not the correct answer. Sentence 1 is an appropriate transition between the two paragraphs: paragraph 1 discusses one "effect" being that *physical album sales have decreased by more than 70%,* and paragraph 2 discusses the *growing popularity of independent artists.* Eliminate (A). Choice (B) is not the correct answer. Sentence 2 is relevant to the discussion of the *growing popularity of independent artists.* This paragraph contrasts the historical necessity of *physical album sales and radio play* with the ability of today's consumers *to discover artists that may not have the benefit of any record company resources.* Eliminate (B). Choice (C) is not the correct answer. Sentence 3 is relevant to the discussion of the *growing popularity of independent artists.* This paragraph contrasts the historical necessity of *physical album sales and radio play* with the ability of today's consumers *to discover artists that may not have the benefit of any record company resources.* Eliminate (C). Choice (E) is not the correct answer. Sentence 5 is relevant to the discussion of the *growing popularity of independent artists.* The action of *uploading a self-produced video to the internet* is mentioned as an example of digital music services contributing to the success of independent artists. Eliminate (E).

8. **D** The statement that primarily supports this answer is that digital music services *have allowed consumers to build their music collections one song at a time, instead of having to purchase full albums.* Since consumers "had" to purchase full albums, it follows that this was the *primary way to purchase music.* Choice (A) is not the correct answer. Although the passage refers to the *growing popularity of independent artists,* there is no indication that *independent artists did not have any significant presence in the music industry.* In other words, we do not know how popular independent artists were in this period; we only know that their popularity is now *growing.* This answer is much stronger than the language in the passage. Eliminate (A). Choice (B) is not the correct answer. Although the passage states that *physical album sales have decreased by more than 70%,* there is no evidence that the sales were *continually increasing* before this time. The passage does not reveal the trend of physical album sales prior to the early 2000s, only that there has been a decrease since then. Eliminate (B). Choice (C) is not the correct answer. The passage discusses *peer-to-peer file sharing services* and *online retailers,* but does not reveal the origin of digital music itself. It is quite possible that digital music formats existed for a long time; the passage only discusses the increased popularity of related services since the early 2000s. Eliminate (C). Choice (E) is not the correct answer. This answer states that the sound quality was *inferior;* however, there is no such comparison made in the passage. The passage does not discuss *sound quality* of music formats, only popularity. Eliminate (E).

9.   **D**   The text that best supports this answer is the statement that *independent practice… is an important component of student learning.* The passage then continues with additional reasoning in favor of independent practice. Select (D). Choice (A) is not the correct answer. The passage does not indicate that *students will struggle to learn without the guidance of the teacher.* Eliminate (A). Choice (B) is not the correct answer. Although the passage states that independent practice is *an important component of student learning,* the author does not express thoughts on how much homework teachers *do,* or *should,* assign. Eliminate (B). Choice (C) is not the correct answer. The passage does not make reference to *multiple learning modalities.* Eliminate (C). Choice (E) is not the correct answer. The passage does not indicate circumstances in which homework may be *unnecessary.* Eliminate (E).

10.   **C**   This plan would meet all of the requirements listed. The best approach for this type of question might be to read each requirement one at a time, and eliminate answers that do NOT meet the requirement. Choice (A) is not the correct answer. This plan does not meet the requirement in the fourth bullet (regarding courses). This candidate would take two Fine Arts courses, and one Science course, but these would be from two different emphases, and the requirement is to take *three courses in chosen emphasis.* Choice (B) is not the correct answer. This plan does not meet the requirement in the third bullet (regarding hours in intermediate grades). This candidate will have completed only 400 of the 500 required hours in intermediate grades. Choice (D) is not the correct answer. This plan does not meet the requirement in the first bullet (regarding the Early Childhood Workshop). This candidate will have taken the workshop in his or her third semester; however, the requirement is to take the workshop *during the first or second semester.* Choice (E) is not the correct answer. This plan does not meet the requirements in either the third or fifth bullets. This candidate will have completed zero of the 500 required service hours in intermediate grades, and he or she will not have passed the Teacher Competency Exam.

11.   **D**   This sentence suggests an event that led to the creation of the Food, Drug, and Cosmetic Act in 1938. The sentence states that *additional regulatory authority was needed,* which indicates that this was a catalyst for the expanded regulation in 1938. Choice (A) is not the correct answer. Although the passage indicates that Elixir Sulfanilamide *killed over 100 people,* the author does not hypothesize that *lives would have been saved if the 1938 act had been passed sooner.* This is a speculation that is not reflected in the text of the passage. Eliminate (A). Choice (B) is not the correct answer. The passage does not indicate that the incident with Elixir Sulfanilamide was the *first mass tragedy involving pharmaceuticals in the United States.* There could have been other previous events. Eliminate (B). Choice (C) is not the correct answer. The passage does not suggest that the *Act signed in 1938 was mostly indistinguishable from the one signed in 1906.* Although they may have had similarities, the word "indistinguishable" is far too strong. Eliminate (C). Choice (E) is not the correct answer. The author does not reveal his/her feelings about the regulations, nor suggest that *expanded regulation is needed in the future.* Eliminate (E).

12. B To approach this question, look for an answer that best matches the passage in content, vocabulary, tone, and level of detail. Choice (B) fits well in the context of a brief summary of the legislation discussed. Choice (A) is not the correct answer. Since the passage is about *food and drug* regulations, a sentence about the Federal Highway Administration would be off topic. Eliminate (A). Choice (C) is not the correct answer. The informal vocabulary in this sentence (*really, nowadays*) does not match the moderately academic tone of the passage. Eliminate (C). Choice (D) is not the correct answer. This sentence adds a precise detail that would not fit well in the scope of the passage, which is structured as a brief overview. Eliminate (D). Choice (E) is not the correct answer. Since the passage is mainly concerned with providing a brief overview of the legislation discussed, the definition of *cosmetic* is not very relevant and would be out of place. Eliminate (E).

13. A A *brief essay discussing regulations in US food and drug industries* would fit the content, tone, and scope of the passage. Choice (B) is not the correct answer. The information in sentences 3-5 regards legislation under a different president. It would not be relevant in a biography of Theodore Roosevelt. Eliminate (B). Choice (C) is not the correct answer. The passage is structured as a brief overview. A manual of legislation would have significantly more detail. Eliminate (C). Choice (D) is not the correct answer. The passage is structured as a brief overview. A dissertation would have significantly more detail. Eliminate (D). Choice (E) is not the correct answer. This passage does not present an argument on the matter of safety regulations. It is a brief overview of some specific food and drug legislation. Eliminate (E).

14. C The chart does not reveal information about full time employee income compared with part-time employee income. Note the word EXCEPT in the question stem. Select (C), since this information is NOT shown in the chart. Choice (A) is not the correct answer. See that the average income is provided, as well as the highest income. It is therefore possible to determine that at least some employees earn less than the average. In other words, if some employees earn higher than the average, then it must be true that some employees earn lower than the average. This confirms that some employees earn less than $67,292 in income. Eliminate (A). Choice (B) is not the correct answer. See the portion of the chart that lists "Job Status," which indicates that 74% of employees work full time, and 26% work part time. This confirms that a greater percentage of employees work full time than work part time. Eliminate (B). Choice (D) is not the correct answer. See the portion of the chart that lists "Employees by Department." Of the departments listed, the Executive department has the fewest employees. Eliminate (D). Choice (E) is not the correct answer. See the portion of the chart that lists "Gender of Employees," which states that 57% of employees are male and 43% are female. This confirms that there are more male employees than female employees. Eliminate (E).

15. E The information that students use the computer lab *for 40 minutes per week* supports the argument that *students need to spend more time with technology,* and the conclusion that *an increase in the technology budget* is well warranted. Choice (A) is not the correct answer. The first sentence is not an opinion; rather, it is a statement of information. The author does not state his/her feelings about the situation until later in the paragraph. Eliminate (A). Choice (B) is not the correct answer. The

first sentence does not *highlight a contrast with the final sentence*. Rather, it is offered in support of the final sentence, and the argument that students need more access to technology. Eliminate (B). Choice (C) is not the correct answer. The information that students use the computer lab *for 40 minutes per week* supports the argument that *students need to spend more time with technology.* It is not *an unnecessary detail that distracts from the author's purpose.* Eliminate (C). Choice (D) is not the correct answer. The statement that *students have access to the shared computer lab for 40 minutes per week* would not be considered vivid imagery. Rather, it is straightforward information. Eliminate (D).

16. **D**   The definition of a calorie would be out of place in a brief editorial discussing the causes and effects of obesity in the United States. Such an editorial would be expected to be more general in breadth, without going into the level of detail that would include scientific definitions. Since this would be LEAST likely to include the excerpt, select (D). Choice (A) is not the correct answer. The definition of a calorie would be useful in an introductory text on physical science. Such a text would be reasonably expected to explain the terms that are used. Eliminate (A). Choice (B) is not the correct answer. The definition of a calorie would be useful in a glossary of scientific terms. Eliminate (B). Choice (C) is not the correct answer. The definition of a calorie would be useful in a beginner's guide to nutrition. Note that the calorie is also referred to as a "nutritional calorie" in the excerpt. A nutrition guide would explain how calories are relevant to nutrition. Eliminate (C). Choice (E) is not the correct answer. The definition of a calorie is likely to be found in an encyclopedia, under the entry "calorie" or related topics. Eliminate (E).

Part III
Cracking the Mathematics Section

Sounds somewhat intimidating, doesn't it? The Mathematics Section. When you consider the number of topics that could appear on a math test, your head may start to spin. Not to worry. The writers of the CBEST focus on a limited number of topics, all of which will be covered in detail in the next three chapters. According to the writers of the test, the CBEST "assesses basic skills and concepts that are important in performing the job of an educator." Not sure what this means? Let's take a look.

WHAT THE CBEST TESTS

The CBEST Mathematics Section contains 50 multiple-choice questions. There is no specific time limit, as you have four hours to complete the entire exam. We recommend, however, that you spend about eighty minutes on the Mathematics Section (some students will find they need to adjust this time—see Chapter 2 for a review on pacing). The writers of the CBEST test three major skill areas:

1. **Estimation, Measurement, and Statistical Principles**
   30% (approximately 15 questions)
   • Standard units of length, temperature, weight, and capacity
   • Measure length and perimeter
   • Estimation of answers using arithmetic
   • Statistical principles such as averages, ratios, and proportions
   • Basic probability
   • Interpret meaning of standardized test scores

2. **Computation and Problem Solving**
   35% (approximately 17–18 questions)
   • Basic operations of addition, subtraction, multiplication, and division with integers, fractions, decimals, percentages, positive, and negative numbers.
   • Solve arithmetic word problems.
   • Solve algebraic problems.
   • Determine whether enough information is given to solve math problems.
   • Recognize multiple methods of solving a word problem.

3. **Numerical and Graphic Relationships**
   35% (approximately 17–18 questions)
   • Recognize relationships in numerical data.
   • Recognize the position of numbers in relation to each other.
   • Use the relations less than, greater than, or equal to and their associated symbols to express a numerical relationship.
   • Identify numbers, formulas, and mathematical expressions that are equivalent.
   • Understand basic logical connectives.

The CBEST Mathematics Section will test you on topics that you may not have studied for several years! We'll get you caught up in the chapters ahead.

- Identify or specify a missing entry from a table of data.
- Use information presented in tables, spreadsheets, and graphs to solve math problems.

You need to answer approximately 60% of the questions correctly in order to pass the Mathematics Section of the CBEST.

WHAT THE CBEST DOESN'T TEST

The CBEST does not test any math you may have taken in college—no complex statistics, linear algebra, or calculus. In fact, most of the material tested on the CBEST was covered in your basic high school math classes. Even the geometry that is tested is very basic (in Chapter 5 we cover all the geometry you need)—no proofs, no theorems, no complex figures.

You won't see any complex math questions from trigonometry, calculus, or advanced statistics.

We aren't saying that the Mathematics Section should be easy—many CBEST test takers have not taken a math class in five, ten, maybe twenty years. If you haven't had math in a long time, pay close attention to the information presented in the upcoming chapters. It may take some time to relearn this information.

> ### NO CALCULATOR
>
> Calculators are not allowed on the test. To prepare for test day make sure to practice completing the problems without a calculator. Some of the techniques covered will help you with this.

POE—MATHEMATICS STYLE

In Chapter 2, and in the reading chapters, we discussed the key technique to eliminating answer choices—Process of Elimination. POE also works very well on the Mathematics Section. As we go through the examples in this book, you may find that we aren't using traditional methods to solve a problem. We won't cite rules of advanced mathematics. We'll be showing you how to use the answer choices to work your way through the problem.

ELIMINATION BY BALLPARKING

Take a look at the following question:

> The area of a gymnasium floor is 3,675 square feet. If the basketball court covers 2,100 square feet, what percent of the gymnasium floor does the basketball court occupy?

If you aren't sure how to set up this question, what would you do? You'd probably have to leave it blank and move on to another question. Without any answer choices, guessing doesn't really work, does it? Well, you could choose a number, and hope for the best. (If you aren't sure how to do a percent question, don't worry. We will review percent questions in detail in Chapter 5.)

On the CBEST, they give you five answer choices to choose from. At worst, you would have a one in five chance of getting the question correct. Let's take a look at the question again, this time with answer choices:

> The area of a gymnasium floor is 3,675 square feet. If the basketball court covers 2,100 square feet, approximately what percent of the gymnasium floor does the basketball court occupy?
>
> A.   14 percent
>
> B.   43 percent
>
> C.   50 percent
>
> D.   57 percent
>
> E.   74 percent

At first glance, this may not seem very different from our original problem. However, we now have a lot more to work with—the five answer choices. Sure, we could make a guess right now, and we'd have a one in five chance of getting the question correct. But let's not stop there. Let's see what the answer choices tell us. The first thing you need to ask is:

Does the Answer Choice Make Sense?

The basketball court covers 2,100 square feet out of a possible 3,675 square feet. Try to picture this in your head. Would the basketball court only take up a very small portion of the gymnasium? Would it take up half? More than half? If you estimate, you can tell that 2,100 square feet is more than half the total 3,675 square feet.

Proven Techniques
Ballparking is a tried-and-true Princeton Review technique that will help you tackle tough math problems quickly. At the very least, Ballparking enables you to eliminate unrealistic answer choices efficiently.

Eliminate Answer Choices That Are Out of the Ballpark

Okay, we know that the basketball court will take up more than half the space in the gymnasium. If we think about this in terms of percentages, we know that the basketball court covers more than 50 percent. Look at (A), (B), and (C). We know that these cannot be correct. So what should we do? Eliminate them! Now, we will choose between (D) and (E)—a 50 percent chance of getting the question correct. This is much better than the original one in five chance. (If you chose (D), you were correct.)

Ballparking is a tool for more than just percentage questions. It can be used for most mathematics questions on the CBEST. In fact, once you read a problem, the first thing you should ask yourself is "Do the answer choices make sense?" You'll find that you can eliminate many incorrect answer choices without doing numerous calculations. You may wonder why the CBEST authors include answer choices that we can eliminate using Ballparking. You can also eliminate partial choices, which CBEST authors often include, and which provide a common trap that students often fall into. Here is an example of a question involving partial answer choices:

Eliminate answer choices on the Math Section by Ballparking the correct answer.

> Brian has $250 a month in spending money. If Brian spends
> 20 percent on movies, and 15 percent of the remaining
> amount on baseball games, how much money does Brian
> have to spend after movies and baseball games?
>
> A. $30.00
>
> B. $50.00
>
> C. $80.00
>
> D. $163.50
>
> E. $170.00

Before we go straight to calculating the answer, let's Ballpark. Brian is starting with $250, and we need to find out how much money he will have after movies and baseball games. Let's approximate. Is he spending over half his money? No. Thus, we should be able to eliminate (A), (B), and (C).

Here is how the CBEST writers incorporate partial answer choices into a question. This question requires several steps. Let's take the information we are given one step at a time.

Brian spends 20 percent of his money on movies. 20 percent of $250.00 = $50.00. Notice that answer choice (B) is a partial answer choice. If you lost track of what you needed to solve, you'd see that $50.00 number in your scratch work. However, we aren't done with this question!

Next, he spends 15 percent of the remaining amount at baseball games. The remaining amount is also a concept that CBEST writers love to use. What is the remaining amount? Brian started with $250.00; now, after spending $50.00, the remaining amount is $200.00. Thus, we need to find 15 percent of $200.00 (not of the original $250.00). 15 percent of $200.00 = $30.00. Notice again that this is a partial answer choice—eliminate (A).

Our final step is to find the amount of money Brian has left. He started with $250.00, spent $50.00 on movies, and $30.00 on baseball games. If we subtract, we find

$$
\begin{array}{r}
\$250.00 \\
-\ \$50.00 \\
-\ \underline{\$30.00} \\
=\ \$170.00
\end{array}
$$

(E) is the correct answer. Why did the CBEST writers include three answer choices that we were able to eliminate immediately? Because they wanted to provide partial answer choice traps. We already mentioned how (A) and (B) are answer choice traps. (C) is the total amount that Brian spent on the two activities. CBEST writers want to give you the opportunity to select a number that you've probably written down.

Can Partial Answer Choices Help You?

Absolutely. Because partial answer choices will appear on many of the mathematics questions on the CBEST, you need to learn to take advantage of them. First, if you recognize a partial answer choice as you are going through the problem, it probably means that you are doing the question correctly. Keep working! Second, it is generally a safe bet to eliminate any number you come up with as you are working through the steps of a problem. This will help you eliminate more answer choices.

When Should You Use Ballparking?

All the time. Even if you are absolutely sure how to set up a problem, evaluating the answer choices will give you some clues. Ballparking helps bring some clarity to a problem before you work too hard to find the exact answer. Ask yourself, "Do the answer choices make sense?" If they don't, eliminate them. If you find that your calculations lead you to one of these answer choices, you will know you've made an error. Take a step back, reread the problem, and start again.

Applied Strategies
Even if you aren't sure how to solve a math question, eliminate as many answer choices as possible by Ballparking.

Common Sense Is Your Friend

Students often get so caught up trying to solve a problem that they simply forget to think. If you have a problem, and aren't sure of the specific formula or the exact method to solve the question, take a step back. Start by looking at the answer choices, and try to Ballpark.

Even if you have no idea how to do a problem, don't simply guess and move on. Ballparking is most essential when you don't know how to solve a problem. In the previous examples, we demonstrated the value of being an intelligent guesser. The difference between guessing from among two or three possible choices, as opposed to five, will greatly affect your final mathematics score. Ballparking will help you to avoid careless errors, eliminate partial answer traps, and improve your chances of guessing correctly.

TAKING THE CBEST MATHEMATICS TEST

As we discussed in Chapter 2, there is no order of difficulty presented in the Mathematics Section. It is perfectly natural to start with question number one, then do question number two, question number three, and so on. However, as you proceed through the test, you will find that some questions are harder than others. You will want to maximize your time and effort on the easier questions, and spend less time on the harder questions.

NO ONE QUESTION MAY BEAT YOU

On most tests, there is always that one question that seems to haunt you. No matter how hard you work, you just can't seem to get it right. There are a number of reasons for this: You can't exactly remember the formula, you are miscalculating, or maybe it's just a mental block. We understand how frustrating this can be, especially when deep down inside you just know you can do the problem. Some students will spend unlimited time on a question that stumps them, just to "prove" to themselves they can do it.

Unfortunately, this stubbornness can really hurt your overall score. Precious minutes pass, leaving you rushed to complete the remaining questions. At some point, you will probably need to let a question go. Don't fret. You may have lost that battle, but you can still win the war. In fact, this is so important that we've designed a technique to help you avoid this trap.

Tailor your test toward your strengths—if you love algebra questions, make sure you have time to solve all algebra questions. If you hate geometry, save those as second-pass questions.

FIRST PASS, SECOND PASS

As we've mentioned, you need to get about 60 percent of the mathematics questions correct in order to pass the section. This leaves you with a lot of room to pick and choose the questions you want to spend time on. Of course, regardless of how many questions you do, you will be registering an answer for every question. By focusing on the questions you can handle, you will improve your accuracy and your score. Here is how to use this technique:

On your first pass, start at the beginning and do every problem that, after reading it, makes sense to you right away. If you get to a question that you have no idea how to solve, then you should leave the question and move on. In order to keep track of these questions, so you can come back to them later, put a little mark next to the question number on your bubble sheet. Once you complete the section and answer all the first pass questions, you'll then go back to the questions that you've skipped.

Why go through all this trouble? We want to make sure that you are using your time to maximum efficiency. If you find that you can't answer all of the mathematics questions in the time you have, at least you've answered all the problems you know you can do.

Sometimes, when you start your second pass, you'll figure out exactly how to get one of the problems that stumped you on the first pass. Of course, there may still be some questions that, no matter how many times you read them, seem impossible to answer. But remember, no matter how bad a question may be, under no circumstances should you leave it blank. Let's say that one more time:

> **You may not leave a problem blank!**

There is a big difference between leaving a question for later, and simply leaving a question blank. If you have no idea how to do a second-pass question, be sure to use Ballparking as a technique to eliminate answer choices. Eliminate what you can, and then select an answer choice. Before you turn in your bubble sheet, check to make sure that you have selected an answer for every question.

Avoid careless mistakes by writing down all calculations.

MATH ON PAPER, NOT IN YOUR HEAD

If you haven't taken a math class for years, or if you usually rely on a calculator or spreadsheet to do your work, it may take you a while to get comfortable working with numbers again. It is crucial that you do all your work on paper, and not in your head. Writing down your calculations will do more than improve your accuracy—you'll be able to eliminate partial answer choices based on the numbers you've written in your test booklet as you go through the steps for each problem.

There is no need to worry about keeping your test booklet clean. In fact, you should be using your test booklet constantly. Whenever you eliminate an answer choice, cross the answer out, leaving no doubt that it is an incorrect answer choice. That way, if you need to guess, you'll clearly know which answer choices remain.

PRACTICE CORRECTLY

It is important that you practice these math problems in the same way you will be taking the test. Don't practice using a calculator. Be sure to do calculations in this book, and to mark off incorrect answer choices. It takes a while to adapt, and you don't want to be trying these things for the first time during the actual test. The two tests in the back of this book should provide excellent practice.

Summary

Here are some general points to remember throughout the entire Mathematics Section:

o   The CBEST Mathematics Section contains 50 questions on only a few areas of math:
    • Estimation, Measurement, and Statistical Principles—30%
    • Computation and Problem Solving—35%
    • Numerical and Graphic Relationships—35%

o   Complicated math topics, such as trigonometry, calculus, proofs, and theorems are not tested on the CBEST.

o   A type of POE, called Ballparking, enables you to eliminate answer choices that don't make sense because they are either too big or too small.

o   Ballparking will help you recognize and avoid partial answer choices.

o   Do the Mathematics Section using the first-pass, second-pass system:
    • Use the first pass for the problems you recognize and know how to solve.
    • Leave questions you are unsure of until the second pass.

o   You must answer every question. There is no penalty for guessing.

o   There is guessing, and then there is guessing! Always ask yourself if you can eliminate any answer choices.

o   To practice getting ready for the CBEST without the help of a calculator, write all of your calculations on paper.

Chapter 6
Basic Math

MATHEMATICS REVIEW

Before we start reviewing the specific types of questions tested on the CBEST, you should be certain that you are familiar with some basic terms and concepts that you will need to know for the CBEST. This material is not very difficult, and the sample problems are not representative of actual CBEST questions. However, you must know this information backward and forward. If you don't, you'll lose valuable points on the test and have trouble setting up problems correctly.

Math Flashbacks

Is zero a positive number? Is zero an integer? While these may seem more like trivia questions than crucial CBEST information, knowing the basics helps us understand and correctly set up problems. The difficulty, however, is that you learned some of this information in the third grade! We understand that you may be a little rusty, so, let's flash back to the basics. We think you'll be surprised by the number of times you say "Oh yeah, I remember that."

The Number Line

The number line is a two-dimensional way of looking at positive and negative numbers.

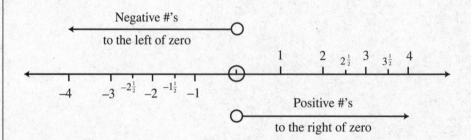

Facts about zero:
Zero is neither positive nor negative.

A positive number is defined as any number greater than zero—that is, any number located to the right of zero on the number line. A negative number is any number less than zero—that is, any number located to the left of zero on the number line. What about zero? Zero is neither positive nor negative.

Numbers get larger the farther they move toward the right on the number line. For example, 15 is larger than 2, since it is farther to the right on the number line. Numbers get smaller the farther they move toward the left on the number line. This means that, –4 is smaller than –3. It may seem contradictory that a 4 is smaller than a 3, but remember, –4 is farther to the left than is –3.

Combining Positive and Negative Numbers

What's 4 + 3? Seven, of course. We can use the number line to help us add. When you add two positive numbers, you are simply counting to the right on a number line. In our example, we count 4 spaces to the right, and then another three spaces, giving us 7 total spaces to the right. 4 + 3 = 7.

Well, that was probably the silliest paragraph you've read so far. But stay with us. The number line can also help us to add positive and negative numbers together. What if we wanted to find the sum of 6 and –2? To do this, count 6 spaces to the right of zero on the number line (positive 6). Next, to add –2, count over 2 spaces to the left. Where did you stop? 4? Perfect.

Thus, 6 + (–2) = 4.

Adding a negative number is the same thing as subtracting a positive number. We could rewrite the addition problem above as the following:

$$6 - 2 = 4$$

Visualize the number line to help you work with positive and negative numbers.

Positive and Negative Numbers—Multiplication Rules

Here are a few rules to remember when multiplying positive and negative numbers together:

1. positive × positive = positive
2. negative × negative = positive
3. positive × negative = negative

Integers

Integers are a specific type of number. Examples of integers are:

1, 2, 3, 4, 400, 389, 27, –912...

Zero is also an integer. Therefore, we can break up the group of integers into positive integers (1, 2, 3, 4, and so on); negative integers (–1, –2, –3, –4, and so on), and zero. There are an infinite number of integers. So what isn't an integer? Here are a few examples:

$$332.7, -\frac{33}{2}, 27.246857, \pi ...$$

More Great Books
Do you need to brush up on your math basics? Check out these other Princeton Review books: *MathSmart*
MathSmart II

Facts About Zero:
Zero is an integer.

Essentially, integers are numbers that do not contain fractions or decimals. If a number can only be expressed as a fraction or decimal, it is not an integer.

Odd and Even Numbers

The terms odd and even are used to describe certain types of integers. Even numbers are integers that can be divided evenly by 2. Examples of even numbers are:

$$-24, -2, 0, 4, 8, 12, 416...$$

One way to tell if a number is even is to look at the last digit. An integer is even if its last digit is even. That is, any integer that ends in 0, 2, 4, 6, or 8 is an even number. The number -357982 is even, because the last digit (2) is an even number. However 2.4 is not an even number. Even though the last digit (4) is even, 2.4 is not an integer. Only integers can be classified as even or odd.

Odd numbers are integers that cannot be divided evenly by 2. If an integer isn't an even number, it's an odd number. Examples of odd numbers are:

$$-25, -3, 1, 3, 5, 7, 9, 9245...$$

One way to tell if a number is odd is to look at the last digit. An integer is odd if its last digit is odd. For example, $-444,225$ is an odd number, because the last digit (5) is an odd number.

Notice that zero is an even number (even though zero is neither positive nor negative).

Here are some rules that deal with the results of combining even and odd numbers:

1. even × even = even
2. odd × odd = odd
3. even × odd = even
4. even + even = even
5. odd + odd = even
6. even + odd = odd

While it is helpful to have these rules memorized, you can always recreate them by trying them yourself. For example, if you multiply 2 and 4 (two even numbers) together, you get 8 (an even number). Therefore, you know that the product of two even numbers is always an even number. These rules hold true no matter what values you choose.

Places and Digits

What are the digits? (We aren't talking about your fingers and toes here.) There are ten digits: 0, 1, 2, 3, 4, 5, 6, 7, 8, 9

Digits are used to create numbers, just like the alphabet is used to create words. The number 324,856 is made up of six different digits. Each of these digits is in a "place." A place indicates where the digit is located within the number. Let's use the following number below to review the places of a number:

243.789

The 2 is in the *hundreds* place. Its value is 2×100 or 200

The 4 is in the *tens* place. Its value is 4×10 or 40

The 3 is in the *units* place. Its value is 3×1 or 3

The 7 is in the *tenths* place. Its value is $\frac{7}{10}$, or .7

The 8 is in the *hundredths* place. Its value is $\frac{8}{100}$, or .08

The 9 is in the *thousandths* place. Its value is $\frac{9}{1000}$, or .009

Adding all the numbers together gives you 243.789

Another term to describe the "units" place is the "ones" place.

Arithmetic Operations

There are only a few arithmetic operations that are tested on the CBEST:

1. addition ($4 + 8 = 12$)

2. subtraction ($12 - 8 = 4$)

3. multiplication ($4 \times 8 = 32$ or $8 \times 4 = 32$)

4. division ($32 \div 4 = 8$)

5. raising to a power ($2^2 = 4$)

6. finding a square root ($\sqrt{25} = 5$)

(Note that these last two operations, raising to a power and finding a square root, rarely appear on the CBEST. There will be a brief review on the basics of these operations in the next few pages.)

You are probably very familiar with the first four math operations. When you use these operations, there is a special name for each result. These are listed below:

1. The result of addition is a **sum.**
2. The result of subtraction is a **difference.**
3. The result of multiplication is a **product.**
4. The result of division is a **quotient.**

PEMDAS

Let's say we wanted to find the result of the following expression:

$$6 + 10 \div 5 - 3 \times 2 + (3 \times 5)$$

There are a number of different operations that we will need to perform in order to simplify this expression. In fact, you will see many CBEST questions that ask you to solve a problem using many different operations. There is a specific order in which these operations must be performed in order to simplify the expression correctly. What is the order? Just remember one thing:

PEMDAS

Many students have learned this as "Please Excuse My Dear Aunt Sally" (although no one seems to remember the story behind the phrase). This acronym stands for the following math operations: Parentheses, Exponents, Multiplication, Division, Addition, and Subtraction. In a complex expression, the first thing you solve should be the operation inside parentheses; next, reduce any term with exponents; then, perform all multiplication and division at the same time, going from left to right in the expression; finally, perform all addition and subtraction, again going from left to right in the expression.

Most CBEST questions will be designed to give you a clear understanding of the order in which you must perform the operations. However, if you are unsure of exactly the order in which to solve a problem, be sure to use the rules of PEMDAS.

Let's go back to the previous expression, and solve it using the rules of PEMDAS:

$$6 + 10 \div 5 - 3 \times 2 + (3 \times 5)$$

Step 1: Solve all work inside the parentheses. $3 \times 5 = 15$, so our problem now looks like:

$$6 + 10 \div 5 - 3 \times 2 + 15$$

Step 2: There are no exponents, so we move to multiplication and division, moving from left to right in the expression:

$$6 + 2 - 6 + 15$$

Step 3: We finish the problem by using addition and subtraction, moving from left to right in the expression:

$$8 - 6 + 15$$
$$2 + 15$$
$$17$$

ARITHMETIC DRILL

Here are some additional problems to practice the correct order of operations. Answers can be found on page 130.

1. $310 + (200 - 194) = $ _____

2. $(5 + 3) \times 7 = $ _____

3. $(5 \times 7) - (3 \times 5) = $ _____

4. $2 \times [7 - (6 \div 3)] = $ _____

5. $12 - 5 \times 3 + 7 = $ _____

Factors

Factors are defined as numbers that divide evenly into your original number. For example, the factors of 24 are: 1, 2, 3, 4, 6, 8, 12, and 24.

If you are asked to find the factors of a number, the best way to make sure you don't leave any out is to find them in pairs. For instance, if you are asked to find the factors of 36, count in pairs, starting with (1×36).

Then move to the next pair (2×18); then (3×12); then (4×9); 5 doesn't work; (6×6); 7 doesn't work; 8 doesn't work; when you get to 9—you've already written it down, so you know you're done. Thus, the factors of 36 are 1, 36, 2, 18, 3, 12, 4, 9, and 6.

Factors = the smaller numbers that divide into your original number

Multiples

Multiples are defined as numbers that your original number will divide into evenly. For example, the multiples of 4 are 4, 8, 12, 16, 20, 24, etc. One way to remember multiples is to think of your "times tables." To find the multiples of 4, start with $4 \times 1 = 4$, then $4 \times 2 = 8$, $4 \times 3 = 12$, and so on.

Students often have trouble remembering the difference between factors and multiples. When you think of factors, think of fractions, or the smaller pieces of a number; when you are asked to find multiples, think of multiplying, and use the times tables in order to calculate the multiples.

Multiples = the larger numbers (think multiply) Factors = the smaller numbers (think fractions)

- What are the *multiples* of the number 12? 12, 24, 36, 48, and so on.
- What are the *factors* of the number 12? 1, 2, 3, 4, 6, 12.

Fractions

Fractions = Division

A fraction is defined as a part of a whole. A fraction is just another way of expressing division. $\dfrac{x}{y}$ is the same thing as x divided by y. The expression $\dfrac{1}{2}$ is the same thing as 1 divided by 2. The top part of the fraction (x in the example above) is known as the **numerator**. The bottom part of the fraction (y in the example above) is known as the **denominator**. These terms aren't tested on the CBEST, but you should be familiar with them for the explanations that will follow.

Reducing Fractions

A fraction can be expressed in many different ways. For example:

$$\frac{50}{100} = \frac{25}{50} = \frac{10}{20} = \frac{4}{8} = \frac{2}{4} = \frac{1}{2}$$

When you add or multiply fractions, you will often end up with a big fraction that may not appear in the answer choices. In order to find the correct answer, you will need to know how to reduce a fraction to its simplest value.

To reduce a fraction, divide both the numerator and the denominator by the same factor. This process may take several steps. While it may save time to find the largest number that will divide into both numbers, try to keep your pencil moving. Don't worry about whether two numbers will both divide by 24! Start with nice, small numbers. See if both parts of the fraction can be divided by 2, 3, or 5. If you find that you need to reduce again, fine. You'll get to the final result in no time.

Take, for example, the fraction $\frac{12}{60}$. What can we divide numerator 12 and denominator 60 by? If you saw that they are both divisible by 12, great! The fraction will reduce to $\frac{1}{5}$. If you didn't see that right away, don't panic. Start with an easy number. Both 12 and 60 are even, so start with 2. This will result in $\frac{6}{30}$. Try reducing by 3—now we're down to $\frac{2}{10}$. Divide by 2 again, and you've got $\frac{1}{5}$. This might take a few more steps, but it will get you the correct answer nonetheless.

If possible, try to reduce fractions before performing operations with them. This will help you save time, and avoid errors that come up when you start to manipulate large numbers.

Adding or Subtracting Fractions with the Same Denominator

In order to add two or more fractions with the same denominator, simply add the numerators of each fraction. The denominator will be the common denominator in each fraction. Here is an example:

$$\frac{3}{4} + \frac{1}{4} = \frac{3+1}{4} = \frac{4}{4} = 1$$

Subtraction works in exactly the same way:

$$\frac{3}{4} - \frac{1}{4} = \frac{3-1}{4} = \frac{2}{4} = \frac{1}{2}$$

Converting Mixed Numbers to Fractions

The CBEST loves to use mixed numbers—that is, a number that contains both a whole number and a fraction. An example of a mixed number is $3\frac{4}{5}$. When you come across a mixed number, you should usually convert it into a fraction (often referred to as an improper fraction, since the numerator will be greater than the denominator). Let's convert $3\frac{4}{5}$ into a standard fraction.

First, convert the integer part of the number into a fraction with the same denominator as the fraction part of the number. In this example, we want to turn the integer 3 into a fraction with a denominator of 5:

$$3 = \frac{3}{1} = \frac{15}{5}$$

Next, add the two fractions with a common denominator together:

$$\frac{15}{5} + \frac{4}{5} = \frac{19}{5}$$

Often, CBEST questions will require you to perform operations involving two different mixed numbers. Converting mixed numbers into fractions will help make your calculations easier.

The Bowtie

Unfortunately, not all fraction problems will contain fractions with the same denominator. There is a way to add and subtract fractions with different denominators. Remember the phrase "least common denominator?" This is the method used most often to teach fractions. To use it, you need to find the smallest number that is a multiple of both denominators. This generally involves a lot of counting (the multiples of 4 are 4, 8, 12, 16, 20...; the multiples of 5 are 5, 10, 15, 20...), and is occasionally a frustrating experience.

Welcome to the Bowtie. The Bowtie is a powerful tool to help simplify the process of adding, subtracting, and comparing fractions. The example below will show you how the Bowtie is used:

$$\overset{4}{\frac{1}{3}} \diagdown\!\!\!\!\!\diagup \overset{9}{\frac{3}{4}} \; = \; \overset{13}{\frac{13}{12}}$$

The first step is to multiply in the direction of each arrow. Write each number on top of the fraction at the top of the arrow. Next, use the sign (in this case, addition) to combine the two numbers you just wrote down. In the example above, we added 4 and 9 together, giving us 13 as the numerator. Finally, in order to find the denominator, multiply the two denominators together. The resulting fraction is $\frac{13}{12}$.

The beauty of the Bowtie is that you don't have to sit there trying to come up with a common denominator. Simply multiply, add, and you're done!

Multiplying Fractions

To multiply fractions, line them up and multiply straight across:

$$\frac{4}{5} \times \frac{5}{6} = \frac{20}{30} = \frac{2}{3}$$

We performed one multiplication problem above another. Across the top of the fractions, we multiplied 4 and 5; across the bottom of the fractions, we multiplied 5 and 6.

However, there is an even easier way to solve the fraction problem above. When multiplying two fractions, always look to see if you can reduce either or both of the fractions. In the problem above, we could cancel out the five in each fraction—that would leave us with a 4 on the top left and a 6 on the bottom right. We can reduce these numbers by two, leaving us with $\frac{2}{3}$, the final answer. In general, your calculations will be easier if you take a moment to reduce before you multiply.

Dividing Fractions

Dividing fractions requires one additional step. To divide one fraction by another, flip the second fraction over, and multiply (in fancier terms, multiply by the reciprocal of the second term). Here is an example:

$$\frac{4}{5} \div \frac{3}{10} =$$

$$\frac{4}{5} \times \frac{10}{3}$$

Now we can reduce the 10 and the 5, and get the final result $\frac{8}{3}$.

Make sure that you reduce only after you have flipped the second fraction. Sometimes students get confused when whole numbers are involved, such as

$$\frac{6}{\frac{2}{3}}$$

Rewrite a fraction division problem by flipping the second fraction and multiplying.

Remember, a whole number can be a fraction, by placing the whole number over 1.

In this problem, we have $\dfrac{\frac{6}{1}}{\frac{2}{3}}$, which is the same as $\dfrac{6}{1} \div \dfrac{2}{3}$. Now, we can flip the

second fraction, giving us $\dfrac{6}{1} \times \dfrac{3}{2}$. The final result is $\dfrac{18}{2}$, or 9.

Comparing Fractions

The CBEST sometimes contains problems that require you to identify which of two fractions is larger. When fractions have the same denominator, it is easy to tell which amount is bigger. For example, which fraction is larger, $\dfrac{1}{4}$ or $\dfrac{3}{4}$? The answer is $\dfrac{3}{4}$. 3 parts out of 4 is clearly larger than 1 part out of 4. When two fractions have the same denominator, simply choose the fraction with the largest numerator.

Comparing fractions becomes somewhat more difficult when the fractions do not

The Bowtie can also be used to compare two fractions.

have a common denominator. Which fraction is greater, $\dfrac{4}{7}$ or $\dfrac{3}{5}$? The most efficient way to compare these fractions is to use the Bowtie again. Here, we'll use the first step of the Bowtie—cross multiply as the arrows indicate below:

$$^{20}\dfrac{4}{7} \quad \times \quad \left(\dfrac{3}{5}\right)^{21}$$

The result of 4×5 is 20, so we write this above the fraction $\dfrac{4}{7}$; the other arrow gives us a result of 21. Now, compare the two products we just calculated. Which one is bigger? 21. Since 21 is the larger product, the fraction underneath, $\dfrac{3}{5}$, is the larger fraction!

Once again, the Bowtie will save you time when working with fractions. This is much more efficient than turning these fractions into decimals, or finding a common denominator.

Those Tricky Fractions

The CBEST writers specifically state that you will have to answer questions that deal with the manipulation of fractions. We've reviewed how to perform all the basic operations with fractions, and even how to compare fractions. By using the Bowtie, you can add, subtract, and compare fractions with ease. We've also reviewed the rules of multiplication and division with fractions.

Occasionally, you will be asked questions about identifying the largest fraction, or identifying a result when combining fractions. Sometimes, the end result of a fraction problem isn't always obvious. Here are a few things to remember with fractions:

- **Multiplying two fractions will yield a product less than the original fractions.** Generally, when we think of multiplying two numbers, we think of the product being larger than the original numbers (for example, $10 \times 7 = 70$). But with fractions, the product is smaller than the original numbers $\frac{1}{10} \times \frac{1}{7} = \frac{1}{70}$, a number much smaller than $\frac{1}{10}$ or $\frac{1}{7}$.

- **Pay careful attention before identifying the larger fraction.** It is easy to recognize that 6 is greater than 2. Remember, though, that is $\frac{1}{6}$ much less than $\frac{1}{2}$. If you are unsure which fraction is larger, remember to use the Bowtie to compare.

FRACTION DRILL

Answers can be found on page 130.

1. $\dfrac{6}{4} \times \dfrac{5}{9} =$ _____

2. $\dfrac{22}{45} \times \dfrac{15}{33} =$ _____

3. $\dfrac{7}{12} \div \dfrac{28}{3} =$ _____

4. $\dfrac{\frac{3}{5}}{\frac{9}{10}} =$ _____

5. $\dfrac{2}{9} + \dfrac{3}{4} =$ _____

6. $\dfrac{5}{4} - \dfrac{1}{3} =$ _____

7. $\dfrac{7}{9} + \dfrac{5}{2} - \dfrac{5}{6} + \dfrac{2}{3} =$ _____

8. $2\dfrac{3}{8} - 1\dfrac{4}{5} =$ _____

Decimals

As we mentioned earlier, fractions are simply a way to indicate division. Fractions can also be expressed as decimals. Any fraction can be converted into a decimal, and vice-versa. You probably know some already ($\frac{1}{2} = .5; \frac{1}{4} = .25, etc$). In order to find the decimal equivalent of a fraction, simply divide the numerator by the denominator. For example,

$$\frac{3}{4} = 3 \div 4 = .75$$

Adding and Subtracting Decimals

In order to add or subtract decimals, you must align the decimal places of all the numbers. Then simply add or subtract. Some examples are:

$$
\begin{array}{r}
2.72 \\
+\,3.46 \\
\hline
=6.18
\end{array}
\qquad
\begin{array}{r}
8.19 \\
-\,1.54 \\
\hline
=6.65
\end{array}
$$

If you are trying to add or subtract two decimals, and the two numbers do not have the same number of digits, you will need to add zeros to fill out the places in each number. For example, if we want to find the difference between 8.3 and 2.784, we first need to set up the problem:

$$
\begin{array}{r}
8.3 \\
-\,2.784 \\
\hline
\end{array}
$$

To make the problem complete, add zeros to the end of the first number (in the hundredths and thousandths places). The problem should look like:

$$
\begin{array}{r}
8.300 \\
-\,2.784 \\
\hline
=5.516
\end{array}
$$

Multiplying Decimals

The best way to multiply decimals is to ignore any decimal points until you have completed the multiplication. Once you complete the problem, count the number of digits that are located to the right of all decimal points. Then place the decimal point that number of places to the left of the final result. Let's look at the following example:

$$
\begin{array}{r}
2.45 \\
\times\,\,3.2 \\
\hline
=\,490 \\
+\,7350 \\
\hline
7840
\end{array}
$$

Now, there are three numbers located to the right of the decimal point, so we need to move the decimal three places to the left. Starting with the 0, count over three places to the left. The final result is 7.840.

Align the decimal points before adding or subtracting decimals.

Before dividing decimals, make sure the denominator is a whole number.

Dividing Decimals

When diving decimals, you need to make sure that the divisor (the number you are dividing by) is a whole number. For example, if you are given the problem:

$$1.86 \div .3$$

The easiest way to solve this is to put it into fraction form:

$$\frac{1.86}{.3}$$

Now we must first turn the divisor (.3) into a whole number. In order to make .3 a whole number, we move the decimal point one place to the right. Whatever you do to the bottom part of the fraction, you must do to the top part. So, we need to move the decimal point in 1.86 one to the right, resulting in 18.6. Now, our division problem looks like:

$$\frac{18.6}{3} = 6.2$$

DECIMAL DRILL

Answers can be found on page 131.

1. $8.654 - 3.27 = \underline{\hspace{1cm}}$

2. $1.354 + 8.207 = \underline{\hspace{1cm}}$

3. $12.9 \times 25.8 = \underline{\hspace{1cm}}$

4. $12.8 \div 6.25 = \underline{\hspace{1cm}}$

5. $21.6 \div 8 = \underline{\hspace{1cm}}$

6. $\dfrac{12.9 \times 3.1}{0.3} = \underline{\hspace{1cm}}$

PERCENTAGES

Percentages are very similar to fractions and decimals. In fact, a percent is really just a fraction whose denominator is 100. The word "percent" means "out of 100."

A percent is a number out of 100.

$$50\% = \frac{50}{100} = .5$$

$$47\% = \frac{47}{100} = .47$$

As you can see, percentages can be converted into fractions and decimals, and vice versa. In order to convert a fraction into a percentage, usually the easiest thing to do is to first convert the fraction into a decimal. Then, multiply the decimal by 100 in order to get the percentage. For example:

$$\frac{3}{4} = 3 \div 4 = .75\,(\times 100) = 75\%$$

$$\frac{6}{10} = 6 \div 10 = .6\,(\times 100) = 60\%$$

This process will work for any fraction. However, it does require a few steps. There are a few fractions that show up often on the CBEST and are worth memorizing. Review the chart on the following page.

Fraction	Decimal	Percent
$\frac{1}{100}$	.01	1%
$\frac{1}{8}$	.125	12.5%
$\frac{1}{5}$	.2	20%
$\frac{1}{4}$	.25	25%
$\frac{1}{3}$	.333	33%
$\frac{2}{5}$	.4	40%
$\frac{1}{2}$	.5	50%
$\frac{3}{5}$	.6	60%
$\frac{2}{3}$	.667	66%
$\frac{3}{4}$	.75	75%
$\frac{4}{5}$	.8	80%

Quick and Easy Percent Calculation

Break down a complex percent question into easy percentage calculations.

Percent problems can often be solved by calculating "easy" percentages such as 1% and 10%. Instead of immediately doing detailed calculations, break down the work into these "easy" percentages. For example,

What is 23% of 520?

We can answer this question by first finding 20% of 520, and then adding 3% of 520. To find 10% of a number, simply move the decimal point one place to the left. In our example, 10% of 520 = 52. Since we are looking for 20%, simply multiply by 2 to get 20% = 104.

To find 1% of any number, all you have to do is move the decimal point of that number over two places to the left. In our example, 1% of 520 = 5.2. Since we want 3%, multiply by 3 to get 15.6.

Now, we can combine the values to find the correct answer. 20% of 520 = 104, and 3% of 520 = 15.6. So, 23% of 520 = 104 + 15.6, or 119.6.

With a little practice, you'll find that you'll be able to solve percentage questions with minimal calculation.

———————————○———————————

1. A school district is proposing a 15% decrease in the number of students per classroom. Currently there are 20 students per classroom. How many students per classroom would there be with the proposed decrease?

   A. 23 students
   B. 19 students
   C. 18.5 students
   D. 17 students
   E. 16 students

Here's How to Crack It

We need to find 15% of 20. Using the techniques discussed above, we can break 15% down into 10% and 5%. 10% of 20 is 2. Half of that is 1. Thus, 15% is 2 + 1, or 3 students. Since the school district is proposing to decrease the number of students, subtract 3 from 20. The new total would be 20 − 3 = 17. Choice (D) is the correct answer.

———————————○———————————

Translating Percentages

Many percent questions will be in the form of a word problem. In order to set up the problem correctly, you'll need to be able to translate words into their mathematical equivalents. Here are some key terms to translate:

> **Of** = Multiply ("$\frac{1}{3}$ of 24" translates to: $\frac{1}{3} \times 24$)
>
> **Percent** = # out of 100 ("30%" translates to: $\frac{30}{100}$)
>
> **What** = Variable ("30% of what" translates to: $\frac{30}{100}x$)
>
> **Is, Are, Were** = Equals Sign ("$\frac{1}{3}$ of x is 12" translates to: $\frac{1}{3}x = 12$)

Applied Strategies
Tip! Translate percent word problems into their mathematical equivalents.

2. Teresa took a science test with 40 questions. If she missed 7 questions, and left 9 unanswered, what percent of the questions did Teresa answer correctly?

A. 9%
B. 16%
C. 27%
D. 40%
E. 60%

Here's How to Crack It

In order to set up a math equation for the above problem, translate the last sentence.

"What percent" translates to: $\dfrac{x}{100}$.

"Of the questions" translates to: $\times 40$

"did she answer correctly" translates to: $= 24$ (the number of questions she answered correctly can be found by subtracting 7 and 9 from 40). Thus, the equation reads:

$$\frac{x}{100} \times 40 = 24$$

Now, we can manipulate the equation to find the percent.

$$\frac{x}{100} \times 40 = 24$$

$$\frac{x}{100} = \frac{24}{40}$$

$$\frac{x}{100} = \frac{3}{5}$$

$$x = \frac{300}{5}$$

$$x = 60$$

Choice (E) is the correct answer. Notice that there are several partial answer choices, including 40% (the amount of questions Teresa did *not* answer correctly).

Don't forget that Ballparking, as always, is helpful on this problem. If you recognized that Teresa answered over half of the questions correctly, then only (E), will work.

———————————○———————————

Percent Change

Some CBEST questions will ask you to find a percent increase or decrease between two values. Whether you're solving for percent increase or percent decrease, you should use the percent change formula:

$$\% \text{ Increase or Decrease} = \frac{\text{Difference}}{\text{Original Amount}}$$

———————————○———————————

3. In 1995, Company X sold a total of 40,000 computers. In 1996, Company X sold a total of 50,000 computers. By what percent did sales of computers increase for Company X from 1995 to 1996?

A. 20%
B. 25%
C. 50%
D. 65%
E. 80%

Here's How to Crack It

The question asks for a percent increase, so we need to use the percent change formula. Your equation should look like:

$$\% \, \text{Increase} = \frac{10,000}{40,000}$$

It can often be confusing to determine which of the following numbers is defined as the original amount. An easy rule to remember is this: If the question asks for a percent decrease, the original amount is the *higher* number. If the question asks for a percent increase, the original amount is the *lower* number. In this case, we are asked to solve a percent increase, so our original amount is the lower number (the number from 1995).

Once we've set up the problem as above, we can reduce our fraction 1 to $\frac{1}{4}$, which is the same as 25%. Choice (B) is the correct answer.

―――――――――――――――○―――――――――――――――

Beware of partial answer choices! Notice that 20% is also an answer choice. If you incorrectly made 50,000 the original amount, you would have gotten 20% as the correct answer. Be careful on these questions—CBEST writers will always include the incorrect answer choices.

MEASUREMENT

According to the authors of the CBEST, you will be required to "understand and use standard units of length, temperature, weight, and capacity in the U.S. measurement system." In order to solve measurement questions, you will need to learn two things: conversions, and how to set up a conversion equation. First, here are a number of common measurements that you should know for the test:

Length:	12 inches	=	1 foot
	3 feet	=	1 yard
Therefore,			
	36 inches	=	1 yard

Temperature: In any temperature question, the equation $F = \frac{9}{5}C + 32$ will be provided. Common temperature questions will give you a temperature in one scale, and ask you to find the temperature in the other scale.

Weight:	16 ounces	=	1 pound
	2,000 pounds	=	1 ton
Capacity:	2 cups	=	1 pint
	2 pints	=	1 quart
	4 quarts	=	1 gallon
Time:	60 seconds	=	1 minute
	60 minutes	=	1 hour
	24 hours	=	1 day
	7 days	=	1 week
	52 weeks	=	1 year

Now that you've learned these conversions, let's see how to solve a typical conversion problem:

----

4. Kathleen jogs for $1\frac{1}{2}$ hours per day. How many seconds does Kathleen spend jogging each day?

   A.   90
   B.   150
   C.   1,800
   D.   3,600
   E.   5,400

When converting units, make sure your units cancel correctly.

Here's How to Crack It

We are given an amount of time expressed in hours and need to convert it to seconds. In order to eliminate hours, we need to multiply by a "conversion fraction." Look at the following expression:

$$1.5 \text{ hours} \times \frac{60 \text{ minutes}}{1 \text{ hour}} = 90 \text{ minutes}$$

We multiplied 1.5 hours by the fraction (60 minutes/1 hour). This is called a "conversion fraction." We aren't changing the number at all, we're simply changing the units that we use to express the time. In order to cancel the units of hours, we put 60 minutes in the top part of the fraction, and 1 hour in the bottom part of the fraction. The "hours" unit cancels, leaving us with minutes. Now, let's go the final step and turn this number into seconds:

$$90 \text{ minutes} \times \frac{60 \text{ seconds}}{1 \text{ minute}} = 5,400 \text{ seconds}$$

When converting units, make sure your units cancel correctly.

Since we want the final answer in seconds, we multiply by a conversion fraction that allows the "minutes" units to cancel out. The final answer is 5,400 seconds, and (E) is the correct answer.

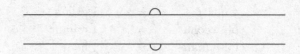

5. Fiona is preparing her favorite appetizer. If the recipe calls for 4 pounds of ground beef for one serving, how many ounces of ground beef will she need for two servings?

A. 12
B. 16
C. 64
D. 128
E. 140

Here's How to Crack It

First, convert pounds to ounces, using the conversion fraction below:

$$4 \text{ pounds} \times \frac{16 \text{ ounces}}{1 \text{ pound}} = 64 \text{ ounces}$$

We've converted pounds to ounces. However, we aren't done! The question asks for the amount we need for *two* servings. If we multiply this amount by 2, we find that the correct answer is 128 ounces. Choice (D) is the correct answer.

When faced with a measurement question, first write down the conversion fraction, then set up your problem so that you can eliminate unwanted units.

GEOMETRY

This title probably made you cringe. Relax, the most difficult parts about geometry —proofs, theorems, and complicated formulas—will *not* be tested on the CBEST. There are a few basic rules you will need to relearn in order to handle the two to four questions you will see on the test. All of the formulas and rules will be covered below. However, the key to geometry is Process of Elimination! It is easy to recognize bad answer choices in geometry questions. Even if you aren't sure how to get the correct answer, try to eliminate as many incorrect answer choices as possible.

We've reduced the size of the geometry review from prior editions of *Cracking the CBEST* because students are no longer tested on area and volume. Instead, you will be asked questions that require you to "measure length and perimeter." Below, we'll review common geometric shapes that appear on the CBEST and how to calculate the length/perimeter of each one. Therefore, don't panic if you don't see some of the formulas you used to use in geometry—they simply won't be covered on the actual exam!

There will be no proofs or theorems on the CBEST.

Triangles

Angles

Every triangle contains 180 degrees.

The word triangle means "three angles," and every triangle contains three interior angles. The sum of their angles will always be 180 degrees.

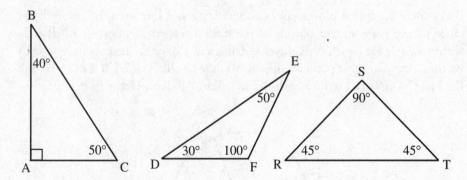

Perimeter

The perimeter of a triangle is the sum of the lengths of its sides.

Finding the perimeter of a triangle is quite simple—add up the lengths of the three sides.

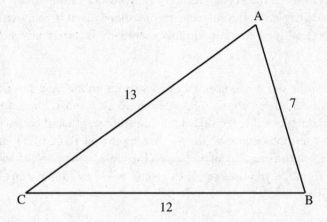

In the figure above, the perimeter of triangle ABC is 32 (7 + 12 +13).

Circles

Degrees

Circles contain 360 degrees.

Tip! Finding the radius is the key to answering any "circle" question.

Every circle, regardless of size, contains 360 degrees. A line from the center of the circle to any point on the outside of the circle is called a radius, or *r*. All radii within a circle are equal. A diameter is defined as a line that reaches from a point on the circle to another point on the circle, while traveling through the center. The diameter, or *d*, is twice the length of the radius. All diameters within a circle are equal.

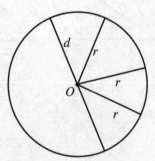

The key to any circle question is to know the value of the radius. You will need this value to find the circumference of a circle.

Circumference

The circumference of a circle is $2\pi r$, or πd, where r is the radius of the circle and d is the diameter.

Circle Formulas:
Circumference = $2\pi r$

Problem: O is the center of the circle. Find the circumference of the circle below:

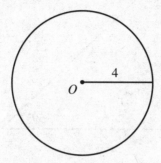

Solution: The radius of the circle is 4. With the radius, we can find the circumference:

$$2\pi r = 2\pi(4) = 8\pi$$

Rectangles and Squares

Angles

All of the angles in rectangles and squares are right angles.

In addition to having all right angles, rectangles and squares both have equal opposite sides. All opposite sides are parallel to one another. A square is a rectangle that has 4 equal sides.

Perimeter

The perimeter of a rectangle or a square is the sum of the lengths of its sides. Just add them up.

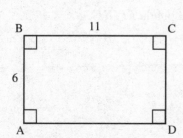

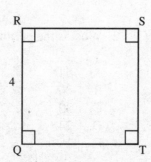

In the figures above, the perimeter of the rectangle is 34 and the perimeter of the square is 16.

GEOMETRY DRILL

Answers can be found on page 131.

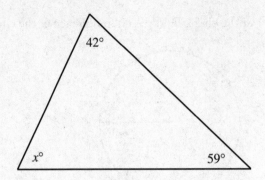

1. In the figure above, what is the value of *x*?

    A.   101
    B.   90
    C.   86
    D.   79
    E.   17

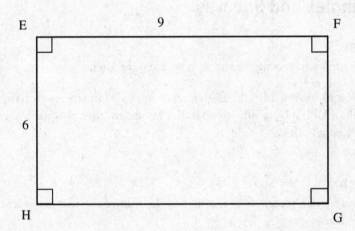

2. What is the perimeter of rectangle *EFGH*?

    A.   54
    B.   36
    C.   30
    D.   24
    E.   15

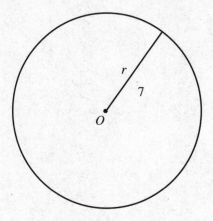

3. What is the circumference of the circle?

    A.   14
    B. 14π
    C. 28π
    D. 49π
    E. 98π

ANSWERS TO DRILLS

Arithmetic Drill
From page 107

1. 316

2. 56

3. 20

4. 10

5. 4

Fraction Drill
From page 114

1. $\dfrac{5}{6}$

2. $\dfrac{2}{9}$

3. $\dfrac{1}{16}$

4. $\dfrac{2}{3}$

5. $\dfrac{35}{36}$

6. $\dfrac{11}{12}$

7. $3\dfrac{1}{9}$

8. $\dfrac{23}{40}$

Decimal Drill

From page 116

1. 5.384

2. 9.561

3. 332.82

4. 2.048

5. 2.7

6. 133.3

Geometry Drill

From page 128

1. **D** The sums of the angles in a triangle must add up to 180. Two angles are given to us. The calculation is $180 - 59 - 42 = 79$ degrees.

2. **C** The perimeter of a rectangle is twice the length plus twice the width. For rectangle *EFGH*, the perimeter is $6 + 9 + 6 + 9 = 30$.

3. **B** The circumference of a circle is $2\pi r$. The circumference is $2 \times \pi \times 7 = 14\pi$.

Summary

o PEMDAS helps us remember the order of operations in a sequence. Simplify anything found in the parentheses; then solve any exponents; then multiply and divide, from left to right; finally, add and subtract, from left to right.

o **Factors** are numbers that divide into your original number evenly. When counting the number of factors, use factor pairs so that you don't leave any out.

o **Multiples** are numbers that your original number will divide into evenly. When finding multiples, think of multiplication tables, and remember to start by multiplying the number by 1.

o Use the Bowtie to help you add, subtract and compare fractions.

o A percentage is a number out of 100.

o Use translation techniques to turn percentage word problems into math expressions.

o Review the basic measurements of length, weight, capacity, and time.

o The **perimeter** of a triangle is the sum of its three sides.

o The **circumference** of a circle is $2\pi r$.

o The **perimeter** of a rectangle is twice the length plus twice the width.

Chapter 7
Estimation, Measurement, and Statistical Principles

ESTIMATION

CBEST writers state that there may be some math questions where you will need to "estimate the results of problems involving addition, subtraction, multiplication, and division prior to computation." This should sound familiar. In Part III, we discussed how Ballparking can help you eliminate answer choices. Sounds like the CBEST authors want to give us a few free points here! Before we move on to some more complicated statistical principles, let's take a look at a few questions where estimation will be the key to quickly finding the correct answer.

Applied Strategies
Tip! Always look at the answer choices to see if you can Ballpark without doing any calculations.

1. Oliver sells the following items at his coffee shop:

   $3.00 for a quesadilla
   $1.25 for a cup of coffee
   $1.75 for nachos

   Laura purchases 3 quesadillas, 2 orders of nachos, and 2 cups of coffee. How many quesadillas would Leo have to purchase in order to spend the same amount of money as Laura?

   A. 1

   B. 2

   C. 3

   D. 5

   E. 10

Here's How to Crack It

This is one of the easier math questions that you would find on the CBEST. Therefore, the key to this question is doing your work accurately and quickly. If you look at the answer choices before doing numerous calculations, you will recognize that this question can be solved without any work. Can we eliminate any answer choices immediately? Yes. Choices (A), (B), and (C) won't be the correct answer. Laura ordered three quesadillas, and additional food. Thus, Leo will need to order more than the three Laura ordered. Immediately, we are down to two answer choices—5 and 10. Ten quesadillas would equal $30, which seems much more than Laura's total cost. Choice (D) is the correct answer.

STATISTICAL PRINCIPLES

Averages

There are a number of ways to describe an average—you may see the terms average, arithmetic mean, or mean. They all describe the same thing. An average is defined as follows: in a set of *n* numbers, the average is the total of the numbers divided by *n*. Let's make that a little easier. There are three parts to an average: the total, the number of things, and the average. To solve average questions, use the average circle:

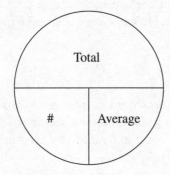

When you get an average question, fill out the circle. You will be given two pieces of information—your job is to find the third. The average circle helps you see how to get the correct answer.

Example 1

> You take three tests and score a 90, 80, and an 82.
> What is your average score for the three tests?

Solution: Fill in what you know. The total, or sum, is 252. The number of things is 3. *To find the average, divide the total by the number of things.* 252 ÷ 3 is 84.

Example 2

> You score an average of 84 on five tests. What is
> the sum total of all five tests?

Solution: You can fill in the average (84), and the number of things (5). *To find the total, multiply the two numbers together.* 84 × 5, or 420, is the correct answer.

Example 3

You score an average of 74 in your history class, and have a total of 296 points. How many tests did you take?

Solution: Here, we can fill out the total (296), and the average (74). *To find the number of things, divide the total by the average.* 296 ÷ 74, or 4 is the correct answer.

Some average questions will require more than one step, or ask for information that won't be contained in the average circle; regardless, always find the third piece of your average circle. Here is a more challenging average question:

Example 4

If Paula-Ann scored an average of 86 on her first 5 tests, what is the minimum she must score on her 6th test in order to have an overall average of 88?

A. 84

B. 88

C. 90

D. 96

E. 98

Solution: Like the previous examples, let's fill out our average circle first. We have the average and the number of things, so we need to find the total. Multiplying 5 by 86 gives us a total of 430. Next, let's fill in another average circle with the information we want in the second part of the question. There are six things, and we want an average of 88. The total here is 528. The difference between the totals on the first five tests and all six tests is 98 (528 − 430). (E) is the correct answer.

Take all average problems one step at a time, and always fill out the average circle.

Ratios

A ratio is a form of comparison. At first, it may seem that ratios are just like fractions. However, a fraction compares part of something to the whole thing. A ratio compares part of something to another part. Ratios can be written in three formats. The ratio of a to b can be written as:

When expressing a ratio, order matters. 16:20 is different from 20:16

$$\frac{a}{b}$$, or the ratio of *a* to *b*, or *a:b*

To understand the difference between ratios and fractions, let's work with the following example: In a third-grade class, there are 20 boys and 16 girls.

The ratio of *boys* to *girls* can be written as $\frac{20}{16}$, or 20:16.

Ratios, like fractions, can also be reduced, or turned into decimals or percentages. The ratio of *girls* to *boys* is not 20:16 but 16:20. Be careful with the order of the ratio. A ratio of 20:16 is different from a ratio of 16:20.

What fractional part of the class is boys? To find a fraction, we are looking for the part over the whole. There are 20 boys, and a whole, or total, of 36 students. Thus, the fractional part of the class which is boys is $\frac{20}{36}$, which may be reduced to $\frac{5}{9}$.

The Ratio Box

If we know that a class has a ratio of boys to girls of 2:1, do we know how many people are in the class? No, since the class could be made up of 20 boys and 10 girls, or of 200 boys and 100 girls. The ratio alone does not help us determine the actual number of students there are. We need more information. If we were told that the class had a total of 90 students, we could then find the number of boys and girls in the class. How? Use the ratio box below.

	Boys	Girls	Whole
Ratio (parts)	2	1	3
Multiply By			
Actual Number			90

If we treat the initial ratio as "parts," we could find the total number of parts. In this example, we know the class is composed of 2 parts boys and 1 part girls, for a total of 3 parts. We filled in the "whole" number as 3.

Our next step is to determine how we can make the jump from 3 parts to the whole class of 90 students. In order to solve this, we need to find out what number we need to multiply by in order to transform 3 into 90. You can see that we need to multiply by 30. Therefore, let's fill in every space in the second row with the number 30 (the second row will always contain the same number—we multiply evenly across all parts of the ratio):

	Boys	Girls	Whole
Ratio (parts)	2	1	3
Multiply By	30	30	30
Actual Number			90

Use the ratio box to turn an initial ratio into actual numbers.

Our final step is to determine the actual number of boys and the actual number of girls in the class. We can do that by multiplying the two numbers in the boys column (2 × 30), and the two numbers in the girls column (1 × 30). The completed ratio box appears below.

	Boys	Girls	Whole
Ratio (parts)	2	1	3
Multiply By	30	30	30
Actual Number	60	30	90

From our work, we have found that in a class of 90 students, with a ratio of 2 boys to 1 girl, there are 60 boys and 30 girls in the class. Here are a few points on how to use the ratio box:

- Always use the Ratio Box on ratio questions— you will be given an initial ratio, and one "actual number."
- Start by filling in the initial ratio and the actual number; take the sum of the initial ratio to get the whole number of "parts"; determine the multiply number, and write that number in for every column.
- Find the actual numbers by multiplying down each column.

The Ratio Box helps you keep track of all the information you need for any type of ratio question. Practice using the ratio box, and ratios will be a breeze. Here is a final example:

1. CORE Education services produces two types of products—notebooks and binders. If CORE has an inventory of notebooks and binders in a 3:2 ratio, and a total of 100 products in stock, how many notebooks does CORE have in inventory?

   A. 5

   B. 30

   C. 40

   D. 60

   E. 80

Solution: After reading the question, here is what the initial ratio box should look like:

	Notebooks	Binders	Whole
Ratio (parts)	3	2	5
Multiply By			
Actual Number			100

Next, we need to find the multiplier. What do you multiply 5 by in order to get 100? The answer is 20. Here is what the completed ratio box looks like:

	Notebooks	Binders	Whole
Ratio (parts)	3	2	5
Multiply By	20	20	20
Actual Number	**60**	40	100

The correct answer is (D), 60. Be careful not to select 40, which is the total number of binders in inventory.

Proportions

Some CBEST questions will define a relationship between two things, and ask you to use this relationship to find other proportional values. Let's take a look at a sample proportion question:

2. If Chris can iron three shirts in 18 minutes, how long will it take him to iron 12 shirts?

   A.   1 hour 4 minutes

   B.   1 hour 12 minutes

   C.   1 hour 18 minutes

   D.   1 hour 44 minutes

   E.   3 hours 18 minutes

Here's How to Crack It

Every proportion question will contain two relationships—one that is given to you, and one with a missing piece of information. In this example, we're given the relationship:

$$\frac{3 \text{ (shirts)}}{18 \text{ (minutes)}}$$

Set this relationship equal to the one we want to find:

$$\frac{3 \text{ (shirts)}}{18 \text{ (minutes)}} = \frac{12 \text{ (shirts)}}{x \text{ (minutes)}}$$

Make sure your units match when calculating a proportion.

In order for a proportion equation to be correct, notice that the units must be in the same order (in this example, both fractions contain shirts over minutes). Further, the units must always be the same (you can't have minutes in one fraction and hours in the other). Now, we can cross multiply to solve the question:

$$3x = (12)(18)$$
$$x = (4)(18)$$
$$x = 72 \text{ minutes}$$

Thus, it takes Chris 72 minutes to iron 12 shirts. While 72 minutes is not an answer choice, we can reduce to find the correct answer of 1 hour, 12 minutes. Choice (B) is the correct answer.

PROBABILITY

The CBEST will test your knowledge of basic probability. Below, we'll show you everything you need to know about probability for purposes of this test. Probability can get quite complicated (some schools offer yearlong courses that explore probability in great detail), but we'll keep it simple by breaking down the four basic things you need to know for the CBEST.

Probability is Expressed as a Fraction Between 0 and 1

Probability defines the likelihood that an event will occur. A probability of 0 means that there is no chance the event will occur. A probability of 1 means that it is certain that an event will occur. Outside of these extremes, probability is expressed as a fraction between 0 and 1.

Probability is a fraction in which:

$$\frac{\text{\# of desired outcomes}}{\text{total \# of outcomes}}$$

Let's look at a few examples. What if we want to find the probability of throwing a single six-sided die and getting a 4? There are a total of 6 **possible** outcomes for one such roll—1, 2, 3, 4, 5, and 6. There is just one **desired** outcome—that we get a 4. Thus, the probability of rolling a 4 is $\frac{1}{6}$. What about the probability of flipping a coin and having it turn up heads? Here, the probability is $\frac{1}{2}$. There are two possible outcomes—heads or tails, and our one desired outcome is that we flip heads.

An event is defined as **independent** if it is not affected by previous events.

Let's talk about rolling a die again. Let's say you throw the die and it comes up a 4. Does this mean that the probability of a 4 appearing next time will be less than $\frac{1}{6}$? Absolutely not! The probability of rolling a 4 on the next turn is still $\frac{1}{6}$, since the two rolls are independent events and one does not affect the outcome of the other.

Multiply the probability of independent events to find the combined probability.

To find the probability of more than one independent event occurring, multiply the probability of each event together.

What is the probability of throwing a 4 two times in a row? Well, the probability of throwing a 4 is $\frac{1}{6}$. This probability does not change on the second throw. Thus, the probability is $\frac{1}{6} \times \frac{1}{6}$, or $\frac{1}{36}$.

The following examples are sample questions that will test the concepts you need to know for the test.

---

3. David throws a six-sided die and gets a 3. What is the probability that his next throw will NOT be a three?

    A. $\frac{1}{6}$

    B. $\frac{1}{4}$

    C. $\frac{1}{2}$

    D. $\frac{5}{6}$

    E. 1

Here's How to Crack It

The probability of not getting a three is $\dfrac{5}{6}$. There are five rolls which would not give us a three—namely, if we were to roll 1, 2, 4, 5, or 6. There is a total of six possible outcomes. The probability is not affected by the fact that David rolled a 3 on his previous throw. Choice (D) is the correct answer.

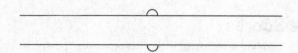

4. A bag of marbles contains 8 red marbles, 6 blue marbles, and 4 green marbles. If one marble is chosen at random from the bag, what is the probability that this marble will be blue?

    A. $\dfrac{2}{9}$

    B. $\dfrac{1}{3}$

    C. $\dfrac{4}{9}$

    D. $\dfrac{1}{2}$

    E. $\dfrac{3}{4}$

Here's How to Crack It

There are a total of 18 marbles (the total number of **possible** outcomes). There are 6 blue marbles (the number of **desired** outcomes). Therefore, the probability of selecting a blue marble is $\dfrac{6}{18}$, which reduces to $\dfrac{1}{3}$. Choice (B) is the correct answer.

STANDARDIZED TEST SCORES

As you know, tests can be graded and evaluated in a number of ways. We've all experienced different grading systems—letter grades, percentile scores, and scores specific to a test (like the CBEST scores of 20-80 in this section!). Below, we will review the two most common types of standardized test scores. Your job is to interpret these scores, and understand how individuals performed relative to other students.

Percentile Scores

Percentile scores provide a measure of how a test taker performs relative to other test takers. Percentiles can be understood as a rank within 100, and percentile scores range from 1 to 99 (the highest percentile is 99, and the lowest is 1). For example, if a student scored in the 78th percentile on a test, that student achieved a score that is higher than 78 percent of the other students who took the test (and lower than 21 percent of the students who took the test). So, if 200 students took the test, the student in the 78th percentile scored higher than 156 students who also took the same test. A score in the median (or middle) of all scores would receive a score in the 50th percentile.

Do not confuse percentile with percentage correct scores. Percentile scores allow you to compare one student's scores with those of a group of students who took the test. If a student scores in the 75th percentile, it does NOT necessarily mean that the student got 3 out of every 4 questions correct on the test! In fact, without more information, we have no idea how many questions the student answered correctly—all we know is that the student performed better than 75 percent of the students who took the exam.

Below is an example of how you may be tested on interpreting percentile scores:

5. On a recent statistics quiz, Lisa scored in the 82nd percentile. Her friend Kendra scored in the 65th percentile. The quiz contained 150 questions, and Lisa answered 111 questions correctly. Which of the following statements must be true?

A. Kendra answered 39 questions correctly.

B. Kendra answered 94 questions correctly.

C. 17 students received scores between Lisa and Kendra

D. Kendra's score is greater than the score of 65 other students

E. Kendra answered fewer than 111 questions correctly.

Here's How to Crack It

The correct answer is (E)—because Kendra scored in a lower percentile than Lisa, she must have answered fewer questions correctly than Lisa did. Thus, she answered fewer than 111 questions correctly. Let's look at the other answer choices. First, do we know how many questions Kendra answered correctly? We do not. All we are given is her percentile score. We have no idea how many questions Kendra got right (only that the number is less than 111). That eliminates (A) and (B). Next, do we know how many test takers there are? We do not. Choices (C) and (D) assume that there are 100 test takers. We are not given this information anywhere in the statement above.

Stanine Scores

"Stanine" is short for standard nine. The name comes from the fact that stanine scores range from a low of 1 to a high of 9. So while percentile scores range from 1 to 99, stanine scores range from only 1 to 9. Stanine scores provide less detail for students about test performance relative to other students than do percentile scores. Stanine scores often are given with verbal descriptions of the student's performance. A stanine score of 1, 2, or 3 is below average; 4, 5, or 6 is average; and 7, 8, or 9 is above average. The median (or middle) score is a 5.

Relating Stanine Scores to Percentile Scores

How is it determined who gets a stanine score of 4, and how many students will receive such a score? Stanine scores assume a normal distribution, meaning that for a particular stanine score, you can approximate the range of percentile scores that equate to that score. Look at the normal distribution curve below:

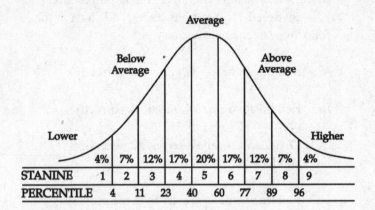

Approximately 17% of test takers will receive a stanine score of 4—and this number corresponds to a percentile score between 23% and 40%. Notice that the same number of students will receive a 4 as will receive a 6; the same is true for 3 and 7; 2 and 8; and 1 and 9.

---

6. Brent received a stanine score of 5 on the Chemistry exam. Angie received a stanine score of 4 on the same exam. Which of the following statements must be true?

   A. Brent received a percentile score at least 10 points higher than Angie.

   B. Brent answered 20% of the questions correctly.

   C. Brent received the exact average score of all test takers.

   D. Over 50% of the test takers received a higher stanine score than Angie.

   E. Brent scored in the 50th percentile on the exam.

Here's How to Crack It

Let's evaluate each statement one at a time. Statement (A) is possible, but it does not have to be true. For example, Brent could receive a score in the 42nd percentile, and Angie could receive a score in the 38th percentile. Statement (B) is false—we have no information about how he did on the questions themselves. We don't know if he got most of the test questions right or wrong! Statements (C) and (E) are possible, but a stanine score of 5 indicates a wide range of scores (40th percentile to 60th percentile). Statement (D) is true. According to the chart, 60 percent of the test takers will receive a stanine score of 5 or higher. Choice (D) is the correct answer.

Summary

o   Estimating the correct answer can solve some questions on the CBEST. Use Ballparking techniques to eliminate answer choices and avoid needless calculations.

o   Use the average circle to find any of the three parts of an average—the number of things, the total, and the average.

o   A ratio compares a part to a part. Use the ratio box to solve most ratio questions.

o   To find a proportion, set the equation you are given equal to the one you want to find.

o   Probabilities are expressed as fractions between 0 and 1. Probability is defined as the number of desired outcomes over the total number of possible outcomes.

o   Percentile scores and stanine scores describe the performance of a test taker relative to the performance of other test takers who took the same exam. Remember that these scores do not indicate the number of questions a student answered correctly— they simply place a student's score in relation to all other scores.

Chapter 8
Computation and Problem Solving

Approximately 35 percent of the questions on the Mathematics Section will fall under the category of computation and problem solving. Of these questions, we've already covered two important areas:

- Questions that require you to add, subtract, multiply, or divide whole numbers.
- Questions that require you to add, subtract, multiply, or divide fractions, decimals, and percentages.

In addition to solving word problems using the order of operations, you will have to solve questions involving algebra. You may not like algebra. You may remember, with sadness, the last time you sat through an algebra class. Well, there is some good news. In the pages ahead, we'll show you how to solve algebra questions without having to write an equation! Here is an outline for the algebra concepts that will be covered in this chapter:

- Manipulating an equation. Okay, so there will be some algebra. We'll show you what to do if you are asked to solve an equation.
- Solve an inequality. We'll show you how to handle an equation that has a > or < sign, instead of an equals sign.
- Backsolving. Worried about trying to turn a word problem into an equation? Don't be. With this technique, we'll show you how to solve an algebra question without algebra!
- What numbers are needed? We'll show you how to crack a specific algebra question on the CBEST by identifying the numbers you'll need to use to solve a problem.
- What can be determined? Some CBEST questions will ask you to identify what, if anything, can be known given certain pieces of information.
- There's got to be another way. Some math questions will require you to find an alternative method of solving a problem.

MANIPULATING AN EQUATION

Believe it or not, you've already set up a number of algebraic equations. In the last chapter, we set up equalities when using proportions. When we set up a proportion, we had several numbers and one unknown, or variable. A sample equation question could look something like the following question.

1. If $3x + 18 = 24$, what is the value of x?

   A. 2

   B. 6

   C. 14

   D. 15

   E. 45

Here's How to Crack It

The question can be asked in many ways: "what is the value of x," "solve for x," "x equals?" No matter how the CBEST authors phrase the question, you have to do one thing—isolate the variable x from all the other numbers. This means getting the variable on one side of the equation, and all the numbers on the other side of the equation. In order to do this, you need to know **the golden rule of equations:**

Whatever you do to the left side of the equation, you have to do the same to the right side of the equation.

Let's take a look at how to solve the equation above.

First, the variable is found on the left side of the equation. Thus, we need to get all the values on the right side of the equation. The first step is to move any numbers, in this case, the 18.

$$
\begin{array}{r}
3x + 18 = 24 \\
-18 \quad -18 \\
\hline
3x - \ 0 = \ 6
\end{array}
$$

In order to move the 18, we needed to subtract 18 from the left side of the equation. Therefore, we also need to subtract 18 from the right side of the equation. After simplifying each side of the equation, you can see that there is no longer a value on the left side of the equation (there is no need to write the zero, simply eliminate it from the equation). Our new equation is:

$$3x = 6$$

The golden rule of equations—whatever you do to one side of the equation, you must do to the other side of the equation.

Next, we need to move the number 3 from the variable x. Currently, 3 and x are to be multiplied together. In order to eliminate the 3 from the left side of the equation, we need to divide by 3. Following the golden rule, we also must divide the right side of the equation by 3.

$$3x = 6$$
$$\div 3 \quad \div 3$$
$$x = 2$$

The number 3 cancels out on the left side of the equation and we are left with the variable x. On the right side of the equation, we can simplify the operation 6 divided by 3. Our final equation is that $x = 2$; answer choice (A) is the correct answer.

———————○———————

Occasionally, you will be presented with an equation that has more than one variable. Don't worry. You won't be asked to try to solve for multiple variables. Instead, the CBEST writers will give you a value to enter into the equation, as in the following example:

———————○———————

2. If $4a + 2b = 32 - a + b$, find the value of a when $b = 12$.

A. 2

B. 4

C. 6

D. 10

E. 12

Here's How to Crack It

Start this problem by rewriting the equation, substituting the number 12 wherever you see b:

$$4a + 2(12) = 32 - a + (12)$$

Next, using the order of operations, simplify the equation:

$$4a + 24 = 32 - a + 12$$

$$4a + 24 = 44 - a$$

Now you can solve this equation using the same techniques we described in the previous example. Isolate the variable a from all the other numbers. In this case, both the left side and the right side of the equation contain the variable a. While you can choose to put the variable on either side of the equation, it is usually easier to move the smaller value. In this example, we'll move the $-a$ to the left side of the equation:

$$\begin{aligned} 4a + 24 &= 44 - a \\ +a \quad\quad\; &\quad\; +a \\ 5a + 24 &= 44 \end{aligned}$$

Next, move the number 24 away from the variable to the right side of the equation:

$$\begin{aligned} 5a + 24 &= 44 \\ -24 \;\; &\;\; -24 \\ 5a &= 20 \end{aligned}$$

Finally, divide by 5:

$$\begin{aligned} 5a &= 20 \\ \div 5 \;\; &\;\; \div 5 \\ a &= 4 \end{aligned}$$

Choice (B) is the correct answer.

If you have questions with more than one variable, the CBEST authors will need to give you additional information in order to solve the equation. Most often, they will simply give you the value of one of the variables, and ask you to find the other. The following drill includes additional equations that will allow you to practice manipulating and solving.

EQUATION DRILL

Answers and explanations can be found on page 174.

1. If $6y - 3 = -9$, then y equals

   A. -2

   B. -1

   C. 1

   D. 2

   E. 6

2. If $n + 2b + p = h - r$, what is the value of h when
   $n = 8$, $b = \dfrac{1}{2}$, $p = \dfrac{3}{4}$, and $r = 6$?

   A. $9\dfrac{3}{4}$

   B. 15

   C. $15\dfrac{1}{2}$

   D. $15\dfrac{3}{4}$

   E. $18\dfrac{3}{4}$

3. If $8c - 12 = 12$, what is twice the value of c?

   A. 0

   B. 3

   C. 6

   D. 32

   E. 96

4. If $5z = 10 + 2z$, what is the value of $9z$?

   A. $\dfrac{10}{3}$

   B. 10

   C. 16

   D. 21

   E. 30

INEQUALITIES

Inequalities are very similar to equations. Instead of providing a specific value for a variable, an inequality defines a range of values for a variable. For example, an inequality may tell you that $x < 5$. You don't know exactly what the value of x is, but you do know its range. It could be any value less than 5.

Let's review the symbols for inequalities. These will be helpful not only for solving inequalities, but also for relating numbers to one another (covered in Chapter 7):

>	**greater than**	$9 > 5$	"9 is greater than 5"
<	**less than**	$5 < 9$	"5 is less than 9"
$\geq$	**greater than or equal to**	$x \geq 5$	"x is greater than or equal to 5"
$\leq$	**less than or equal to**	$y \leq 9$	"y is less than or equal to 9"

Let's use a variation of our first example to see how to solve an inequality:

---

1. If $3x + 18 > 24$, which of the following expressions gives all the possible values of x?

    A. $x > 2$

    B. $x < 6$

    C. $x > 14$

    D. $x < 15$

    E. $x \geq 45$

Here's How to Crack It

When solving an inequality, treat the inequality like an equal sign. Remember to use the golden rule of equations (whatever you do to one side, you must do the other side).

$$
\begin{aligned}
3x + 18 &> 24 \\
-18 \quad & -18 \\
3x \quad &> 6 \\
\div 3 \quad & \div 3 \\
x &> 2
\end{aligned}
$$

Choice (A) is the correct answer.

———————○———————

As you can see, an inequality is just like an equation, with one notable exception:

> **If you are multiplying or dividing by a negative number, you must flip the sign of the inequality.**

Here is an example that illustrates this rule:

———————○———————

2. If $-7a + 3 < 24$, then which of the following expressions gives all the possible values of a?

A. $a = 3$

B. $a < -3$

C. $a > -3$

D. $a > \dfrac{27}{7}$

E. $a = -3$

Here's How to Crack It

With any inequality or equation, try to isolate the variable from all the other numbers. In this case, start by subtracting 3 from both sides of the equation; this leaves us with the inequality:

$$-7a < 21$$

At this point, we need to divide by –7 in order to isolate the variable:

$$\frac{-7a}{-7} < \frac{21}{-7}$$

Here, we are dividing by a negative number. Thus, we must proceed with division as normal, but flip the sign:

$$a > -3$$

Choice (C) is the correct answer. Be careful when selecting your answer choice! The CBEST writers will almost always include an answer choice that looks correct, except that the sign is pointing in the wrong direction.

Remember that when you multiply or divide by a negative number you must flip the inequality sign.

INEQUALITY DRILL

Answers and explanations can be found on page 174.

1. If $-3x + 6 \geq 18$, which of the following must be true?

   A. $x \leq -4$

   B. $x \leq 6$

   C. $x \geq -4$

   E. $x \geq -6$

   F. $x = 2$

2. If $5x + 3 < 28$, then which of the following expressions gives all the possible values of x?

    A. $x < 5$

    B. $x < -5$

    C. $x > 0$

    D. $x > 5$

    E. $x = -5$

3. If $-5x - 21 < 14$, which of the following must be true?

    A. $x > 7$

    B. $x > -7$

    C. $x < 7$

    D. $x < -7$

    E. $x = 7$

BACKSOLVING

Let's take a look at a typical algebraic word problem.

1. Marcello has 34 more dimes than nickels. If he has a total of 76 coins, how many nickels does Marcello have?

    A.   21

    B.   40

    C.   42

    D.   84

    E.   110

Yuck—an algebra question. The traditional way to solve this problem is to set up a system of equations. You could assign a variable for dimes, another variable for nickels, and so on. In this particular question, traditional algebra would take a while. In fact, you would need to create two equations, each with two variables. Isn't there a better way?

The problem asks us for the number of nickels that Marcello has, and presents us with five possible answer choices. If we were to set up the equations properly, we'd find one of those five answer choices.

The correct answer will be one of the five answer choices. Our job is to test each answer choice to see if it fits the problem.

But what if we use those answer choices to our advantage? The answer has to be one of those five, right? Rather than try to create our own equations, we should try one of the answer choices and plug it into the problem to see if it works. If it doesn't work, we can keep trying until we find the answer choice that does work.

This technique is called Backsolving. Whenever you are presented with an algebra question and there are numbers in the answer choices, try plugging in the answer choices to see which one is correct.

Let's solve the sample problem above, using this Backsolving technique.

We'll start with (C), 42 nickels (we'll explain why we started with (C) in a minute). Let's see if we can work back through the problem, assuming that Marcello has 42 nickels.

The first statement tells us that Marcello has 34 more dimes than nickels. If Marcello owns 42 nickels, then he has 76 dimes, for a total of 118 coins. The problem indicates that Marcello has a total of 76 coins, so is (C) the correct answer? No! Using the value of 42 nickels, we did not find the problem worked correctly. Therefore, we can eliminate (C).

Answer choices will appear in either ascending or descending order.

If you take a look at the answer choices, you can see that they are in order from smallest to largest. In general, the answer choices on the CBEST will be in ascending or descending order. We started with (C), the middle value. In the example above, we know that (C) is not correct. Can we also tell if we'll need a larger number or a smaller number? Sure! When we tried the value of 42 nickels, we found a total number of coins much larger than we wanted. Therefore, the correct answer will be fewer than 42 nickels. In this case, we can eliminate (D) and (E), since they will provide even larger totals, and move to the next smaller answer choice, (B).

Choice (B) tells us that Marcello has a total of 40 nickels. If this were the case, this would mean that Marcello has 74 dimes. This gives him a total of 114 coins, a number much larger than we're looking for. Eliminate (B).

This leaves us with only one answer choice. At this point, without doing any more work, feel free to select (A). But for purposes of this example, we'll finish the problem. Choice (A) says that Marcello has 21 nickels. If he has 21 nickels, then he must have 34 more dimes, or 55. This gives us a total of 76 coins, exactly what we're looking for! Choice (A) is the correct answer.

If (C) is incorrect, try to determine if you need a larger value or a smaller value. If you aren't sure, just choose another answer choice and keep working.

Let's take a minute to summarize what we just did. First, we identified a specific type of algebra question—one which had numbers in the answer choices. We can take these numbers, plug them back into the problem, and see which one works. In order to be most efficient, we started with (C), the middle value. This helps us decide which way to go if (C) is incorrect. Once we identified the correct way to go, we eliminated the impossible answer choices, and kept working until we found the answer that worked.

Backsolving turns difficult algebra questions into arithmetic problems. Rather than worry about creating equations, sometimes with more than one variable, focus on using the answer choices to your advantage.

We'll cover two more typical Backsolving questions to be sure you're familiar with this technique.

Proven Techniques
Tip! When Backsolving, always start with choice (C), the middle number.

2. Adam is half as old as Bob and three times as old as Cindy. If the sum of their ages is 40, what is Bob's age?

   A.   3

   B.   6

   C.   12

   D.   18

   E.   24

Here's How to Crack It

Again we have an algebra question with numbers in the answer choices. Backsolve! The answer choices tell us Bob's age. We start with Bob's age at 12, (C). If Bob is 12, then Adam is 6, and Cindy is 2. The sum of their ages is 20. We're looking for the sum of their ages to be 40, so eliminate (C).

Now which way should we go? Should we increase Bob's age to 18 (answer choice (D)) or decrease his age to 6, (B)? When we tried Bob at the age of 12, the sum of their ages was much less than we wanted. We need to increase the total of the three individuals. Therefore, we should increase Bob's age to 18, and try (D). Before trying (D), eliminate (A) and (B)—they will give us even smaller totals.

If Bob is 18, then Adam is half his age, or 9. Cindy is a third of Adam's age, so she is 3. If we take the sum of their ages, we get 18 + 9 + 3 = 30. But the sum of their ages should be 40, so (D) is not correct. Eliminate it.

We're left with only one answer choice, so (E) must be the correct answer. Want to see the work? If Bob is 24, then Adam is half his age, 12. Cindy is a third of Adam's age, so she is 4. The sum of their ages, 24 + 12 + 4, equals 40. We have correctly solved the problem.

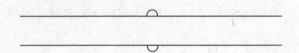

3. If there are four times as many women as men employed by the Acme Insurance Company, then how many of the 75 workers are women?

   A. 80

   B. 75

   C. 60

   D. 45

   E. 15

Here's How to Crack It

Did you recognize this question as a Backsolving problem? We have a statement in which an algebraic equation could be written, as well as numbers in the answer choices. Before Backsolving, be sure to use another great math technique, Ballparking. The question tells us that there are a total of 75 workers. Thus, (A) and (B) don't make sense. We can't have the number of women in the company greater than or equal to the total number of employees.

In general, we have always said to start with (C). In this case, since we have eliminated (A) and (B) due to Ballparking, start with the middle remaining value, in this case (D). By using the remaining middle value, we'll be as efficient as possible when solving this question.

Choice (D) tells us that there are 45 women in the work force. If there are 45 women, and a total of 75 employees, then there must be 30 men (75 – 45). Are there four times as many women as men? In this case, 45 is not 4 times 30. We can eliminate (D). There needs to be a greater number of women in order to make a ratio of 4 times as many women as men. Let's move to (C), which has more women.

Choice (C) tells us that there are 60 women in the work force. If there are 60 women, and a total of 75 employees, then there must be 15 men (75 – 60). Are there four times as many women as men? Yes. 60 is four times greater than 15. Choice (C) is the correct answer.

Will Backsolving Work for Every Question?

Unfortunately, no. Many questions on the CBEST will have to be solved by manipulating the information that is given to you in the question. Backsolving is just one of a number of techniques we have shown you throughout these math chapters. Remember the keys to identifying a Backsolving question:

- Numbers in the answer choices.
- Does it seem like an algebra question? That is, do you feel like you need to start writing an algebraic equation in order to solve the problem traditionally? If so, you've probably identified a Backsolving question.
- The question asks for a specific amount. Backsolving questions will typically end in concrete statements, such as "what is the value of *x*," "how many tools does Bill have," or "how many tickets were purchased?"

How to Recognize a Backsolving Question:
1. Numbers in the answer choices.
2. The question is a word problem.
3. The question asks for a specific amount.

BACKSOLVING DRILL

Answers and explanations can be found on page 175.

1. Kathleen and Elizabeth jog a total of 23 miles today. If Kathleen jogs 5 more miles than Elizabeth, how many miles did Elizabeth jog?

   A. 5

   B. 9

   C. 14

   D. 16

   E. 18

2. Forty-two people have registered for a raffle. If there are twice as many children as adults signed up, how many children are registered for the raffle?

   A. 14

   B. 18

   C. 20

   D. 28

   E. 32

3. If $2x - 7 = 3$, then $x =$

   A. 1

   B. 2

   C. 3

   D. 4

   E. 5

IDENTIFY THE NUMBERS NEEDED

So far in this chapter, we've talked about how to solve algebraic equations and inequalities. We've also talked about how to solve an algebra word problem without setting up an equation by using Backsolving. In this next type of algebra question, we'll need to identify the numbers that are needed to solve an equation. Try asking yourself "Which of the numbers in the problem is (are) needed to solve the problem?" in the following example:

---

1. Tom planted 40 roses and 30 tulips in his garden. There is a 4 to 7 ratio of roses to daffodils. Which of the following number (numbers) in the problem are needed to find the total number of daffodils that Tom has planted?

   A.   40 only

   B.   40 and 30 only

   C.   40, 4, and 7 only

   D.   30, 4, and 7 only

   E.   40, 30, 4, and 7

Here's How to Crack It

You should be able to identify this question as a ratio question. We're given an initial ratio of roses to daffodils, and are asked for the actual number of daffodils. We have the actual number of roses. Remember the ratio box? In order to find the actual number of daffodils, you need the initial ratio, plus one actual number. The initial ratio of roses to daffodils is 4 to 7, and the actual number is the number of roses, or 40. You do not need the fact that there are 30 tulips in Tom's garden. This piece of information does nothing to help you solve the ratio box involving roses and daffodils. Choice (C) is the correct answer.

On these types of questions, you may find it helpful to set up a problem, but be sure *not* to solve it. All you are looking for is the numbers that are *needed* to solve the problem, *not* the correct answer to the problem. You'll lose valuable time trying to find the correct answer.

Tip! If you are asked to identify the numbers needed in a problem, you do not need to solve the problem.

Solving the problem won't get you any bonus points. Try asking yourself the same question for the following example:

2. Tom performs 8 experiments in his lab each day of the week. Over the course of one week, Tom averaged 5 successful experiments per day. On Thursday, Tom performed 6 of his 8 experiments successfully. Which of the following number (numbers) in the problem are needed to find the total number of successful experiments that Tom performed over the entire 7-day week?

A. 8, 5 only

B. 5, 7 only

C. 8, 5, 1 only

D. 8, 5, 6, 1 only

E. 8, 5, 6, 1, and 7

Here's How to Crack It

First, try to identify exactly what the question is asking for. This is an average question, and we're looking for the total number of successful experiments that Tom performed during the week. As you know from the lesson on averages, if we are looking for the total, we need two pieces of information—the number of things, and the average.

We are given the number of things (in this case the number of days, 7) and the average (an average of 5 successful experiments per day). Using the average circle below, we can fill in the information we need to find the correct answer:

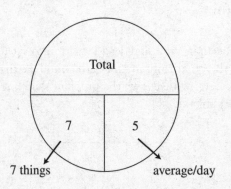

The only two numbers needed for this problem are 5 (the average) and 7 (the number of things). Choice (B) is the correct answer. The information given to us about Tom's performances on Thursday and Friday are unnecessary. While this information may be useful, it is not needed to find the total number of successful experiments.

When asked to identify the number(s) needed to solve a problem, remember the following keys:

1. Identify the type of question. Chances are good that the question will fall into a category you are familiar with. Is it a ratio? A percentage? An average? Once you identify the question, try to set up the problem.
2. Do **not** actually solve the problem. You only need to identify the numbers that are **needed** to solve the problem. Solving the problem will waste time and distract you from your focus on the answer choices.
3. Look out for misleading information. There will usually be some numbers given to you in the question that are not needed to find the correct answer.

WHAT CAN BE FOUND?

Another type of question on the CBEST asks you to identify what kind of information you *could* solve for given the information in a question. You can recognize these questions by the phrase "What can be determined?" If you see this phrase in the question, you won't need to worry about doing any formal calculations—you'll simply need to identify what could be known based on the information you are given. Let's take a look at the following example to better understand these types of questions.

Each of 51 students is asked to select one and only one class as an elective. There are 13 spaces available in music, 18 spaces available in football, and 30 spaces available in art. As of 3:00 P.M., 21 of the total spaces have been filled.

3. Which of the following facts can be determined from the information given above?

 A. the number of students that selected music

 B. the number of girls selecting football

 C. the total number of students at the school

 D. the ratio of boys to girls in art

 E. the number of students in the group that have not yet chosen an elective class.

Here's How to Crack It

There are two key things to remember when solving these types of questions:

1. **Process of Elimination.** Of course! Often the best way to choose the correct answer is to eliminate answer choices that you know are wrong. With these types of questions, evaluating the answer choices will also give you a clue as to what the CBEST writers are looking for.

2. **Stay focused *only* on the information presented.** The biggest trap on these questions is to make assumptions that are not contained in the information (much like the trap of making assumptions in the Reading Section of the test). A correct answer must be proven by the information you are given. You cannot bring in any outside information—stick to what is written!

Let's use these two techniques to solve the example above. What information are we given? We know that each member of a group of students needs to choose one elective class from the following: music, football, and art. We also know that by 3:00 P.M., 21 of the spaces have been filled. What don't we know? We don't know how many students are in each class, nor do we know anything about the boys and girls in each class. Choice (A) is incorrect because we aren't given any information about the number of students that have selected music as the elective class.

Choices (B) and (D) are incorrect—we know nothing about the percentage of boys and girls in the class (in fact, this is never mentioned). Choice (C) is incorrect, since we know nothing about how many students attend the school—we only know about the particular group of students being discussed. Choice (E) is correct—we know that 21 spaces have been filled, and that there are a total of 51 students—and thus we can determine how many students still need to choose an elective.

———————————○———————————

Let's try one more example:

———————————○———————————

> Dave and Melissa travel from their home to the theater, each taking a different route. Dave makes it to the theater in 25 minutes. Melissa travels 7 miles, and makes it to the theater in 42 minutes.

4. Which of the following facts can be determined from the information given above?

  A. The speed at which Dave made the trip, in miles per hour

  B. Whether Dave or Melissa arrived at the theater first

  C. By what percent the duration of Melissa's trip exceeded that of Dave's trip

  D. The time it took Dave to return home from the theater

  E. None of the above can be determined

Here's How to Crack It

First, summarize the information that you are given. We know that Dave and Melissa are each traveling to the theater—Dave takes 25 minutes (we do *not* know how many *miles* he traveled), and Melissa took 42 minutes to go 7 miles. Choice (A) asks for Dave's speed—a calculation that would require knowing both the time and the distance. Since we do not know the distance Dave traveled, we can eliminate (A). Choice (B) is tricky—it *seems* like Dave would arrive at the theater first, but we are not told that the two left for the theater at the same time. Therefore, while (B) may be true, we cannot prove it, so we must eliminate (B). Choice (C) is a percent increase question. Since we have both the time it took Dave and the time it took Melissa, we could set up an equation to find this percentage. Choice (C) is correct. Choice (D) is incorrect because we are told nothing about the return trip home from the theater. And finally, since we have an answer that works, (C), choice (E) is not correct.

So, we know that the correct answer in the problem above is (C). By the way, what is the percentage difference in the duration of the two trips? Don't know? Good! Don't worry about doing formal calculations on these questions. Your job is simply to determine what information can be found, not to actually solve the problem. Solving will only waste time.

Choice (E) in the above example may appear as an answer choice on some questions you encounter on the CBEST. Only select this answer choice once you've eliminated all the others, and be careful! It is very tempting to pick this answer choice if the question is difficult. Make sure you've evaluated all other answer choices before selecting the "It cannot be determined" answer choice.

—————————————◯—————————————

There's Got to be Another Way—Alternative Solution Questions

Some questions on the CBEST will ask you to identify an alternative method to solving a question. In the question, the authors will present one formula for solving a desired problem, and ask you to identify another possible way of setting up the equation. Before we talk about the keys to solving these problems, let's take a look at what one looks like.

5. Joe buys a hot dog with ketchup, mustard, and relish. A hot dog costs $1.75, and toppings are $.35 each. Joe pays with a five-dollar bill. Joe uses the following expression to calculate the amount of money he should receive back for the purchase:

$5.00 – ($1.75 + $.35 + $.35 + $.35)

Which of the following expressions could Joe have also used?

A. $3 \times ($5.00 – $1.75 – $.35)$

B. $3.25 – 3 \times $.35$

C. $1.75 + (3 \times $.35) – 5.00

D. $.35 – $5.00 + 1.75

E. $3($5.00 – $.35) + ($5.00 – $1.75)$

Here's How to Crack It

Before we solve the problem, let's talk about how the problem is structured. First, you will be given a description of the problem. Then, you will be given one correct method of solving the problem. Finally, you will be asked to identify an answer choice that gives you an alternative way of solving the problem.

So, how do you approach this type of question? First, you may be able to identify or set up your own equation after reading through the information. This may help you immediately identify the correct answer. However, if you aren't sure about how to set up the problem, you can still get the correct answer because:

**The Value of the Correct Answer Will Equal the
Value of the Given Equation!**

Make sure your answer choice equals the expression given in the problem.

If you aren't sure how to identify the other equation, no problem! Simplify the initial equation, solve each answer choice, and select the answer choice that gives you the same result as the initial equation. Let's do this for Example 1.

If we solve the equation given to us, we have $5.00 – $2.80 = $2.20. Therefore, the correct answer needs to produce a value of $2.20. Choice (A): 3 × ($5.00 – $1.75 – $.35) = 3 × $2.90 = $8.70, so we can eliminate (A).

Choice (B): $3.25 – 3 × $.35 = $3.25 – $1.05 = $2.20. Perfect! This equation yields the same value as the given equation, so (B) is the correct answer.

Of course, you will save more time if you are able to recognize the correct alternative equation without doing calculations. In this case, the total amount of change that Joe will receive back is $5.00 minus the total cost of the hot dog with the toppings. In the given equation, each additional cost is subtracted from $5.00. Choice (B) simplifies this equation by subtracting the cost of the hot dog from the $5.00.

———————————○———————————

In summary, if you can identify the alternative equation, great. If not, don't worry. Solve each answer choice, and stop when you find one that equals the result of the given equation. Here is one more example:

———————————○———————————

6. Oliver makes business trips between San Diego and San Francisco. Within the last year, Oliver took 6 trips by train, and 6 trips by plane. The cost of a train ride is $53, and the cost of a flight is $102. Oliver uses the following expression to calculate the amount of money he spends on these trips:

    (6 × $53) + (6 × $102)

    Which of the following expressions could Oliver have also used?

    A.   6 ($53 + $102)

    B.   (12 × $53) + $102

    C.   36 × $155

    D.   (6 + 6)($53 + $102)

    E.   12 ÷ $153

Here's How to Crack It

In order to find the total cost Oliver spent on travel, we need to multiply the number of trips by the cost of each trip. The given equation does this for us by taking the sum of the cost of 6 plane trips and 6 train trips. If you look at the expression, you may be able to tell that this expression can be factored (you might even shout out "the distributive property!").

Yes, the expression can be simplified by removing the 6 from each individual expression:

$$(6 \times \$53) + (6 \times \$102)$$
$$= 6(\$53) + 6(\$102)$$
$$= 6(\$53 + \$102)$$

Choice (A) is the correct answer. If you were not familiar with this factoring method, don't worry. Solve the expression:

$$(6 \times \$53) + (6 \times \$102)$$
$$= 318 + 612$$
$$= 930$$

Then go to the answer choices, and find a value that gives you 930. You'll find that only (A) will equal 930 (you should stop as soon as you find the first equation that yields the same result).

Try to manipulate the given expression to fit an expression in the answer choices.

ANSWERS TO DRILLS

Equation Drill
From page 154

1. **B** First, add 3 to each side of the equation: $6y = -6$

    Now, divide each side of the equation by 6: $y = -1$.

2. **D** Here is the equation we are given: $n + 2b + p = h - r$

    Now, substitute the values we are given for n, b, p, and r:

    $$8 + 2(\frac{1}{2}) + \frac{3}{4} = h - 6$$

    $$8 + 1 + \frac{3}{4} = h - 6$$

    $$9\frac{3}{4} = h - 6$$

    $$15\frac{3}{4} = h$$

3. **C** If you got answer choice (B), reread the question! The question asks for twice the value of the variable c. Solve to find that c is 3; twice c is 6, which is the correct answer.

4. **E** Rewrite the equation as $3z = 10$. Since we are asked to find the value of $9z$, multiply the equation by 3 to get $9z = 30$. 30 is the correct answer.

Inequality Drill
From page 168

1. **A** Simplify the inequality to get $-3x \geq 12$. Divide by -3 to get that $x \leq -4$. Remember that the sign will change when multiplying or dividing by a negative number.

2. **A** Subtract 3 from both sides of the equation to get $5x < 25$. Divide by 5 to get $x < 5$.

3. **B** Add 21 to each side of the equation to get –5x < 35. Divide by –5 to get x > –7.

Backsolving Drill
From page 164

1. **B** Start with (C). If Elizabeth jogs 14 miles, then Kathleen jogs 19. This total of 33 is too high, so eliminate (C), (D), and (E), and move to (B). If Elizabeth jogs 9 miles, and Kathleen jogs 14, then the total is 23.

2. **D** Start with (C). If 20 children register for the raffle, then 10 adults register. Since this total does not equal 42, the number of children is too small. Eliminate (C), (B), and (A), and move to (D). If 28 children are registered, then 14 adults are registered. This gives us the total of 42 we are looking for.

3. **E** It is possible to backsolve on equations. If you ever have a complicated equation, simply backsolve to find the correct value of the variable. In this case, starting with (C) will yield you a negative value, not the value of 3. Eliminate (C), (B), and (A). Choice (D) is also too small. Choice (E) gives us the correct value of x.

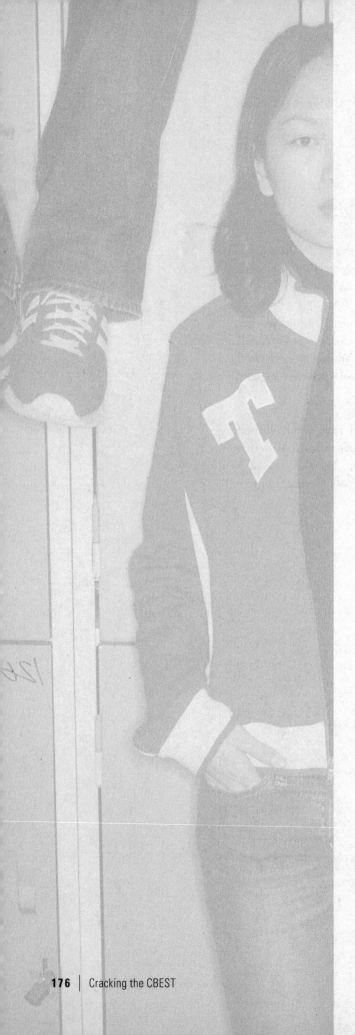

Summary

o When manipulating an equation, remember the golden rule of equations: Whatever you do to one side of the equation, you must do to the other side.

o When manipulating an equation, isolate the variable from all numbers.

o Treat inequalities just like equations, with one exception: Whenever you multiply or divide by a negative number, you must flip the sign.

o Backsolving is a powerful technique on algebra questions; rather than setting up your own equation, try Plugging In the answer choices to see which one "fits" the problem.

o You can backsolve on any algebra question that has the following features:
   • numbers in the answer choices
   • a question that asks for a specific amount

o When Backsolving, start with the middle answer choice (C). If this answer choice does not work, you will often have a clue as to whether the correct answer will be smaller or larger.

o Use POE in conjunction with Backsolving to automatically eliminate answer choices that cannot work in the problem.

o When asked to identify the numbers needed to solve a problem, don't worry about solving the problem—simply set up the equation and identify the needed numbers.

o When given a "Which of the following can be determined" question, be sure to not make any assumptions about what you can solve—stick to only the provided information.

o There are two ways to solve an alternative method problem. You can set up another equation, or you can calculate the value of the given equation, and see which one of the answer choices gives you the same value.

Chapter 9
Numerical
and Graphical
Relationships

About 35 percent of the mathematics problems on the CBEST will involve the question types described below. Some information, especially the logic rules, may be new to you. Don't worry—there will be very little information to memorize in this chapter. The following topics will be covered:

- Numerical relationships. Recognizing the position of numbers in relation to each other.
- Rounding. Using the rules of rounding when solving problems.
- Solving problems with graphs. Taking information contained in tables and graphs to solve math problems.
- Recognizing trends in information presented in graphs.
- Finding missing information in graphs.
- Rules of logic. Understanding and applying basic logical connectives.

POSITION OF NUMBERS

In the review chapter, we discussed the number line and how numbers are plotted on the line. On the CBEST, you will often be asked to recognize the position of numbers in relation to each other. Sample types of questions are:

- Which of the following numbers is greatest?
- Which of the following numbers is closest to zero?
- Which of the following numbers, when multiplied by 3, would yield the smallest product?

In order to handle these types of questions, here are a few rules to remember about the position of numbers.

FRACTIONS

If two fractions have the same numerator, the fraction with the largest denominator is the *smaller* fraction. For example, of $\frac{1}{4}$ and $\frac{1}{3}$, which fraction is largest? The larger fraction is $\frac{1}{3}$ (it has the smallest denominator).

What about trying to find the larger of two fractions with different numerators and denominators? Remember, when trying to determine which fraction is larger, use the Bowtie. The Bowtie is especially useful when two fractions have different numerators and denominators.

Remember to use the Bowtie to compare two fractions.

1. Which of the following fractions is between $\frac{1}{4}$ and $\frac{1}{2}$?

    A. $\frac{1}{6}$

    B. $\frac{2}{3}$

    C. $\frac{1}{3}$

    D. $\frac{3}{4}$

    E. $\frac{1}{8}$

Here's How to Crack It

Before looking at the answer choices, take a look at the two fractions that we are given in the question. Which one is larger? $\frac{1}{2}$. Which one is smaller? $\frac{1}{4}$. So, we need to find an answer choice that is larger than $\frac{1}{4}$ and less than $\frac{1}{2}$. (If you are more comfortable with decimals, you may choose to look for a number that is greater than .25 and less than .5. However, this will require much more time, as you'll need to translate all of the answer choices into decimals as well). First, eliminate any answer choice that is not greater than $\frac{1}{4}$. We can eliminate (A) and (E). Next, eliminate any answer choice that is greater than $\frac{1}{2}$. From this step, we can eliminate (B) and (D). Choice (C), or $\frac{1}{3}$ is the correct answer.

NEGATIVE NUMBERS

When comparing two negative numbers, the larger value is the number that is closest to 0 on the number line.

For example, which number has the larger value, –12 or –3? While we generally think of a value of 12 being larger (it just seems bigger), remember that the negative sign makes it smaller than –3. The number –3 is closer to zero on the number line than is –12.

2. Which of the following numbers is smallest:

A. $-\dfrac{12}{5}$

B.   –4

C. $\dfrac{2}{3}$

D.   0

E. $-\dfrac{19}{3}$

Here's How to Crack It

First, Ballpark using the answer choices. Eliminate any number that is not negative—(C) and (D). Next, we need to compare the remaining answer choices to each other, using the Bowtie. – 4 is smaller than $-\dfrac{12}{5}$. (Using the Bowtie, we get –20 above – 4, and –12 above $-\dfrac{12}{5}$.) Eliminate (A). Next, compare – 4 to $-\dfrac{19}{3}$. Using the Bowtie, you can tell that $-\dfrac{19}{3}$ is the smallest number. (E) is the correct answer.

DECIMALS

When comparing decimals, start by comparing numbers using the largest place. For example, which decimal is greater, 2.461 or 2.409? To find the correct answer, we start with the units digit. Each number has a units digit of 2, so move to the next greatest place, the tenths place. Each number has a tenths digit of 4, so move to the next greatest place, the hundredths place. In this place, the number 2.461 has a larger value than 2.409 (a 6 compared to a 0). Therefore, 2.461 is the larger decimal. Once you find a difference, the problem is solved (there's no need to compare the values in the thousandths place).

---

3. If the value of y is between .0045 and .023, which of the following could be the value of y?

    A.   .0036

    B.   .06

    C.   .0261

    D.   .018

    E.   .0236

Here's How to Crack It

First, eliminate any answer choice that is not greater than .0045. This will eliminate (A). Next, eliminate any answer choice that is not less than .023. This will eliminate (B), (C), and (E). The remaining choice, (D), is the correct answer. The number .018 is located between .0045 and .023.

When asked about the position of numbers, remember the rules of fractions, negatives, and decimals. Further, POE is the key tool to solving these questions. Use the answer choices to help you eliminate incorrect answers, and to thereby find the correct answer.

ROUNDING NUMBERS

The CBEST test writers will sometimes ask you to round a number. Sample questions might read "...rounded to the nearest thousand" or "...if the result is rounded to the nearest tenth." Whenever you are asked to round a number, use the following rules:

To round to the nearest

10	10–14, round down to 10 15–19, round up to 20
100	from 100–149, round down to 100 from 150–199, round up to 200
1,000	from 1,000–1,499, round down to 1,000 from 1,500–1,999, round up to 2,000

For decimals, use the following rules:

To round to the nearest

10th	from .1–.14, round down to .1 from .15–.19, round up to .2
100th	from .01–.014, round down to .01 from .015–.019, round up to .02

Rounding rules: If the following value is 5 or greater, round up. If the following value is 4 or lower, round down.

In general, look at the digit in the place next to the digit you are rounding (for example, if you are asked to round to the nearest tenth, look at the hundredths digit). If the digit is from 0–4, round down. If the digit is 5 or higher, round up to the nearest value.

Here is a sample question that you might see on the CBEST:

---

4. Students scored an average of 73.4861 on a recent test. What is the average score of the students, rounded to the nearest hundredth?

   A.   100

   B.   73.5

   C.   73.49

   D.   73.486

   E.   73.48

Here's How to Crack It

First, eliminate (A), (B), and (D). None of these answer choices are rounded to the nearest hundredth. To round 73.4861 to the nearest hundredth, we need to look at the digit in the thousandths place. The digit is 6. Rounding tells us that if a digit is 5 or greater, round up. Thus, we need to round the digit in the hundredths place from 8 up to 9. The correct answer is 73.49, (C).

ONLY ROUND ONCE!

It is important that you wait until all calculations have been finished before you round the numbers off. Rounding too early can lead to an incorrect answer choice. Here is an example in which rounding too early will lead to a mistake:

Perform all calculations with complete numbers before rounding the final result.

5. When the sum of 1.324 and 3.743 is rounded to the nearest tenth, the result is:

    A.   5.0

    B.   5.067

    C.   5.07

    D.   5.08

    E.   5.1

Here's How to Crack It

First, the answer must be rounded to the nearest tenth, so eliminate (B), (C), and (D). Next, add the two values together. Do *not* round yet! We're looking to round the **sum**, not the individual numbers. The equation: 1.324 + 3.743 yields a result of 5.067. Now we can round to the nearest tenth; the 6 digit in the hundredths place indicates that we need to round up. The correct answer is 5.1, (E). (Note that if you rounded each number initially, the values would be 1.3 and 3.7, and the sum would be 5.0—(A). Be careful!

ROUNDING DRILL

Answers and explanations can be found on page 196.

1. What is 2.019 rounded to the nearest tenth? To the nearest hundredth?

2. What is 438,172 rounded to the nearest hundred?

3. What is 173,893 rounded to the nearest thousand?

4. What is .4954 rounded to the nearest hundredth?

5. To the nearest ten, what is 186?

GRAPHS

The size of a graph will not indicate the level of difficulty of the questions. Don't let a large graph intimidate you!

Most types of math questions on the CBEST are presented as word problems. The CBEST writers will also ask you to solve various math problems using graphs. These graphs can take many forms—a table of information, a bar chart, a line chart, or a pie chart.

Often, questions using graphs can be intimidating to students, simply because of the size or amount of information presented in a graph. Yet graph questions are no more complicated than any other type of math question. Simply find the information that you need from the graph, use that data for any necessary calculations, and you're done. Finally, some students feel that the more complicated the graph, the more difficult the problem will be. This simply isn't true. Don't let the size of a graph intimidate you! Let's use the chart on the next page to evaluate the questions that follow.

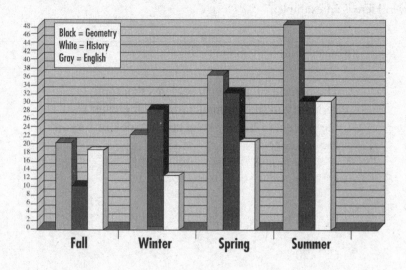

Black = Geometry
White = History
Gray = English

Fall   Winter   Spring   Summer

1. How many more students took geometry in the winter than took history in the fall?

A. 3

B. 10

C. 18

D. 19

E. 28

Here's How to Crack It

In this graph question, we are asked to find the difference between two values on the graph. First, locate the value of each group. As you can see, 28 students took geometry in the winter and 18 students took history in the fall. After finding these two pieces of information, the problem is straightforward. Subtract 18 from 28 to get 10, or (B), as the correct answer. (Note: partial answer choices will always appear on problems using graphs, so be careful!)

As you can see, graph questions are not that complicated once you identify the type of information you need from the graph. In the example above, all the numbers we needed to use were presented in the graph. On some more challenging graph questions, you may need to do a few extra steps before finding the correct answer. Here is an example:

_____○_____

2. The percent of geometry students that took geometry in the spring is how much greater than the percent of history students that took history in the spring?

   A.   7%

   B.   12%

   C.   20%

   D.   30%

   E.   32%

Here's How to Crack It

This question asks us to compare two percents. In the graph above, no percentages are given, so we'll need to calculate the percentages first. To find the percent of geometry students that took geometry in the spring, we need two pieces of information—the total number of geometry students for the year, and the number of geometry students in the spring.

If we add up all geometry students for the year, there are 100. 32 took geometry in the spring. To express this as a percentage, we have $\frac{32}{100} = 32\%$.

If we follow the same procedure to determine the percent of history students that took history in the spring, we get:

$$\frac{20}{80} = \frac{1}{4} = 25\%$$

The difference between the two values is 32% –25%, or 7%. Choice (A) is the correct answer. Again, watch out for the numerous partial answer choices.

_____○_____

RELATING DATA FOUND IN GRAPHS

In the previous two examples, we had to take information from the graph and perform certain operations on the numbers. On some CBEST questions, you will be asked to compare numbers to each other. Sample questions include:

- "What was the percent increase from Year x to Year y?"
- "In order to equal the amount of sales of Company x, Company y needs to increase its sales by what percent?"
- "What year saw the greatest increase in production for Company x?"

Remember the percent change formula? This formula is often helpful when asked to compare data within a graph. Using the graph from the previous page, let's examine one of these types of questions.

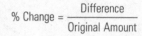

$$\% \text{ Change} = \frac{\text{Difference}}{\text{Original Amount}}$$

---

3. Which class saw the largest percent change in enrollment from spring to summer?

   A. English

   B. Geometry

   C. History

   D. English and History have the same percent increase

   E. It cannot be determined by the information given

Here's How to Crack It

We need to find the largest percent change from the spring term to the summer term. In order to find a percent change, use the percent change formula:

$$\text{Percent Change} = \frac{\text{Difference}}{\text{Original Amount}}$$

For English, the percent change is

$$\frac{(48-36)}{36} = \frac{12}{36} = \frac{1}{3} = 33\frac{1}{3}\%$$

For Geometry, the percent change is

$$\frac{(32-30)}{30} = \frac{2}{30} = \textit{less than } 10\%$$

For History, the percent change is

$$\frac{(30-20)}{20} = \frac{10}{20} = \frac{1}{2} = 50\%$$

From these calculations, you can see that (C) is the correct answer choice.

FILL IN THE MISSING DATA

Another type of graph question asks you to supply information that has been left off of a graph. Some graphs may leave off totals, subtotals, etc. When asked to find the "missing piece," first try to identify any pattern in the data. This will help you ballpark your answer, as well as give you clues as to how to calculate the correct answer.

Use the table below to answer the question that follows:

Day	Starting Price of Stock x	Ending Price of Stock x
Monday	$3\frac{1}{2}$	6
Tuesday	6	$8\frac{1}{2}$
Wednesday	$8\frac{1}{2}$	11
Thursday	11	
Friday		16

4. The chart above shows the starting price and ending price of stock x for one week. If the same growth occurs throughout each day of the week, what was the starting price of stock x on Friday?

A. 11

B. $12\frac{1}{4}$

C. $13\frac{1}{2}$

D. $14\frac{1}{2}$

E. 16

Here's How to Crack It

Each day the stock gains $2\frac{1}{2}$ units. If we add this to Thursday's starting price, the ending price on Thursday will be $13\frac{1}{2}$. This is also the same starting price as the start total on Friday. Therefore, (C) is the correct answer.

LOGICAL CONNECTIVES

You may see a few questions dealing with fundamental rules of logic. While these questions may be unfamiliar to you, they aren't very complicated. There are only a few rules that will be tested on the CBEST, and we'll review them all.

If-Then Statements

An "If-Then" statement is a type of logical claim. It can be abbreviated "If A, then B." Consider the following statement:

> "If the children do their homework, then they will receive ice cream."

This statement can be broken into two parts. The "If" portion of the statement is "If the children do their homework" (the part of the statement represented by "A"). The "Then" statement is "they will receive ice cream" (the part of the statement represented by "B").

Only one other statement logically follows from an If-Then statement. This is called the contrapositive. If we have a statement of the form

If A, then B

the contrapositive form is

If not B, then not A

If we translate this to our statement above, the contrapositive tells us "If the children did not receive ice cream, then they did not do their homework."

Memorize the contrapositive rule: Given If A, Then B, we know that If Not B, then Not A must be true.

On the CBEST, you may be asked to identify an answer choice that logically follows from a prior statement. The way to do this is always to find the contrapositive.

As an aside, you may be wondering if there are other possible truths in the statement above. Other statements, like "If the children did not do their homework, they did not receive ice cream" may seem correct, but cannot be proven (maybe someone decided to give them ice cream anyway). Also, the statement "The children received ice cream, so they must have done their homework" does not logically follow. All we know for certain is that if the children did not receive ice cream, they did not do their homework.

A common problem with these types of questions is that students try to use too much information to solve the problem. Don't think of examples in everyday life, or whether or not children should get ice cream for doing their homework! Simply identify the contrapositive, and find it among the answer choices.

Here are some more example of If-Then statements:

5. Consider the following statement: If Ben scores a goal, his team will win. Which of the following answer choices must be true?

   A. Ben's team won, so he must have scored a goal.

   B. Ben's team lost, and he scored a goal.

   C. If Ben does not score a goal, his team will lose.

   D. If Ben's team lost, he didn't score a goal.

   E. Ben is the only member of his team who can score a goal.

Here's How to Crack It
The statement is an If-Then statement. Identify the contrapositive. In this example, the contrapositive is (D). Choice (D) is the correct answer. Choice (A) is incorrect, because it is not necessary that Ben score in order for his team to win. Choice (B) is incorrect, because our statement tells us that if Ben scores his team will win. Choice (C) is incorrect (it takes the form If not A, then not B—which is not always true). And (E) is out of scope.

6. Consider the following statement: If Paula orders tacos for dinner, she will not eat a salad. Which of the following statements must be true?

A. Paula ate tacos and a salad for dinner.

B. If Paula ate a salad for dinner, she did not order tacos.

C. If Paula did not eat a salad, she must have ordered tacos.

D. Paula will eat a salad for dinner.

E. Paula does not like salad.

Here's How to Crack It

Again, you have been given an If-Then statement. This one is a little tricky since the second part of the argument is negative (If tacos, then *not* salad). Still, find the contrapositive to identify the correct answer. The contrapositive is: If salad, then no tacos. Choice (B) says exactly this, and is the correct answer. Choice (A) is impossible according to the information in the question. Choices (C) and (D) are possible, but cannot be proven. Choice (E) is a silly answer choice. Expect to see one of these per logic question, and be sure to eliminate it!

QUANTIFIERS—SOME, ALL, NONE

If-Then statements are not the only type of logic question that you may see on the CBEST. Other logic questions will involve quantifiers—terms that describe the members of a group. We'll take the three main quantifiers—all, some, and none, individually in the examples below.

On an "all" question, use the same rules that you would in a contrapositive question to find the correct answer.

All

Consider the following statement: "All integers are numbers." This statement tells us that every integer is also a number. But it does not follow that all numbers are integers. (In fact, we know that is false. There are other numbers, like decimals and fractions, which are not integers.)

So, if you are asked a question which includes the term "all," treat the statement the same way you would treat an If-Then statement. Use the contrapositive to find what logically follows.

---

7. Consider the following statements: "At Sequoia High School, all members of the basketball team are at least six feet tall."

Which of the following statements must be true?

A. Everyone at Sequoia High School is at least six feet tall

B. All students at Sequoia High School who are at least six feet tall are on the basketball team.

C. Students at Sequoia High School who are under six feet tall are not on the basketball team.

D. Some students at Sequoia High School are under six feet tall.

E. The tallest students at Sequoia High School are members of the basketball team.

Here's How to Crack It

We are told that all members of the basketball team are at least six feet tall. With an "all" quantifier, find the contrapositive. The contrapositive tells us that if a student is under six feet, then he or she is not a member of the basketball team. Choice (C) states the contrapositive, and is the correct answer. Choice (D) may seem correct, and is probably very likely, but it does not logically follow from the information in the question.

Some

Questions with the quantifier "some" are another type of logic question. Let's evaluate the following statement:

> "Some of the students are wearing red shirts today."

"Some" tells us that at least one item fits a particular category.

What can we logically deduce from this statement? We could speculate about what the other students are wearing. We might speculate about the popularity of red shirts at school. However, the only thing we know for *certain* is that *at least one* of the students is wearing a red shirt. The quantifier "some" tells us that certain members of the group fit into one category. Here is an example:

8. All students must enroll in one math class. This year, students may choose between calculus, geometry, or statistics. Some of the students are enrolled in calculus. Which of the following must be true?

   A.   Some students are enrolled in geometry.

   B.   Some students are enrolled in statistics.

   C.   All students are taking calculus.

   D.   More students are taking calculus than geometry or statistics.

   E.   Not all of the students are enrolled in statistics.

Here's How to Crack It

We are given the statement that some students are enrolled in calculus. Therefore, all we know is that at least one student is taking calculus. We don't know whether any students at all are enrolled in geometry or statistics, or how many are enrolled in each subject. In fact, it is possible that *all* of the students are taking calculus, but we can't be certain— therefore, eliminate (C). Choices (A) and (B) could be true, but we don't know whether students are enrolling in other subjects. Choice (D) is incorrect—we don't know the exact number of students enrolled in each subject. Choice (E) simply restates what we are told in the problem—if some of the students take calculus, we know that at least one student is studying calculus. Therefore, *all* students cannot be taking statistics. Choice (E) is correct.

None

A final type of quantifier you may see is "none." Consider the following example:

> "At a reception, none of the soft drinks are diet sodas."

What do we know for certain given this statement? All we can deduce is that, of all the soft drinks at the reception, none of them are diet sodas. This is equivalent to saying that *all* soft drinks at the reception are *not* diet sodas.

Below is a sample question using all types of quantifiers.

9. Mitch has a collection of marbles. None of his marbles are colored green. Some of the marbles are colored red. The marbles are colored red, blue, orange, or yellow; but no marble has more than one color on it.

   Which of the following statements must be true?

   A. Mitch has more marbles colored red than any other color.

   B. Mitch has more blue marbles than green marbles.

   C. Mitch has more red marbles than green marbles.

   D. Mitch's favorite marble is colored orange, red, and yellow.

   E. If Mitch has a blue marble, then he has an orange marble.

Here's How to Crack It

The sample question has provided us with several statements about Mitch's collection of marbles.

Look at each answer choice, and eliminate those that are incorrect. Choice (A) might seem likely, but we are not given any information about the number of red marbles that Mitch has (or the number of marbles of any other color). We can't prove (A), so eliminate it. Next, we don't know if Mitch has any blue marbles at all, so eliminate (B). Choice (D) is incorrect—we are told in the problem that each marble has only one color. Choice (E) tries to trap you (it's an If-Then statement) but nothing like this is stated in the question. Choice (C) is true—it restates the two facts we are given in the problem. Mitch has at least one red marble, and has no green marbles. Therefore, he has more red marbles than green marbles.

ANSWERS TO ROUNDING DRILL
From page 184

1. 2.0, 2.02

2. 438,200

3. 174,000

4. 0.50

5. 190

Summary

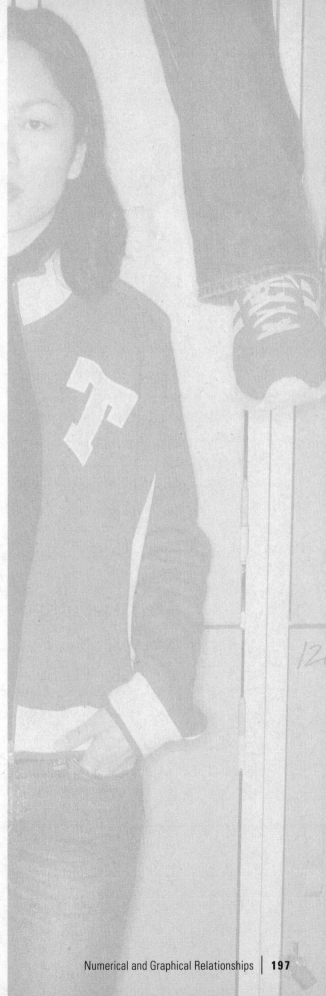

○ Topics presented in this chapter will account for approximately 35 percent of the questions you see on the Mathematics Section of the CBEST.

○ Use the number line as a guide to the position of numbers in relation to each other. Be sure to review the rules of negative numbers, fractions, and decimals—often the CBEST writers will use these types of numbers in these types of questions.

○ When rounding, look at the digit beyond the place to which you are to round. If the digit is from 0–4, round down. If the digit is 5 or greater, round up.

○ Only round numbers *after* all calculations have been performed. Rounding numbers before working with them can lead to rounding errors and incorrect answers.

○ Questions involving graphs are no more complicated than other math questions. Find the information you need to do the problem. The size or complexity of the graph does not relate to the difficulty of the problem.

○ You will often need to use the percent change formula on graph questions.

○ Look for a pattern in order to identify how to calculate any missing information in a graph.

○ When given an If-Then statement, the only logical deduction you can make is the contrapositive.
  - Logic: If *a*, Then *b*.
  - Contrapositive: If Not *b*, Then Not *a*.

○ The CBEST will include quantifiers, such as "all," "some," and "none" in logic questions. Use POE on all questions to find the correct logical answer choice.

○ Use the rules of If-Then statements when given a question that has an "all" quantifier.

○ When you see the quantifier "some" (i.e., "some of *x* are *y*"), then the only conclusion you can draw is that at least one member of *x* belongs to *y*.

Part IV
Cracking the Writing Section

INTRODUCTION TO THE WRITING SECTION

You will be asked to compose two essays in the Writing Section of the CBEST. One of the topics asks you to analyze a situation or statement. We'll call this essay the "Issue" essay. The other topic asks you to write about a personal experience. We'll call this the "Experience" essay. There is no specific time restriction for the Writing Section. As we've mentioned, you will have four hours to complete the entire CBEST; our pacing plan allots approximately 30–40 minutes per essay. Your essays MUST be written in pencil. Therefore, when you practice composing essays for the CBEST, be sure to use a pencil.

There is a tremendous difference between writing a good essay for one of your classes and writing a good essay for purposes of the CBEST. Most composition assignments in school require you to write essays that are several pages long. Most require you to demonstrate some specialized knowledge on a particular topic. If a teacher were to assign you a ten-page paper on a specific topic, he or she would probably evaluate your essay on a number of factors—command of the material, insight, analysis, and overall writing ability. Obviously, this same set of criteria won't be applied to the impromptu essays you write for the CBEST.

CBEST scorers have a very specific way of reading and evaluating each of your essays. The scorers who will read and score your essays are usually teachers, trained to read these essays "holistically." Holistic scoring means that the teachers will evaluate your essays not only on the basis of your ideas, but also by the quality of your writing. We'll outline these scoring criteria, and then design a specific approach to each of the two essays on the CBEST.

HOW ARE ESSAYS SCORED?

Two graders will read each of your essays. Each essay will be given a score from 1–4. We'll describe what each of the scores represents in a moment. Graders will evaluate your essays based on the following criteria:

1. **Rhetorical Force**—the clarity with which the central idea or point of view is stated and maintained; the coherence of the discussion and the quality of the writer's reasoning.
2. **Organization**—the clarity of the writing and the logical sequence of the writer's ideas.
3. **Support and Development**—the relevance, depth, and specificity of supporting information.
4. **Usage**—the extent to which the writing shows care and precision in word choice.

5. **Structure and Conventions**—the extent to which the writing is free of errors in syntax, paragraph structure, sentence structure, and mechanics (spelling, punctuation, and capitalization).
6. **Appropriateness**—the extent to which the writer addresses the topic and uses language and style appropriate to the given audience and purpose.

Scoring Description

A score of 4, or pass, describes a well-formed writing sample that effectively communicates a whole message to the specified audience. An essay of this caliber has the following characteristics:

- The author clearly presents a central idea and/or point of view and maintains focus on that topic.
- Ideas or points of discussion are logically arranged.
- Assertions and generalizations are supported with relevant and specific information.
- Word choice is precise and usage is careful and accurate.
- The writer composes well-formed sentences and paragraphs, with only minor flaws in mechanical conventions.
- The response completely addresses the topic and uses language and style appropriate for the given audience.

A score of 3, or marginal pass, is an adequately formed writing sample that communicates a message to the specified audience. An essay that receives a score of 3 has the following characteristics:

- The author presents a central idea and/or point of view and generally maintains focus. The response is adequately reasoned.
- The meaning is generally clear.
- Assertions and generalizations are adequately supported, although sometimes unevenly.
- Word choice and usage are adequate. Some errors are present, but they do not take away from the overall meaning.
- The response may have errors in paragraphing, sentence structure, and/or mechanical conventions, but they are neither frequent nor serious enough to impede overall meaning.
- The response may not fully address the topic.

A score of 2, or marginal fail, is a partially formed writing sample that attempts to communicate a message to the specified audience, and has the following characteristics:

- The writer may state a central idea or opinion, but loses focus. Reasoning may be too simplistic.
- Organization of ideas may be present, but is ineffective, leaving the reader confused.
- Assertions are only partially supported. Some comments may be irrelevant or insufficient.
- Word choice and usage are unclear, and are a distraction to the reader.
- The writer's response may have distracting errors in paragraphing, sentence structure, and mechanical conventions.
- The response incompletely addresses most tasks of the assignment, and/or uses language inappropriate for the audience and purpose.

A score of 1, or fail, is an inadequately formed writing sample that fails to communicate a message to the specified audience. In order to fail, your essay would have the following characteristics:

- The writer fails to state a central idea or opinion. The response lacks coherence and reason.
- Organization of ideas is ineffective and seriously flawed, impeding the meaning throughout.
- Assertions are not supported or are very underdeveloped; the presentation of details is confused.
- Word choice and usage contain serious and frequent errors.
- The response demonstrates little or no understanding of any of the assignment's tasks. Language may be inappropriate for the audience and purpose.

OUR APPROACH TO THE ESSAYS

Throughout the remainder of this chapter, we will show you how to develop a specific plan to compose an essay on the CBEST. We'll identify specific strategies for the Issue essay and the Experience essay. By the end of this chapter, you will have constructed an essay template showing you exactly what you need to do. Further, we will go back to the scoring criteria above, and ensure that you follow the six keys to a strong essay. Finally, we'll point out some of the most common errors and traps that students fall into when writing their essays.

Applied Strategies
We'll help you develop a strategy to construct a format for your essays before you begin writing.

Preparing for the Essay

We've just spent four chapters reviewing the key concepts and strategies you'll need for the Mathematics Section. Many students think there is no way to prepare for the essays, though. They often feel that since they won't know the essay topics in advance, preparation is impossible. After all, are there key concepts and strategies when it comes to an essay?

It is true that you'll see the topic for the first time on the day of the CBEST, however, you CAN walk into the test with a specific plan for how you will compose your essays. You can prepare the structure of your paragraphs, including how they will relate to one another. In short, you will have a blueprint for composing an essay on any topic.

Creating a Template

A template is a blueprint for your essays. It will provide you with an all-purpose system that you will use to construct your essay, regardless of the topic. In the rest of this chapter, we'll show you how to construct a template for both the Issue essay and the Experience essay. We'll start with the Issue essay.

ISSUE ESSAY

There are a number of things you will need to do in order to create a successful Issue essay:

1. **Read the entire topic and question at least once.** Identify what the authors are asking you to discuss. Are you simply asked if you agree or disagree with an issue, or are the writers asking you to respond to a number of questions? Does the question ask you to use examples? If so, do the writers want specific examples (from school, recent events, literature, etc.)?
2. **Take a stand. Are you for or against the issue?** Taking a clear stand on the issue is crucial to the framework of your entire essay.
3. **Support your claim.** Now is the time to come up with examples. Take down notes on your test booklet, and come up with three to five reasons/examples that support your claim. You will need to expand on these in order to explain and defend your thesis to the reader. Spend up to five minutes brainstorming and taking notes. Don't worry just yet about the strength of your examples.
4. **Rank your supporting work.** Choose the best three or four examples/reasons that support your claim.
5. **Compose your essay using the template format.** This step will be discussed in much more detail. In short, you'll be inserting your claim and supporting ideas into your template.

Tip! It is imperative that you take a stand in an "Issue" essay. You must decide if you are for or against the topic.

6. **Review your essay.** Once your essay is complete, you will need to review it to be sure you have avoided the traps and mistakes that students frequently make.

Successful Issue Essays

CBEST authors are looking for an essay that takes a stand. You must take a strong position on the issue. It will not matter which side of an issue you take—there are no "right" or "wrong" answers on these essays. Certainly, you will want to present good evidence to support your position, but authors will never deduct points for choosing a particular position. In addition to taking a stand, authors will grade you on how well you support your position. Finally, the essay must be engaging—well organized, easy to read, and structurally sound.

An Issue Essay Template

As you practice writing, you may find that you want to come up with your own template. No problem. The template presented here is not the only way to write a successful Issue essay. It does, however, provide you with a systematic way to organize and construct a successful essay.

Paragraph 1: The issue of _____

_____

is a controversial one. Some believe that _____

Others believe that _____

_____

After careful thought, I feel that _____

_____

Paragraph 2: One reason for this belief is that _____

_____

Paragraph 3: Another reason for this belief is _____

_____

Paragraph 4: The best reason for this belief is _____

_____

Paragraph 5: In the final analysis, _____

_____

Paragraph 1—The Introduction

Your introduction needs to do the following things:

1. Introduce/restate the issue.
2. Address the two sides of the issue. Clearly state one position, then another, then state where you fall on the issue, in relation to those two camps.
3. State your thesis. A thesis sentence is the sentence that states your overall position on the issue, and tells the readers what you are going to discuss. Use your thesis to state your position, and introduce the supporting reasons that you will use in the paragraphs to follow.

Let's use some sample Issue essay questions in order to practice writing the first paragraph in our essay:

More Great Books
Improve your vocabulary in order to write a stellar essay by checking out *GrammarSmart* and *WordSmart* from your friends at The Princeton Review.

Essay Topic 1

The school board at High School X is considering raising the number of years of required physical education classes. The board will be voting on a proposal to raise the number of years students need to take physical education from one year to three years. Do you think the school board should increase the physical education requirement to three years? Support your opinion with specific examples.

Here is a sample first paragraph that uses the template:

> The issue of increasing the required number of physical education classes in high school is a controversial one. Some believe that physical education classes are a crucial part of the high school experience, where students learn lessons of competition and cooperation. Others believe that physical education activities can be done after the school day in extracurricular activities, and that the increase in the number of required classes would take away from more traditional learning. After careful thought, I believe that the school board should increase the physical education requirement to three years in order to benefit student health, teach general cooperation skills, and provide a necessary break from a long day indoors.

As you can see, we used the template format above to write our introductory paragraph. To finish our essay, we would then use the following paragraphs to develop the reasons we presented in our thesis statement (student health, cooperation skills, and a break from the classroom). Is it possible that we could use this template, but take the other side of the issue? Of course! Here is a sample paragraph that takes the other position:

Notice how the same template can be used to take different stands on an issue. Regardless of what you write about, the template does not change.

The issue of increasing the required number of physical education classes in high school is a controversial one. Some believe that physical education classes are not as important as more traditional subjects like math and history. Others believe that physical education activities help to teach competition and cooperation, skills that students need to learn for their experiences beyond the classroom. After careful thought, I believe that the school board should not increase the physical education requirement to three years because students would lose the opportunity to take other electives, which, unlike physical education, cannot easily be done after school hours.

You may have noticed in the two examples above that in making this particular template work most effectively, "some believe that..." introduces a position that you are ultimately going to support. The "others believe that..." introduces some counter arguments to your position. The sentence beginning "after careful thought..." will return to the point of view you believe in, and is where you will state your thesis.

Now that the first paragraph is complete, we will begin to focus on the next step of the essay—supporting your claim.

Paragraph 2—Support Your Claim

Spend a few minutes listing as many examples and reasons you can think of to support your claim.

You've taken a stand on one side of an issue. Now, you need to support it. Before you begin writing your essay, take notes on your scratch paper, coming up with several examples and reasons to support your position. This is often called brainstorming. Don't worry about the quality of these examples. The goal in brainstorming is to come up with as many examples as possible.

If you are having trouble coming up with reasons, don't panic. Reread the question, and think about the people who would be affected by the issue being discussed. In the example above, who would be affected? Certainly the students would face a new curriculum in school. Administrators, parents, and teachers would also have opinions on the issue. Consider some of the arguments these groups would make. Would they be happy with the position you've taken? Why, or why not?

Once you have spent a few minutes brainstorming, you then need to start going through what you have written to determine which ideas are most compelling. The template we've provided includes three paragraphs to support your claim. In general, three examples are sufficient to support your thesis. Now, plan the order in which you want to present these ideas. Save your strongest example for the final supporting paragraph.

Paragraphs 3 and 4—Your Supporting Paragraphs

Your goal is to make each example as precise and compelling as possible. After you have brainstormed and narrowed your list down to your best examples, spend a couple of moments on each one, describing them with as much detail as possible. Try to add depth and clarity to your examples. Err on the side of thoroughly explaining a statement, rather than simply making assertions without the facts to support them.

Paragraph 5—Writing Your Conclusion

A conclusion paragraph needs to restate your central claim, and leave the reader with a final point to consider. First, summarize your thesis. Although there are some benefits to increasing physical education requirements, the proposal to do so should not be approved. After another sentence or two, leave the reader with a final sentence that states your opinion. Try to make this final sentence powerful, as it is the final thing your reader will see when evaluating your essay. While students may increase their physical fitness, are we willing to decrease their classroom experiences?

The appearance of your essay is important. Be sure you have written neatly, and that paragraphs are properly formatted.

Review Your Essay

Once you've chosen a position, developed a thesis, brainstormed and developed your examples, start composing your essay. Using the template, your essay should flow easily from one paragraph to the next. Once you complete your essay, read it over again. Check for the common traps and errors we'll identify later in this chapter. Do any necessary editing. Then, take a deep breath, and start the next essay.

THE EXPERIENCE ESSAY

There are a number of things you will need to do in order to write an effective Experience essay. You'll already be familiar with some of the steps below from the Issue essay.

1. Read the entire topic and question at least once. Identify what the authors are asking you to discuss. Are you asked to describe an event from your life? Does the essay ask how the event has affected you? Are you asked to identify important people in your life? How did they help influence you?
2. **Choose a topic.** If you can immediately identify an experience (event, person, etc.), move on to step 4. If you don't immediately recognize a topic, move to step 3 to brainstorm.
3. **Develop your story.** Now is the time to come up with an experience to describe. Do not try to make up a story that you feel will reflect what the readers want to read. The questions will be general enough so that you will be able to draw an experience from your life. Your challenge will be to communicate the details, importance, and impact that your experience had on you. Take down notes on your test booklet, and come up with details to support your experience. You will need to describe your experience in detail in order to support and explain your thesis to the reader. Spend up to 5 minutes brainstorming and taking notes.

Most "Experience" essays will ask you about your teaching experience, or your motivation to become a teacher. Spend some time before test day thinking about your teaching background.

4. **Answer a reader's questions.** Before you begin to write your essay, be sure that your essay will answer the following questions:
   - Who was involved?
   - How long did the event last?
   - Why did the event occur?
   - What were your emotions during the event?
   - What were the effects of the event?
   - How has the event changed you?

   These questions, of course, won't apply to all essays. In general, though, be sure that your essay conveys not only what happened, but also your feelings and emotions about the event.

5. **Compose your essay**, using the template format. After spending 5–7 minutes on the steps above, compose your essay using the template format that we will describe on the next page.

6. **Review your essay.** Once your essay is complete, you will need to review it as with the Issue essay to be sure you have avoided the traps and mistakes that students frequently make.

Successful Experience Essays

CBEST authors are looking for an essay that grabs their attention. Try to compose an essay that describes an important or symbolic moment in your life. Writing about how you learned to walk and chew gum at the same time is probably not as compelling as how you learned to overcome your fear of public speaking. When you describe your experience, keep in mind that the reader does not have any background knowledge about the event or people involved in your story. Be sure to fully describe the characters and supporting information in your experience. Finally, like the Issue essay, the Experience essay must be appealing to read—well organized, clearly written, and structurally sound.

An Experience Essay Template

We've covered the basics of a template when we wrote the Issue essay, but the Experience essay requires a different set of criteria. There are a number of different formats that you can use to compose your essay.

Variation 1

Paragraph 1:	Introduction and thesis.
Paragraph 2:	Describe the event.
Paragraph 3:	Describe the immediate effects of the event.
Paragraph 4:	Describe the long-term effects of the event.
Paragraph 5:	Conclusion.

Variation 2

>Paragraph 1: Introduction and thesis.
>Paragraph 2: Describe any background information/events leading up to your experience.
>Paragraph 3: Describe the choices you felt you needed to make.
>Paragraph 4: Describe the results of your actions.
>Paragraph 5: Conclusion.

Any variation will work; just make sure that your essay is constructed in a logical format. In any case, the two most important paragraphs of your essay are the first and last, the introduction and conclusion.

The Introduction

Your introduction needs to do the following things:

1. Introduce/restate the topic.
2. Provide any information that the reader would need in order to understand your thesis.
3. State your thesis. For an Experience essay, a thesis should introduce the event you are about to discuss, and how it may have shaped you as a person.

Let's use a sample Experience essay question in order to practice writing the first paragraph:

Essay Topic 2

At some point in our lives, all of us have faced some sort of rejection or defeat. Write an essay about a time in your life when you experienced such a rejection. How did the experience affect you?

Here is a sample first paragraph, which includes the three steps of the introduction:

>Most people think of rejection as a negative experience. We are quick to become discouraged when we are defeated. However, there are many valuable lessons to be learned in the face of rejection. The state championships in water polo were the occasion of my greatest humiliation and rejection. I suffered many defeats during the water polo playoffs, but these defeats helped me to refocus my efforts and improve my performance considerably.

As you can see, we used the template format above to write our introductory paragraph. To finish our essay, we would then use the following paragraph topics to explain the event: (what happened at the state championships?), the immediate effects (anger, sadness, etc.), and the long-term effects (refocus, improvement, rededication to the sport). Remember to ask yourself the why, what, how, when, and where questions to ensure you are delivering a vivid picture of the event to the reader.

Concluding the Experience Essay

A conclusion paragraph should first summarize the event about which you wrote. "It was devastating to sit on the bench during the playoffs after having been a starter for the entire regular season." After another sentence or two, leave the reader with a final sentence that states your opinion about how the event has changed you or your life. Try to make this final sentence powerful, as it is the final thing your reader will see when evaluating your essay. "I often speculate on what type of player I would be if the coach had let me play on that June afternoon, but I am certain I wouldn't be as dedicated and focused as I am today."

SIX KEYS TO A STRONG ESSAY

So far, we've discussed how to construct templates for each type of essay you will write on the CBEST. Now, let's revisit the scoring criteria to make sure that your essays will include all of the items a reader looks for when evaluating your response.

1. Answer the Question, and Only the Question— Rhetorical Force

As Sergeant Joe Friday would say, "Just the facts, ma'am." In order to compose a successful essay, you must present an essay that answers the question. Make sure your thesis addresses all questions presented to you. If an essay question asks you to describe an experience and the influence it had on you, you must address both parts. Writing only about the experience, and not about the effects of the experience, will lower your score.

Some essay prompts contain more than one question. Be sure your essay answers all of the questions.

Further, do not stray from the topic to add information that does not directly address the question. Sure, sometimes you may need to write a paragraph that provides background information on an issue, but don't write a paragraph that has nothing to do with the question. A strong essay is focused, complete, and to the point. As a final review of your essay, take each paragraph, and make sure it ties back in to your thesis.

2. Organization

Our templates give you a specific framework to present your thoughts in a clear, logical way. Use paragraphs 2, 3, and 4 to explain your topic of choice. Readers will appreciate an essay that flows from one paragraph to the next, and transition sentences help to join two paragraphs together. Your first sentence (which is usually your topic sentence) should identify with the information presented in the previous paragraph. For example, referring to the essay about physical education requirements, the second paragraph could describe the health benefits. The third paragraph could describe the lessons of cooperation and teamwork learned through physical education classes. How could these be tied together? Quite easily. In fact, check out the sentence below.

> The increase in physical education classes would not only improve the general health of a student, but would also improve cooperation and teamwork skills.

This sentence helps to connect one paragraph to the next, and tells the reader what the paragraph will be describing. Transition sentences do not need to be fancy, so don't waste time trying to come up with elegant connections from one point to the next.

3. Development of Ideas

CBEST scorers will want you to provide support for your ideas. Stating an opinion is not enough. The scorers will want to see if you have legitimate explanations for your ideas. On the CBEST scoring criteria, the "depth" of supporting information is important. Compare the following two explanations:

> **No depth:** Under the new requirements, students would miss valuable class time.

> **Depth:** Consider the effects of two more years of physical education classes. Currently, students are able to take only four "elective" classes during their sophomore through junior years. If students need to take two more years of physical education classes, they will lose 50 percent of their elective classes. Most students cite elective classes as the most rewarding classes in school.

Which do you think the CBEST readers prefer? If you are going to state an opinion, be sure you have enough information to explain your reasoning. CBEST scorers will never penalize you for stating an opinion, only for opinions that are not fully explained.

4. Usage

CBEST scorers are looking for two things regarding the composition of your essay: Intelligent word choice, and correct usage of words. Try to vary your word choice when writing your essay. If you have an essay topic that asks you to describe an event that occured when you were happy, do not use the word "happy" fifty times during your response. Further, if you are not sure what a word means, don't use it. An improperly placed word can stall an essay, or contradict a point you are trying to convey. In order to receive a good score on this part of the essay, make sure you avoid the word-choice traps.

5. Structure and Convention

A strong essay will be both grammatically correct and easy to read. One way to make an essay easier to read is by changing the form and look of your sentences. Effective writing mixes up short and long sentences for variety. If you find that all of your sentences are about the same length and tone, try to adjust the sentence length.

6. Appropriateness

You are writing to an experienced group of teachers. Consider your audience when composing your essays.

Finally, a strong essay will appeal to the person evaluating your essays. Since CBEST scorers are veteran teachers who have been trained to grade these essays, consider what you would write to a veteran teacher. In general, if you write within a strong template, and explain yourself, the readers will easily understand your essay. However, be sure to avoid using any jargon, acronyms, or language that may be unfamiliar to the reader.

ESSAY WRITING PITFALLS

Here are some of the most common mistakes that students make when writing essays for the CBEST. Read through them to make sure you aren't doing the same types of things when writing your essays.

The "I Believe" Syndrome

Whenever an essay asks for your opinion on an issue, it is very natural to state "I believe" or "I think." There is no problem with this, as long as you only do it once in a while. However, if you qualify every opinion statement with "I think," the essay will become very dull to read. We know that everything you write is what you think. After all, you're writing the essay.

Big Word Syndrome

Some test takers believe that if they can insert challenging vocabulary into their essays, they will receive a high score. Usually, these attempts fail miserably. Don't panic if you feel you are composing your essay in simple, conversational text. The important thing is how well your essay flows, not if you can insert the words "anthropomorphic" and "catastrophic" into the same sentence.

Redundancy Syndrome

There is nothing worse than reading the same idea over and over again, written in a number of different ways. Economy of words is important on the CBEST. Don't write a sentence unless it has something unique to add to the essay. Don't write a sentence unless it has something unique to add to the essay. Don't write a sentence unless it has something unique to add to the essay.

Ugly Essay Syndrome

CBEST scorers will read several hundred essays at one time. Imagine how your essay will be treated if it is messy, illegible, and without proper indentations. Be respectful to your readers. They appreciate a neat, well-formatted essay. Make sure that you indent each new paragraph, and that you legibly write your essay. If your cursive writing rivals the handwriting of a doctor, consider printing your essays.

Summary

o   You will be asked to compose two essays on the CBEST—one Issue essay and one Experience essay. While there is no specific time limit for each essay, our pacing plan suggests you spend between 30–40 minutes for each.

o   CBEST scorers will evaluate your essays on a number of criteria, and give you an overall score from 1–4 for each essay. Two readers will grade each essay.

o   Have a plan for constructing your essays. Use the template structure so that you will know ahead of time how your essays will be organized.

o   For a successful Issue essay: Step 1: Read the entire topic and question at least once. Step 2: Take a stand. Step 3: Support your claim. Step 4: Rank your supporting work. Step 5: Compose your essay, using the template format. Step 6: Review your essay.

o   For a successful Experience essay: Step 1: Read the entire topic and question at least once. Step 2: Choose a topic. Step 3: Develop your story. Step 4: Answer a reader's questions. Step 5: Compose your essay, using the template format. Step 6: Review your essay.

o   Your thesis statement should be stated in the introductory paragraph of each essay.

o   Avoid the common essay syndromes—"I think," big words, redundancy, and the ugly essay.

Part V
Taking the CBEST

Test day is coming. After all the hours of studying, memorizing math rules and practicing your essays, it is time for the real thing. No problem! By the time you've completed this book, you will have studied all of the types of problems that will appear on this test, learned key strategies and techniques for maximizing the number of questions you can get correct, and taken and reviewed two full-length practice tests. Think about how much more you know about this test now than before you started! In this chapter, we're going to talk about how to get ready for test day—what you'll need, how to handle the day of the test, and what to do after you've completed the test.

THE CBEST CHECKLIST

CBEST Checklist:
- admissions ticket
- pencils
- proper identification

On the night before the exam, you'll want to set aside everything you need for the test. First and most importantly, set aside your admissions ticket. About two weeks prior to your CBEST date, make sure you have received your admission ticket to the test. If you have not received your admission ticket two weeks before the test date or if you lose it, you must contact National Evaluation Systems, Inc., at (916) 928-4001 between 9:00 A.M. and 3:00 P.M. Your admission ticket will indicate the site location and directions to the test center. If you are not sure where the center is located, or how long it will take you to get there, you may want to drive to the center on a morning prior to the test. At the very least, plan on allotting an extra 10 to 15 minutes for your commute. Parking is often very difficult, and you may need to search for your specific room location.

Second, bring several sharpened number 2 pencils to the test site. While most classrooms are equipped with pencil sharpeners, don't be surprised if you don't find one. Remember, you'll need pencils for all sections of the exam, including the essays.

You'll need to bring some type of government identification, such as a driver's license, DMV identification card, passport, or military identification card. If you are unsure whether the identification you have is acceptable, contact NES.

Finally, there are some things you do NOT want to bring. No food or drink is allowed into the testing area. Calculators, or any computing devices are also prohibited. Most important, do not bring a cell phone into the exam. Registration rules indicate that you can be disqualified for bringing in a cellular phone!

The Night Before

Students often try to do something dramatic the night before the CBEST. Don't. You've probably been told to make sure you get lots of sleep the night before the exam. If you are accustomed to sleeping only six hours a night, trying to get twelve hours of sleep the night before will not benefit you. You'll probably be sitting in bed for hours wondering why you're trying to get so much sleep, and won't think about anything except the test! On the other hand, it probably isn't a good idea to party all night prior to the test. You want to be in a sober state of mind when taking the CBEST.

Another common mistake is to "cram" the night before the CBEST. If you've studied the techniques we've presented, and have taken the practice tests, cramming will do absolutely nothing except raise your level of anxiety about the test. If you want to do a few practice problems, great. Go over problems you've already solved. If you think that you can improve your math score by doing 300 math questions the night before, think again.

In short, stick to your normal routine. Have a relaxing evening (maybe rent a good comedy), and you'll be ready to go on test day.

Nerves

It is absolutely natural to be nervous going in to take the test. The CBEST is an important hurdle in your quest to be a teacher and should be taken seriously. It shouldn't scare you, however. We don't want you to get so nervous about passing the test that you just sit there for four hours and stare blankly at the test booklet.

How do you avoid this? Well, you're already doing it. The best way to avoid getting nervous is to become familiar with the test. For this reason, it is extremely important that you take the two practice tests under the exact conditions of an actual CBEST. Give yourself four hours in a quiet environment. Don't watch TV when you take the two tests, and don't break out a calculator for those difficult calculations. Familiarity with the test is a key component to gaining confidence on the CBEST. You'll be able to practice dealing with the fatigue that will set in during the four hours. Sure, the actual CBEST will be somewhat more stressful than the practice tests you take, but you want to be sure you're familiar with how the day will work. You may still be nervous, and that's fine. You just don't want to be panicked.

It is also important to remember that you have learned many techniques and strategies that leave you in control of the CBEST. You control the order in which you complete the sections. You control which questions you want to attack. You can use the tools of Process of Elimination, Scope, and Ballparking to leave you in better control of the answer choices. These techniques will help you greatly increase your chances of solving the problem correctly.

Use the two practice tests to refine your control of the CBEST. In Chapter 2, we talked about the recommended pacing on each section. Make sure to modify this pacing after each diagnostic test so that by test day you'll have a clear plan for how much time you should spend on each section.

The actual CBEST will be just like the practice tests you have taken. Walk into the testing center on test day knowing that you have seen this material before.

Four Hours Is a Long Time

Be sure to use all four hours of the testing period when taking the CBEST. Your pacing plan should allow an extra 10 to 15 minutes to do the following: relax between sections, use the restroom, sharpen pencils, and so forth. Don't feel like you have to continually be working at a furious pace during these four hours. Give yourself "mini-breaks" throughout the test. Closing your eyes, and taking five deep breaths, can often be all that you need to clear your mind before moving on to the next section.

Also remember that this is not a race! You will likely see other test takers leave the room before the end of the four hours. Remember that some test takers will only be taking one or two sections of the exam; others will take the test as quickly as possible. When the room gets half-empty, it can be very tempting to start to rush, with hopes of starting your Saturday afternoon a little early. Stay focused. A few more minutes in the testing room can mean never having to go back to take the CBEST again.

Testing Conditions

As a test taker, you have a right to a fair and accurate administration of your test. If you encounter anything that you feel is unsatisfactory, don't be afraid to ask your proctor or test supervisor to change it. Certain examples of unsatisfactory conditions are: a room with an uncomfortable temperature, excessive noise surrounding the classroom, or incorrect timing of the test. If you feel that your test was not administered in the correct way, be sure to document the incident after the test, and contact NES to discuss your rights as a test taker.

Receiving Your Scores

There are two ways of receiving your CBEST results—over the Internet, and in the mail. Unofficial scores are posted on the Internet approximately 16 days after the exam (results of the Writing Sample appear after approximately three weeks). In order to access your unofficial scores, go to **www.cbest.nesinc.com** and follow the directions online. The information you will need to provide can be found on your registration form. While there are rarely changes from these scores, it is important to note that the scores you will see online are not official scores.

You will receive your official scores approximately three weeks after the test date, and they will be mailed to the address you designated on your registration form. Scores will not be released by phone, fax, or in person. In addition to receiving your scores, you will receive a detailed breakdown of your performance on each of the skills measured by each section of the test.

Should You Ever Cancel Your Score?

It is possible that you may leave the test center feeling that you did not perform as well as you had hoped. Unfortunately, many students in that situation feel that the correct thing to do is cancel their scores. No matter how you think you performed on the exam, **DO NOT** cancel your scores on the CBEST. Here are just a few reasons why:

1. **You only have to pass.** Unlike other standardized tests, where your score can be used as an evaluative measure, you only have to pass the CBEST. Your scaled scores are inconsequential— a 41 equals a pass, as does an 80. So, you shouldn't be concerned about how well you performed, only about whether you passed.

2. **You may pass some (or all) of the sections!** Typically, when students cancel their scores, it is because they feel that they performed horribly on one section. Well, if you cancel your score, you will not receive the results of any section on the test. Remember, if you pass a section of the CBEST, you'll never need to take that section again. For example, if Chris passed the essays and Reading Section, but not the Mathematics Section, he would only need to take the Mathematics Section during the next administration of the CBEST. If he cancels his scores, he would need to take all three sections again.

3. **Your score report can help you in the future.** If you did not pass one of the sections, the information provided on your CBEST score report can help you when you take the test again. When you receive your scores, you will also receive a category breakdown within the Reading and Mathematics Sections. This feedback can help you narrow your focus when you study for a particular section again.

Since you only need to pass the CBEST, we recommend that you do not cancel your scores.

And Finally . . .

Be sure to celebrate after completing the test. You deserve it.

Congratulations! You are on your way to becoming a teacher.

Chapter 10
Practice Test 1

SECTION I: TEST OF READING

Directions: Each statement or passage in this test is followed by a question or questions, based on its content. After reading a statement or passage, choose the best answer to each question from among the five choices given. Answer all questions following a statement or passage on the basis of what is stated or implied in that statement or passage. Be sure to mark all of your answers in the Reading Section of your answer document.

Note: Some passages contain numbered sentences, blank lines, or underlined words that are to be used for your reference in answering the questions that follow those passages.

Read the passage below. Then answer the four questions that follow.

Imagine going to a fast food restaurant a few years from now. You order a burger, and before you receive your order, the burger is placed through gamma-ray treatment. Order some fish, and you'll have to wait for the fish to be placed under a pressure three times higher than the pressure found in the deepest part of the ocean. Why would restaurants go to such lengths? Simply, to make sure your food is safe.

The threat of bacteria entering into our food is at an all-time high. New bacteria such as *Escherichia coli* and *Vibrio vulnificus* have alarmed many food handlers, and have caused an increasing number of food poisoning deaths for the last five years. As a result, food processors are adopting rigorous standards of cleanliness. Food scientists are helping. Many scientists are proposing radical alternatives to common food treatment, such as some of the examples described above. While the new techniques are costly, they are not as costly as the potential lawsuits, bad publicity, and human loss that one outbreak could cause.

The real price to this new technology may not be in dollars, but in overall taste. Scientists admit that tastes may vary in certain foods depending on their processing treatment. As a layman, it seems that placing an oyster under 90,000 pounds of pressure sure seems likely to have some effect on the taste. I just hope that when the gamma rays remove any bacteria, they'll leave me with the wonderful joy of eating a delicious burger.

1. The writer's main purpose in writing this passage is to:

   A. demonstrate his love for hamburgers.

   B. explain why some food processing techniques will change in the future.

   C. perform a cost analysis of a food outbreak.

   D. demonstrate recent scientific advancements.

   E. predict popular foods in the twenty-first century.

2. Which of the following best defines the word "layman" as it is used in the passage?

   A. non-scientist

   B. expert

   C. private citizen

   D. clergyman

   E. carpenter

3. This passage is most likely taken from:

   A. a scientific journal

   B. a cookbook

   C. an economics textbook

   D. a newspaper column

   E. a legal journal

4. Which of the following best describes the author's attitude toward the new food processing techniques?

   A. amazed

   B. concerned

   C. angry

   D. frustrated

   E. whimsical

Read the passage below. Then answer the three questions that follow.

High Definition Television, or HDTV, is finally available to consumers, approximately ten years after most companies promised the systems. Consumers love the new system. More than 10,000 people appeared at a local store on the first day that HDTV became available. The appeal of HDTV is the clearer picture that an HDTV signal produces. The signal holds approximately three times as many horizontal and vertical lines as a standard television, resulting in a picture that rivals movie screens. Further, HDTVs are quite large—current versions range from 56 inches to a 64 inch wide screen unit.

Despite these benefits, consumers who purchase these sets now may be disappointed with the results. There are very few digitally produced programs on television, and the number of these programs is unlikely to increase in the near future. The major networks plan to offer only five hours of digital programming per week next year, and only in the top-ten major markets. It will not be until 2004 that more than 50 percent of network television is broadcast in digital form. Further, cable companies are not under any regulation to switch to carrying digital programming. Since two-thirds of Americans receive their television through cable, the delay may be even longer.

5. The main point of the passage is that:

   A. Current HDTV sets are much larger than most standard televisions.

   B. The arrival of HDTV is much later than expected.

   C. The cable television industry is thriving.

   D. HDTV provides a clearer resolution picture.

   E. HDTV is available, although there is little programming that utilizes HDTV technology.

6. Which of the following would be the best title for the passage?

   A. HDTV Is Here to Stay

   B. Network and Cable Broadcasting

   C. HDTVs Are Here—Is the Programming?

   D. Television in 2004

   E. Why I Love HDTV

7. Which of the following best describes the word "major" in the ninth sentence as it is used in the passage?

   A. officer

   B. large

   C. subject

   D. legal

   E. important

Read the passage below. Then answer the question that follows.

Whenever a major train accident occurs, there is a dramatic increase in the number of train mishaps reported in the media, a phenomenon that may last for as long as a few months after the accident. Railroad officials assert that the publicity given to the horror of major train accidents focuses media attention on the train industry, and that the increase in the number of reported accidents is caused by an increase in the number of news sources covering train accidents, not by an increase in the number of accidents.

8. Which of the following, if true, would seriously weaken the assertions of the train officials?

A. The publicity surrounding train accidents is largely limited to the country in which the crash occurred.

B. Train accidents tend to occur far more often during certain peak travel months.

C. News organizations have no guidelines to help them determine how severe an accident must be for it to receive coverage.

D. Accidents receive coverage by news sources only when the news sources find it advantageous to do so.

E. Studies by regulators show that the number of train accidents remains relatively constant from month to month.

Read the passage below. Then answer the four questions that follow.

In Roman times, defeated enemies were generally put to death as criminals for having offended the emperor of Rome. During the Middle Ages, however, the practice of ransoming, or returning prisoners in exchange for money, became common. Though some saw this custom as a step toward a more humane society, the primary reasons behind it were economic rather than humanitarian.

In those times, rulers had only a limited ability to raise taxes. They could neither force their subjects to fight, nor pay them to do so. The promise of material cooperation in the form of goods and ransom was therefore the only way of inducing combatants to participate in a war. In the Middle Ages, the predominant incentive for the individual soldier was the expectation of spoils. Although collecting ransom clearly brought financial gain, keeping a prisoner and arranging for his exchange had its costs. Consequently, procedures were devised to reduce transaction costs.

One such device was a rule asserting that the prisoner had to assess his own value. This compelled the prisoner to establish a value without too much distortion; indicating too low a value would increase the captive's chances of being killed, while indicating too high a value would either ruin him financially or create a prohibitively expensive ransom that would also result in death.

9. The primary purpose of the passage is to:

   A. discuss the economic basis of the medieval practice of exchanging prisoners for ransom.

   B. examine the history of the treatment of prisoners of war.

   C. emphasize the importance of a warrior's code of honor during the Middle Ages.

   D. explore a way of reducing the costs of ransom.

   E. demonstrate why warriors of the Middle Ages looked forward to battles.

10. From the passage, it can be assumed that a medieval soldier:

    A. was less likely to kill captured members of opposing armies than was a soldier of the Roman Empire.

    B. was similar to a twentieth-century terrorist.

    C. had few economic options and chose to fight because it was the only way to earn an adequate living.

    D. was motivated to spare prisoners' lives by humanitarian rather than economic ideals.

    E. had no respect for his captured enemies.

11. Which of the following best describes the change in policy from executing prisoners in Roman times to ransoming prisoners in the Middle Ages?

    A.   Roman emperors demanded more respect than medieval rulers, and thus Roman subjects went to greater lengths to defend their nation.

    B.   It was a reflection of the lesser degree of direct control medieval rulers had over their subjects.

    C.   It became a show of strength and honor for warriors of the Middle Ages to be able to capture and return their enemies.

    D.   Medieval soldiers were not as humanitarian as their ransoming practices might have indicated.

    E.   Medieval soldiers demonstrated more concern about economic policy than did their Roman counterparts.

12. The author uses the phrase "without too much distortion" in the final paragraph in order to:

    A.   indicate that prisoners would fairly assess their worth.

    B.   emphasize the important role medieval prisoners played in determining whether they should be ransomed.

    C.   explain how prisoners often paid more than an appropriate ransom in order to increase their chances for survival.

    D.   suggest that captors and captives often had relationships.

    E.   show that when in prison a soldier's view could become distorted.

Read the passage below. Then answer the four questions that follow.

In recent years, Americans have gotten the message—eat more vegetables! However, we're still not eating enough of the leafy green vegetables, such as spinach, broccoli, and Brussels sprouts that do the most to promote good health. Currently, half of all the vegetable servings we consume are potatoes, and half of those are French fries.

Research reported at the Nurses Health Study confirms the benefits of leafy greens. Researchers determined that women who daily consumed at least 400 micrograms of folic acid in either leafy green vegetables or multivitamin pills reduced their risk of colon cancer as much as 75 percent over fifteen years. Remember not to simply substitute vitamins for vegetables, because there are thousands of healthy compounds present in vegetables that cannot be duplicated in a pill.

13. The main point of the passage is:

   A. Multivitamin pills contain folic acid, as do leafy green vegetables.

   B. Recent studies help confirm that leafy green vegetables help to promote good health.

   C. Eating more vegetables can reduce the risk of colon cancer.

   D. Important research was just presented at the Nurses Health Study.

   E. Almost half of the vegetables consumed by Americans are potatoes.

14. The author argues that vitamins may not be an ideal replacement for leafy vegetables because:

   A. Increasing dependence on multivitamins can lead to poor nutritional habits.

   B. Multivitamins are not proven to fight against colon cancer.

   C. Folic acid is not contained in multivitamins.

   D. A vitamin supplement may not replace the thousands of compounds found in leafy green vegetables.

   E. Caloric intake may decrease sharply.

15. The passage states that leafy green vegetables are helpful because:

   A. They help to reduce the risk of contracting colon cancer, but little more.

   B. They contain more compounds than potatoes.

   C. They contain folic acid.

   D. They contain numerous compounds that are helpful to the body, such as folic acid.

   E. Multivitamins are not very helpful.

16. Which of the following changes would the author most likely wish to see in the way Americans consume vegetables?

   A. a lower overall consumption in vegetables

   B. an increase in the number of potatoes consumed

   C. an overall increase in the number of leafy green vegetables consumed

   D. a switch from leafy green vegetables to carrots

   E. more spinach and fewer Brussels sprouts

Read the passage below. Then answer the five questions that follow.

One of the most attractive features of the Internet, its ability to customize content instantly, is ironically becoming one of its most sinister: the ability to monitor who you are and what you are doing. Websites now have the ability to track what sites you visit, how long you visit them, and what you download, print, or purchase. Sites are equipped with programs called cookies that can track this information and use it for marketing purposes. If you visit a sports website, don't be surprised if you find unsolicited emails about sporting events and merchandise in your inbox.

Worst of all, most sites are not forthright about informing visitors about what data they are collecting. A recent study by the FTC found that only 14 percent of sites had posted privacy statements. Fortunately, 71 of the 100 busiest sites did. Of the 100 busiest sites, 91 had customer service centers designed to handle questions about privacy issues. Computer industry leaders are attempting to address these privacy concerns. Browsers are being created that will enable you to delete all cookies at any website you visit. Other entrepreneurs are developing software to help you control the information you give out. After all, if anyone is going to make money from your identity, shouldn't it be you?

17. "Cookies" are described in the passage as:

A. traditional desserts.

B. jargon for company private policy statements.

C. tools that allow a computer user to see what sites request personal information.

D. unsolicited emails.

E. tracking devices that follow what you do on the Internet.

18. What is the best title for the passage above?

A. Privacy Concerns on the Internet

B. The Cookie Crumbles

C. The Lack of Posted Privacy Statements

D. Entrepreneurs and the Internet

E. Profiting from your Identity

19. From the statistics presented in the passage about the number of businesses posting privacy statements it can be assumed that:

A. Only large sites are concerned privacy statements.

B. Only large sites attempted to sell personal information about users who visit their sites.

C. Small sites do not feel it is important to post privacy statements.

D. Most of the largest sites are able to provide information about their privacy policies.

E. Large sites without privacy statements will decrease in popularity.

20. Which of the following would the author most likely support as a solution to privacy concerns on the Internet?

   A.   a list of all sites that use cookies

   B.   the ability to request that sites not use your name or profile for marketing purposes

   C.   the ability to choose which sites you want to provide information to, and which sites you do not

   D.   a list of all sites that have posted their privacy statements

   E.   a government law that ends every form of advertising on the Internet

21. The word "sinister" in the first paragraph is used to mean:

   A.   poisonous.

   B.   threatening.

   C.   corrupt.

   D.   unlucky.

   E.   obnoxious.

Read the passage below. Then answer the three questions that follow.

Recent findings from paleontologists have sparked great debate about the possibility of birds evolving from dinosaurs. Two new species of small dinosaur have been found, each of which was clearly covered with feathers. This has led many in the scientific community to believe the increasingly popular theory that birds are descended directly from dinosaurs.

Some have suggested that even the mighty velociraptor may have been covered with its own feathers. If the dinosaur–bird connection was convincing before, it is now almost certain. With any new discovery come skeptics, and this recent finding is no exception. Even these startling discoveries do not impress some scientists. These scientists contend that both birds and dinosaurs evolved from the same older common ancestor. They assert that any similarities between birds and dinosaurs are due to the common parentage, not due to a direct evolutionary relationship.

22. What is the best summary of the passage?

   A. Whenever a new anthropological study is done, it will be subject to controversy and debate.

   B. The velociraptor was covered with feathers.

   C. New evidence lends greater weight to the theory that birds are descended from dinosaurs.

   D. Critics of recent studies contend common parentage links birds and dinosaurs.

   E. Evolutionary relationships are difficult to define with certainty.

23. What is the author's attitude toward the belief that birds are descended directly from dinosaurs?

   A. skeptical support

   B. unwavering conviction

   C. indifference

   D. confident support

   E. utter disbelief

24. Which of the following is the best definition for the author's use of the word "sparked" in the first paragraph?

   A. started

   B. glittered

   C. ended

   D. ignited

   E. burned

Analyze the index below. Then answer the two questions that follow.

Shakespeare, William	59, 199–215, 245–284
Comic plays of	203–207
Films on plays of	179
History plays of	197–98
Poetry of	189 and 193
Romantic plays of	211–13
Tragic plays of	208–211

25. On what pages would you look to find information on Macbeth, which critics call "Shakespeare's best written tragedy"?

    A.   203–207

    B.   197–198

    C.   189 and 193

    D.   211–213

    E.   208–211

26. Which of the following best describes the organizational pattern used in the section of the book dealing with Shakespeare?

    A.   chronological

    B.   alphabetical

    C.   by category

    D.   by literary importance

    E.   from least influential to most influential

Read the passage below. Then answer the three questions that follow.

Despite years of publicity about the problem, the percentage of college students who binge drink, that is, consume five or more drinks in one sitting, has declined only from 44 percent to 43 percent. Further, half of all students who binge drink do so regularly—at least three times within a two-week period. Finally, 33 percent more students admit that they drink just to get drunk. Dangerous drinking is at its worst in fraternities and sororities, where four out of five members acknowledge that they binge.

Public pressure has shown some previous influence regarding students' drinking habits. A University of Michigan researcher says the percentage of drinkers who binged dropped through the late 1980s and early 1990s, largely because of the widespread publicity about the dangers of drunken driving. _____
_____.

27. Which of the following sentences best summarizes the overall message of the passage?

   A. According to statistics, binge drinking is on the decline.

   B. Dangerous drinking remains high on college campuses despite efforts to curb such behavior.

   C. Fraternity and sorority binge drinking is most problematic.

   D. Too many students drink just to get drunk.

   E. Efforts to curb drunk driving seem to be more successful than efforts to curb binge drinking.

28. Which of the following sentences, if inserted into the blank, would best complete the passage?

   A. Currently, there seems to be no way of stopping binge drinking.

   B. Schools should consider using the same messages used in the 1980s in order to curb binge drinking.

   C. Those messages are unfortunately not being given to college students today.

   D. University officials should evaluate how to use public pressure more effectively to help curb the current binge-drinking problem.

   E. If schools first reduce the number of fraternity students who binge drink, the rest of the campus will follow.

29. Which of the following statements, if true, would weaken the claim that publicity efforts helped to curb binge drinking in the late 1980s?

A. Drunk driving convictions decreased 12% over that time period.

B. Students did not watch as much television as other groups, decreasing the number of times they heard those ads.

C. New state laws for drunk driving became much more severe—one conviction went from a suspended license to three years in jail.

D. Binge drinking was listed as a "favorite activity" by many college students.

E. Membership in a designated drivers program at Michigan increased by 500 percent during the late 1980s.

Read the passage below. Then answer the question that follows.

Zinc lozenges have gained great popularity among adults as a means to reduce the duration and severity of colds. Unfortunately, the lozenges do not work for children. _____ _____. Even if they knew and could alter the medicine, children may not be too excited about taking them. Children complain about the taste of the lozenges; many children vomit if taking one on an empty stomach.

30. Which of the following sentences would best complete the passage when inserted into the blank above?

    A.   Scientists are unable to explain why the lozenges do not work for children.

    B.   Nonetheless, children should take them.

    C.   Be careful of products that promote zinc lozenges for children.

    D.   New lozenges are currently being tested for animals.

    E.   The severity of children's colds should be monitored closely.

Read the passage below. Then answer the five questions that follow.

The United States is currently home to an unprecedented 4,000 nonnative plant species and 2,300 alien animal species. These plants and animals arrive by air and by sea from other continents, often in the bilge water of tankers and as stowaways on aircrafts. Previously, very little was done to stop this transport of alien plants and animals. But now, aliens are so out of control that they are threatening the very existence of America's native species. Of the 1,900 imperiled American species, 49 percent are being endangered by aliens. Aliens are currently the leading threat to species populations, next to habitat destruction. In some locations, the influence of aliens is already as bad as it can be. In Hawaii, more than 95 percent of the 282 imperiled plants and birds are threatened by aliens.

In general, a plant or animal is kept in check by species that compete with it, eat it, or sicken it. On new grounds, though, aliens often have no such constraints. Many foreign creatures have flourished in delicate ecosystems. Our environment cannot quickly adapt to a new plant species.

A crucial preventative measure is to outlaw the release of ballast water in ports. Some ports, like the port in San Francisco Bay, are populated by almost 99 percent alien species. Yet, limiting the inclusion of alien species will not be easy. Many new species enter undetected. Further, some alien species provide great help to our environment. America's economy thrives on many of our immigrants—soybeans, wheat, cotton, rye, and fruiting trees all originated on other continents and were brought over by colonists. Without any data or observations, it is difficult to predict if an alien species will be beneficial or harmful to our environment.

31. Which of the following is the best summary of the passage?

 A. The United States is home to over 6,000 alien plant and animal species.

 B. Alien species provide a number of problems to our ecosystems, which do not have easy solutions.

 C. Alien animals and plants can help our environment.

 D. Certain parts of the United States are upset at the number of alien plants species. and animals in our environment.

 E. It is difficult to predict the effects of an alien species in our environment.

32. The author specifically mentions the state of Hawaii in the passage because it has:

 A. benefited the most from alien species.

 B. been greatly hurt by alien species.

 C. been largely unharmed by alien plants or animals.

 D. new laws outlining the entry of alien species.

 E. a port which contains 99 percent alien species.

33. Why does the author suggest outlawing the release of ballast water in ports?

A. Ballast water pollutes the ocean.

B. Ballast filters are costly to port operators.

C. Alien species often enter our environment through ballast water.

D. The San Francisco port does not want any more alien species.

E. Alien species do more harm in the water than on land.

34. Why do scientists fear aliens entering our ecosystems?

A. Alien species will always harm our ecosystem.

B. Alien species have the potential to disrupt our ecosystems, endangering species unique to our country.

C. The cost of damage done by aliens is in the billions of dollars per year.

D. Our ecosystems would always work better without alien species.

E. Alien species multiply much faster in new environments.

35. What would be an appropriate title for the previous passage?

A. Hawaii's Ecological Trouble

B. Bad Ballast Water!

C. Aliens—Changing Our Ecosystems

D. Ecosystems in Trouble

E. Solutions to Alien Invasions

Read the passage below. Then answer the three questions that follow.

Mounting evidence suggests that any musical stimulus, from Beethoven to the Spice Girls, can have therapeutic effects. Whether you've had heart surgery or a bad day at the office, some soothing sounds may help to lessen stress and promote well-being. Music therapy isn't mainstream health care, but recent studies suggest it can have a wide range of benefits. Most studies have been done with patients recovering from various illnesses, such as a stroke and Parkinson's disease.

No one really knows how music helps the body. We do know that listening to music can directly influence pulse, the electrical activity of muscles, and lower blood pressure. Neuroscientists suspect that music can actually help build and strengthen connections among nerve cells. This is probably why listening to Mozart before an IQ test boosts scores by roughly nine points.

36. Which of the following is NOT mentioned as a benefit to listening to music?

   A. relieved stress

   B. increased neural activity

   C. faster recovery

   D. increased coordination

   E. lower blood pressure

37. Which of the following best summarizes the content of the passage?

   A. Music therapy has become so widely accepted, many health care organizations are adding music therapy sessions to their insurance policies.

   B. A detailed analysis on how music helps the body.

   C. Neuroscientists are tracking the neurological effects of music on the body.

   D. Evidence suggests that music therapy helps the body, even if we aren't sure exactly how.

   E. Students can perform better on standardized exams if they listen to more classical music.

38. The author's use of the word "mainstream" in the first paragraph means:

   A. conventional

   B. radical

   C. musical

   D. medicinal

   E. experimental

Read the passage below. Then answer the three questions that follow.

Insulin is a critical hormone that allows individuals to absorb simple sugars (like glucose and fructose) from their food as it is digested. Most individuals produce the right amount of insulin. In fact, most individuals are not aware of the presence of insulin in the bloodstream.

Recently, nutritionists have discovered that foods known as complex carbohydrates—potatoes, carrots, and pasta among them—break down into simple sugars. Sometimes, this breakdown into sugars occurs so rapidly that the sugars may trigger a strong insulin response. This can be a problem, since a high level of insulin will inhibit the breakdown of fatty deposits. Therefore, eating too many carbohydrates leads to too much insulin, which in turn promotes the accumulation of fat. If you want to watch your weight, be sure to watch the number of complex carbohydrates you consume.

39. Which of the following statements, if true, would weaken the argument in the author's last sentence?

    A. Certain foods, like whole grains and cereals, can counteract the tendency of other complex carbohydrates to raise insulin levels.

    B. Weight gain can be countered by more exercise.

    C. Stress is also a factor in the body's ability to break down fatty deposits.

    D. Complex carbohydrates like carrots do not contain many calories.

    E. A combination of proper diet and sleep can decrease insulin levels in the body.

40. What is the best definition for the author's use of the word "trigger" in the second paragraph?

    A. encourage

    B. decrease

    C. inspire

    D. influence

    E. stimulate

41. According to the passage, high levels of insulin may promote weight gain by:

    A. decreasing the heart rate.

    B. inhibiting the ability to break down fatty deposits.

    C. diminishing the health benefit of foods like carrots and pasta.

    D. combining with complex carbohydrates, which then become difficult to break down.

    E. slowing the transport of nutrients in the bloodstream.

Read the passage below. Then answer the four questions that follow.

The koala is one of the most misunderstood animals. Although it is sometimes called a koala bear, or Australian bear, and is somewhat bear-like in appearance, it is not related to true bears. Once abundant, it is now found in much-reduced numbers in Queensland, Victoria, and New South Wales. It has thick, grayish fur, a tailless body 2 to 2 1/2 ft (60–75 cm) long; a protuberant, curved, black nose; and large, furry ears. The five sharply clawed toes on each foot enable it to grasp and climb. A slow-moving, nocturnal animal, the koala has perhaps the most specialized diet of any living mammal. It feeds on leaves and shoots of a particular species of eucalyptus at a specific stage of maturation. The single cub is about 3/4 in (1.9 cm) long at birth and is nursed in the mother's pouch, from which it emerges for the first time at about six months old. Until it is approximately eight months old a koala continues to ride in the pouch, and until about one year of age it is carried on its mother's back or in her arms. The harmless and defenseless koala has been ruthlessly hunted, chiefly for fur but also for food. Disease and the clearing of the eucalyptus forests have also taken a heavy toll. Protective measures have been adopted to prevent the extinction of the koala.

42. An appropriate title for this passage would be:

   A. Koalas Face Extinction

   B. Koala—It's Not a Bear!

   C. The Unique Koala Diet

   D. Get to Know the Koala

   E. Victorian Koalas

43. The following passage would most likely be located in:

   A. a newspaper article.

   B. an editorial column.

   C. a scientific journal.

   D. a doctoral dissertation.

   E. an encyclopedia.

44. Which of the following is NOT one of the reasons the koala is facing extinction?

   A. It is hunted for fur.

   B. It is hunted for food.

   C. Many are isolated as pets, away from other koalas.

   D. Disease in their natural habitat.

   E. Destruction of their natural habitat.

45. Why does the author believe that the koalas are often linked to bears?

   A. Their diet is similar to those of true bears.

   B. Both true bears and koalas raise their young in a pouch.

   C. Both bears and koalas are facing extinction.

   D. Bears and koalas are both nocturnal.

   E. They are often referred to as koala bears or Australian bears.

Read the passage below. Then answer the three questions that follow.

One effect of a moist, warmer-than-usual spring is the increase in the number of ticks. Ticks, no larger than the size of a pinhead, are reason for concern since they can transmit Lyme disease. Lyme disease is spread by ticks that usually live on mice and deer. However, ticks can also attach themselves to other creatures, including people. If a tick bites someone, a large rash will usually appear at the site of the bite within a month. In addition, many will suffer from chills, fever, headache, and mild conditions of arthritis shortly after a rash appears. Untreated, Lyme disease can cause severe arthritis, and an irregular heartbeat.

Antibiotics used to be the only treatment for Lyme disease. Now, recent advances have led to the creation of a vaccine. In order for the vaccine to work, individuals must take three shots over a period of twelve months. Most individuals may find this treatment difficult to administer. A dose of tick-repellent should help the casual outdoor-bound individual avoid the danger of ticks.

46. According to the passage, what is the first

    sign of a tick bite on humans?

    A. an irregular heartbeat

    B. arthritis weather season.

    C. chills and fever

    D. headaches

    E. a large rash

47. Which of the following is the best definition for the word "treatment," used in the second paragraph of the passage?

    A. management

    B. remedy

    C. execution

    D. strategy

    E. processing

48. According to the passage, the vaccine against Lyme disease is appropriate only for those who:

    A. plan on going outside during a warm day.

    B. occasionally spend time hiking and traveling outdoors.

    C. do not like the smell of tick repellent.

    D. live in the Northeastern United States.

    E. are outdoors so often that they must constantly protect themselves against ticks.

Analyze the table of contents below. Then answer the two questions that follow.

49. On what page would you look to find information on how to create a mail merge document?

    A. 208

    B. 212

    C. 215

    D. 216

    E. 228

50. In what way is the table of contents arranged?

    A. alphabetically

    B. by task

    C. chronologically

    D. by age

    E. by level of expertise

SECTION II: TEST OF MATHEMATICS

Directions: Each of the questions in this test is followed by five suggested answers. Select the best answer in each case. Be sure to mark all of your answers in the Mathematics Section of your answer document.

1. Richard can write 2 test questions in 10 minutes. At this rate, how many questions can he write in 2 hours?

   A. 24

   B. 36

   C. 40

   D. 80

   E. 120

2. A delivery driver drove the following distances on Monday: $4\frac{3}{4}$ miles, $5\frac{1}{3}$ miles, 3 miles, $7\frac{2}{3}$ miles, and $5\frac{1}{4}$ miles. What was the average distance the driver drove, in miles, on Monday?

   A. 5

   B. $5\frac{1}{5}$

   C. 6

   D. $6\frac{1}{5}$

   E. 26

3. If n is the average of three numbers x, 12, and 15, what is the value of x?

A. $\left(\dfrac{n}{3}\right) + 9$

B. $3(n - 9)$

C. $3n + 9$

D. $3(n + 9)$

E. $n - 9$

Questions 4 and 5. **Read the information below, then answer the questions that follow.**

> A vending machine contains 42 items. There are 13 candy bars, 14
> bags of pretzels, and 15 packs of gum. After recess, there are 11 items
> remaining in the vending machine.

4. Which of the following facts can be determined from the information given
   above?

   A.   the number of candy bars sold

   B.   the cost of a bag of pretzels

   C.   the total capacity of the vending machine

   D.   the amount of money collected by the vending machine during recess

   E.   the number of items that were sold during recess

5. In order to calculate the total value of the items sold during recess, what
   additional information would be needed?

   A.   the cost of a bag of pretzels, the cost of a candy bar, and the cost of a pack of gum

   B.   the number of candy bars left in the vending machine after recess

   C.   the number of bags of pretzels left in the vending machine after recess

   D.   (A), (B), and (C)

   E.   it cannot be determined without more information

6. A dress that normally sells for $250 is on sale for $175. The sale price is approximately what percent of the original price?

    A. 70%

    B. 60%

    C. 50%

    D. 40%

    E. 30%

7. A bank charges a fee of $4.25 for every $100 that is used for cash advances. What was the amount used for cash advances if the total fee equaled $63.75?

    A. $15

    B. $150

    C. $1,150

    D. $1,500

    E. $1,555

8. Of the following, which is the largest in value?

    A. .02

    B. $\dfrac{3}{14}$

    C. $8\dfrac{3}{4}\%$

    D. .063

    E. $\dfrac{3}{16}$

Use the diagram below to answer the question that follows.

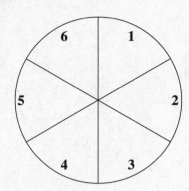

9. The spinner has an equal probability of landing on any number from 1-6. If you spin the spinner two times, what is the probability that the sum of the two numbers will equal 7?

A. $\dfrac{1}{12}$

B. $\dfrac{1}{6}$

C. $\dfrac{1}{4}$

D. $\dfrac{1}{3}$

E. $\dfrac{1}{2}$

10. Consider these two statements:

> Some dolls have brown hair.
> All dolls with black hair have a red bow.

Which of the following statements must also be true?

A. There are no dolls with red hair.

B. No dolls with brown hair have a red bow.

C. Some dolls with red bows have brown hair.

D. Not all dolls have black hair.

E. Not all dolls have red bows.

11. Pam needs to order ribbon to decorate her gifts. Each gift requires 31 inches of ribbon. If she has 22 gifts, what is the total length of ribbon that Pam needs to order?

A. 10 feet, 6 inches

B. 31 feet

C. 56 feet, 10 inches

D. 62 feet, 4 inches

E. 682 feet

12. The length of a rectangle is $4l$ and the width is $7w$. Which of the following expressions represents the perimeter of the rectangle?

A. $22lw$

B. $28lw$

C. $11lw$

D. $4l + 7w$

E. $8l + 14w$

13. Julie can grade 20 spelling tests per hour. If she starts grading tests at 9:00 A.M., which of the following is the best estimate as to when she will be finished grading 134 tests?

   A.   12:30 P.M.

   B.   1:30 P.M.

   C.   2:00 P.M.

   D.   3:30 P.M.

   E.   5:00 P.M.

14. 3 less than 8 times a number is 37. What is the number?

   A.   34

   B.   29

   C.   21

   D.   5

   E.   4

15. $\frac{1}{2}$ is how many times greater than $\frac{1}{4}$?

   A. $\frac{1}{2}$

   B.   2

   C.   4

   D.   6

   E.   8

16. At a certain company, 65% of employees work in the sales department. If the company has 5,020 employees, how many employees do not work in the sales department?

    A. 3,765

    B. 3,263

    C. 2,761

    D. 1,757

    E. 1,255

17. Anne, Sue, and Jen want to go to the amusement park together. They agree to combine their money. Anne has $11.00, Sue has $15.00, and Jen has $16.00. Admission is $21 per person. How much more money will they each need to obtain, on average, in order for everyone to be able to go to the amusement park?

    A. $5.00

    B. $6.00

    C. $7.00

    D. $10.00

    E. $14.00

18. Which of the following expressions is not equivalent to 6 * 52?

    A. $6 + (26 \times 2)$

    B. 12×26

    C. $6 \times (40 + 12)$

    D. 24×13

    E. $(2 \times 3) \times (13 \times 4)$

19. The school library moved some of its books from the first floor to the second floor. If the school originally had 1,035,726 books on the first floor, and if after the move there are 924,192 books on the first floor, approximately how many books were moved to the second floor?

    A. 100,000 books

    B. 75,000 books

    C. 10,000 books

    D. 7,500 books

    E. 1,000 books

20. Jessica's monthly rent is $50 more than $\dfrac{1}{2}$ of Michael's monthly rent.

    If Jessica's monthly rent is $640, what is Michael's monthly rent?

    If r represents Michael's monthly rent, which of the following equations can be used to solve the preceding problem?

    A. $\$640 - 50 = \left(\dfrac{1}{2}\right)r$

    B. $\$640 = 50 + \left(\dfrac{1}{2}\right)r$

    C. $2(\$640) = 50 + r$

    D. $\left(\dfrac{1}{2}\right)\$640 = r - 50$

    E. $640 = 25r$

Questions 21 and 22: Use the chart below to answer the questions that follow.

Population of Town C

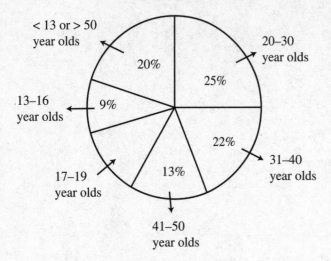

21. What percent of the total population of Town C is made up of teenagers?

    A.   12%

    B.   14%

    C.   17%

    D.   19%

    E.   20%

22. If there are 125,000 people in Town C, how many people are between the ages of 20 and 50, inclusive?

    A.   25,000

    B.   33,575

    C.   50,000

    D.   75,000

    E.   82,500

23. The sum of 3.468 and 7.397, when rounded to the nearest tenth, is:

    A.   11

    B.   10.9

    C.   10.8

    D.   10.0

    E.   3.6

24. If a cafe purchases eggs for $2 per dozen and sells a three-egg omelet for $4, what is the cafe's profit on 4 dozen of these omelets?

    A. $24

    B. $64

    C. $144

    D. $168

    E. $192

Population of State X		
City	1996 population	1997 population
Town A	200,000	250,000
Town B	150,000	150,000
Town C	30,000	60,000
Town D	145,000	160,000
Town E	75,000	65,000

25. Which Town saw the largest percent increase in population from 1996 to 1997?

    A. Town A

    B. Town B

    C. Town C

    D. Town D

    E. Town E

26. By approximately what percent did State X increase in population in 1997 from 1996?

    A. 14%

    B. 25%

    C. 33%

    D. 45%

    E. 85%

27. Howard currently earns $6.00 per hour and works 12 hours per week. If Howard wants to raise his weekly gross pay to $114.00 how many additional hours must he work per week?

A. 4 hours

B. 5 hours

C. 6 hours

D. 7 hours

E. 8 hours

28. Paula-Ann needs to ship two packages. The first package weighs $16\frac{1}{4}$ pounds, and the second package weighs $23\frac{3}{8}$ pounds. What is the total weight of the packages that Paula-Ann needs to ship?

A. $7\frac{1}{8}$ pounds

B. $38\frac{8}{9}$ pounds

C. $39\frac{5}{8}$ pounds

D. 40 pounds

E. $40\frac{5}{8}$ pounds

29. Ben's garden has a collection of roses, tulips, and carnations, in a ratio of 3:2:1. If Ben has a total of 72 flowers in his garden, how many roses are in his garden?

    A.   6 roses

    B.   12 roses

    C.   24 roses

    D.   28 roses

    E.   36 roses

30. If the value of y is between .00268 and .0339, which of the following could be y?

    A.   .00175

    B.   .0134

    C.   .0389

    D.   .268

    E.   2.6

Questions 31 and 32. Use the information below to answer the questions that follow.

- If the distance to a destination is greater than 15 miles from home, Bob will take the bus.
- If the distance to a destination is greater than 4 miles but less than 15 miles from home, Bob will ride his bicycle.
- If the distance to a destination is less than 4 miles from home, Bob will walk.

---

31. If Bob rode his bicycle to Kathleen's apartment, which of the following statements could be true?

    A. Bob's home is 4 miles from Kathleen's apartment.

    B. Bob rode over 30 miles round trip to Kathleen's apartment.

    C. Kathleen's apartment is at least 15 miles from Bob's home.

    D. Kathleen's apartment is within 2 miles from Bob's home.

    E. Kathleen's apartment is 11 miles from Bob's home.

32. Using the information above, which of the following facts could be determined?

    A. the total number of miles Bob rode on his bike on Tuesday

    B. the total number of miles Bob walked on Tuesday

    C. the method of transportation Bob used to get to a destination 20 miles away

    D. the number of miles from Bob's home to any destination

    E. Bob's speed on a bicycle

33. $3x + 12 = 7x - 16$. What is x?

    A. 3

    B. 7

    C. 12

    D. 16

    E. 28

34. Tommy rides his bicycle at a constant rate of 12 miles per hour. How many days will it take him to ride 360 miles?

    A. 1.25 days

    B. 1.5 days

    C. 1.75 days

    D. 2.25 days

    E. 2.75 days 1

35. Multiplying a number by $\frac{1}{2}$ is the same as dividing that number by

    A. $\frac{1}{2}$

    B. $\frac{1}{4}$

    C. 1

    D. 2

    E. 4

36. Marge has a jar of coins (quarters, dimes, nickels, and/or pennies) totaling $24.70. What is the largest number of quarters that Marge could have in her jar?

    A. 247

    B. 118

    C. 98

    D. 49

    E. 24

37. If $3z + 6 = 16$, what is the value of $9z$?

    A. $\dfrac{10}{3}$

    B. 10

    C. 20

    D. 22

    E. 30

Use the information below to answer the question that follows.

Priya was asked to evaluate the expression $(3x + 2)(x + 5)$. Although she was given the value of -5 for x, she was unsure of her answer.

38. If Priya evaluated the expression correctly, what answer should she have given?

    A. -13

    B. 0

    C. 75

    D. 325

    E. 425

39. What is the value of 623,499 rounded to the nearest thousand?

    A. 600,000

    B. 620,000

    C. 623,000

    D. 623,500

    E. 624,000

40. Lara is scheduled to perform 24 surgeries this week. If she performs four surgeries on Monday, how many must she perform each day, on average, to finish by Friday?

    A. 2

    B. 3

    C. 4

    D. 5

    E. 6

41. How long would it take a jogger averaging 6 miles per hour to reach her destination 5 miles away?

    A. 30 minutes

    B. 40 minutes

    C. 50 minutes

    D. 60 minutes

    E. 70 minutes

42. Steve has a jar of coins containing 23 quarters, 15 nickels, 36 dimes, and 42 pennies. Steve removes one quarter from the jar and spends it. What is the probability that the next coin Steve takes from the jar will be a nickel or a dime?

A. $\dfrac{5}{12}$

B. $\dfrac{51}{16}$

C. $\dfrac{10}{23}$

D. $\dfrac{64}{115}$

E. $\dfrac{51}{115}$

Use the table below to answer the following question.

Week 1	−2°
Week 2	17°
Week 3	4°
Week 4	−11°
Week 5	9°
Week 6	22°

43. A website recorded the average temperatures in Springfield for six consecutive weeks. What is the difference between the highest and lowest temperatures recorded during these six weeks?

A. −9

B. −13

C. 33

D. 36

E. 39

44. Mitch makes $2,000 each month. His bills for the month are: $600.00, $250.00, $200.00, $180.00, $140.00, $120.00, and $86.00. If there are four weeks in a month, how much money does Mitch have left each week?

   A. $106.00

   B. $242.00

   C. $318.00

   D. $424.00

   E. $500.00

45. If x is between -1 and 0, which of the following statements must be true?

   I. $x^2 < 1$
   II. $x^2 > 0$
   III. $x^2 < x$

   A. I only

   B. II only

   C. III only

   D. I and II only

   E. II and III only

Questions 46 and 47. Use the table below to answer the questions that follow.

List of Television Shows		
Television Show	**Start Time**	**End Time**
Show A	9:30	
Show B	10:15	10:45
Show C	11:00	11:20
Show D	12:00	12:45
Show E		2:30

46. If Show A is 20 minutes longer than Show C, what time does Show A end?

    A.   9:50

    B.   10:10

    C.   10:20

    D.   10:30

    E.   11:40

47. If Show E is the longest of all five shows, what is one possible start time for Show E?

    A.   2:20

    B.   2:10

    C.   2:00

    D.   1:45

    E.   1:40

48. In Allison's class, there are 23 more boys than girls. If there are a total of 81 students in the class, how many girls are in the class?

A. 23

B. 29

C. 40

D. 52

E. 58

49. Consider this statement:

Every student in Julie's class likes to play chess.

Which of the following statements must also be true?

A. No one in Julie's class likes to play checkers.

B. Everyone that likes to play chess is in Julie's class.

C. Some students in Julie's class don't like to play chess.

D. If a student does not like chess, the student is not in Julie's class.

E. Only students in Julie's class like chess.

50. Given the formula $F° = \dfrac{9}{5}C° + 32°$, where F = Fahrenheit temperature and C = Celsius temperature, which of the following is closest to the temperature in Celsius degrees when the temperature is 95° Fahrenheit?

A. 203°

B. 113°

C. 71°

D. 35°

E. 20°

SECTION III: TEST OF WRITING

Directions: The Writing Section consists of two essay topics. Be sure to write about the assigned topics. Essays on topics of your own choice will not be acceptable. Your written responses should be your original work, written in your own words, and should not be copied or paraphrased from some other work. Since both topics are weighed equally in scoring, you should plan to spend about the same amount of time on each topic.

The essay topics in this test are designed to give you an opportunity to demonstrate your ability to write effectively. Spend some time considering each topic and organizing your thoughts before you begin writing. For each essay, be sure to address all parts of the topic; to support generalizations with specific examples; and to use multiple paragraphs.

You may use any blank space provided in this test booklet to make notes or to prepare a rough draft for each essay. However, your score will be based solely on the versions of your essays written in the space provided in your answer document. Please write as neatly and legibly as possible. To ensure that you have enough space for your entire essay, please do NOT skip lines; do NOT write in excessively large letters; and do NOT leave wide margins.

Topic 1

A local public school system is considering a plan to convert Jefferson High into an all-male school, and Franklin High into an all-female school. Students in the district would be required to attend a same-sex school. Many in the school system think that all-male and all-female high schools would benefit students, and provide a more educational atmosphere. To what extent do you agree or disagree with the supporters?

Support your opinion with specific reasons.

Topic 2

All of us have at some point in our lives had someone whom we've admired, someone we've looked up to. Write about your hero. Identify who the person is, and why he or she is your hero. What qualities does he or she possess that you admire? What have you learned from your hero that has influenced who you are today?

Chapter 11
Practice Test 1:
Answers and
Explanations

ANSWER KEY

Reading

1.	B	26.	C
2.	A	27.	B
3.	D	28.	D
4.	E	29.	C
5.	E	30.	A
6.	C	31.	B
7.	B	32.	B
8.	B	33.	C
9.	A	34.	B
10.	A	35.	C
11.	B	36.	D
12.	A	37.	D
13.	B	38.	A
14.	D	39.	A
15.	D	40.	E
16.	C	41.	B
17.	E	42.	D
18.	A	43.	E
19.	D	44.	C
20.	C	45.	E
21.	B	46.	E
22.	C	47.	B
23.	D	48.	E
24.	A	49.	D
25.	E	50.	B

Mathematics

1.	A	26.	A
2.	B	27.	D
3.	B	28.	C
4.	E	29.	E
5.	D	30.	B
6.	A	31.	E
7.	D	32.	C
8.	B	33.	B
9.	B	34.	A
10.	D	35.	D
11.	C	36.	C
12.	E	37.	E
13.	D	38.	B
14.	D	39.	C
15.	B	40.	D
16.	D	41.	C
17.	C	42.	E
18.	A	43.	C
19.	A	44.	A
20.	B	45.	D
21.	E	46.	B
22.	D	47.	E
23.	B	48.	B
24.	D	49.	D
25.	C	50.	D

SECTION I: TEST OF READING

1. **B** The passage tells us that new steps are being taken to ensure food safety because of the increasing threat of new diseases. Choice (A) is partial—the author's feelings are expressed, but this is trivial to the overall message. Choices (D) and (E) are too broad, and out of scope. Choice (C) is mentioned in the passage, but is not the central point. The author focuses more on a description of new processing techniques rather than the costs associated with an outbreak.

2. **A** The author is using sarcasm in this sentence. The author uses the word to indicate that he does not have a technical understanding of placing an oyster under 90,000 pounds of pressure, but that he assumes something must be happening. Only (A) and (C) are possible definitions of the word. In this case, (A) is a better answer, because it is more specific to the author's intent.

3. **D** This passage includes factual knowledge, as well as the author's opinion and sense of humor. The information is not technical enough to be found in either a scientific journal or a legal journal. While the subject is about food, the passage is unlikely to be found in a cookbook. Finally, the passage does not present enough financial information for it to be found in an economics textbook.

4. **E** The author presents a playful tone within the passage. Choices (B), (C), and (D) all are negative. The author jokes about worrying over the taste of food, but never states that he is in any way against the new techniques.

5. **E** In the passage, the author praises the features of HDTV, but goes on to announce the programming challenges of HDTV. Choices (A), (B), and (D) are all true, but do not address the central theme. Choice (C) might be true, but it is secondary to the main point of the passage.

6. **C** The title correctly addresses the two main issues presented in the passage—the description of what HDTV is, and the analysis of when digital programming will arrive. Be careful about titles that use words or phrases that can be found in the passage. Choice (D) is a perfect example of such a trap choice. However, that title is too broad to be correct—it doesn't mention HDTV.

7. **B** The author uses the word "major" to describe how the large networks will not increase their HDTV programming, thereby limiting the effectiveness of an HDTV set. The words "top ten" also give indication that the use of the word "major" indicates a large amount.

8. **B** This is one of the more difficult questions on this test. First, we need to be very clear about the argument of the railroad officials. They argue that there is in fact no increase in actual mishaps, just an increase in the number of news sources reporting the mishaps. Choices (C), (D), and (E) would all strengthen this claim, so eliminate those three answer choices. Choice (B) weakens that claim by implying that certain months are more likely to have more accidents due to high volume of train rides.

9. **A** This answer choice clearly reflects the overall main idea of the passage. Choice (D) describes the main point of one of the paragraphs, but not of the entire passage.

10. **A** The word "however" in the first paragraph shows the difference between soldiers in the Roman era and those in the Middle Ages.

11. **B** This is a specific question. Look for keywords such as "executing prisoners." In the second paragraph, you can find the correct answer.

12. **A** When asked to find the definition of a phrase, be sure to read a few lines above and a few lines below. In the paragraph, it is mentioned that the device was used to create a value that was neither too low nor too high.

13. **B** The passage discusses the importance of leafy green vegetables, then describes a study that supports the author's claim.

14. **D** Multivitamins do contain folic acid that is contained in leafy green vegetables. However, leafy green vegetables contain many more beneficial compounds.

15. **D** While the passage focuses mostly on the study about colon cancer, the author does state that leafy green vegetables are beneficial for a number of reasons. Part of (A) is incorrect (the phrase "but little more").

16. **C** In the first paragraph, the author is satisfied with the increase in the overall consumption of vegetables, but encourages us to eat more leafy green vegetables.

17. **E** The answer to a specific question is always in the text. Read the line that contains the word "cookies" for a description of what they are.

18. **A** All of the titles contain some word or words found in the passage. However, the overall theme of the passage is about privacy on the Internet.

19. **D** With over ninety sites available to answer questions about privacy, statement (D) is true.

20. **C** The author's concern is that people may be giving information to a site without their consent. Choice (C) allows a user to provide information if they so desire. The user would always know when personal information is being distributed.

21. **B** The author claims that the Internet is both attractive and threatening. "Corrupt" is too strong of a word. The author does not ascribe malicious intent to most Internet sites.

22. **C** The topic sentence of the first paragraph states similar information. Choices (B) and (D) are too specific, while (A) and (E) are too broad.

23.   **D**   The last line of the first paragraph states the author's opinion on the topic. The phrase "almost certain" makes (B) too extreme, while (A) is too wishy-washy. Choice (D) finds a nice balance. Choices (C) and (E) can be easily eliminated.

24.   **A**   The new studies started great debate. If you were unsure of the correct answer, remember to try replacing the answer choices back into the passage.

25.   **E**   *Macbeth* was a tragic play, and tragic plays can be found on pages 208–211.

26.   **C**   The section of the book is broken up into the different types of works that Shakespeare produced. Note that the index lists these sections alphabetically, but the page numbers indicate that his plays are discussed by category, not alphabetically.

27.   **B**   Choice (A) is factually true, but actually contains the opposite message of the passage. Choice (C) is true but too specific; (D) is an opinion that is not the primary focus of the passage. Choice (E) also seems to be true, but the main focus of the passage is on current drinking statistics, not a comparison between eras.

28.   **D**   The second paragraph states that public pressure has worked in the past. The sentence concludes the paragraph by tying it back into the original point—current efforts to curb binge drinking are not successful.

29.   **C**   The researcher claims that public pressure against drunk driving led to a decrease in binge drinking incidents. In order to weaken this claim, you would need to show that another factor helped to decrease binge drinking incidents. Choice (C) does this. Stiff law penalties, not public pressure, may be the primary reason for the decrease in binge drinking.

30.   **A**   At first glance, it appears that a few sentences would fit into the passage. However, make sure you read beyond the blank line. The start of the next sentence, "Even if they knew..." provides a clue that the previous sentence talks about scientists.

31.   **B**   The passage describes the negative effects of alien species in our environment, and explains the difficulty of finding solutions.

32.   **B**   Read a few lines above the word "Hawaii." The author uses Hawaii as an example of an ecosystem that has been ravaged by alien species.

33.   **C**   The author proposes this solution as one way to curb the increasing number of alien species being introduced into our environment. Choice (E) is not stated in the passage.

34.   **B**   Again, not all alien species do harm to our ecosystem, so (A) and (D) are not always true. Choice (C) is a true statement, but scientists are more likely concerned with the environmental impact than a financial impact. Choice (E) is not supported in the passage.

35.   **C**   Choice (A) is too specific. Choice (B) is creative but does not provide enough meaning to the passage. Choice (D) is too general, and (E) is out of scope.

36. **D** All of the other four answer choices can be found within the passage. On a "NOT" question, eliminate an answer choice once you find that it works.

37. **D** The first paragraph states that music therapy helps a number of different people in different conditions. The second paragraph attempts to give some information on how music may help the body.

38. **A** The author uses the word mainstream to point out how music therapy is beyond the normal practices in medicine. This "alternative medicine" is having successful results.

39. **A** The author argues that complex carbohydrates help lead to increased weight gain. The passage supports this claim (insulin levels are raised too high, and are therefore unable to break down fatty deposits). In order to weaken the argument, we need to show that it is possible to counteract the rising insulin levels caused by complex carbohydrates. Choice (A) does this. Others like (B), (C), and (E) may be true, but do not impact the author's warning about complex carbohydrates.

40. **E** The additional sugars in the body will stimulate a rush of insulin into the body. Choices (A), (C), and (D) are all possible definitions for the word trigger. In this passage, however, we want to select the word that shows how sugar levels start, or create, an insulin release.

41. **B** This statement is found directly in the passage, in the second paragraph.

42. **D** Choices (A), (C), and (E) are too specific. Choice (D) is better than (B) since (D) implies that it will provide an introduction about the koala, which is what the passage as a whole is designed to do.

43. **E** The passage is mostly facts, so (B) does not fit. The passage is very general, so (C) and (D) do not fit. The passage is a basic description of a koala, not describing an event involving koalas. Therefore, (E) is the best answer choice.

44. **C** Choices (A), (B), (D), and (E) are mentioned in the next to last sentence in the paragraph.

45. **E** The beginning of the passage mentions that despite their name, koalas are not related to other bears. The similarity of their names is the primary reason for the confusion.

46. **E** In the first paragraph, the author states that the first sign of a tick bite is a large rash. Other conditions may follow after the rash appears.

47. **B** The word treatment is used in a medical sense, and remedy best fits the meaning of the statement.

48. **E** The author encourages the occasional traveler to use traditional methods. Thus, (A) and (B). Choices (C) and (D) are not valid reasons. Choice (E) is an example of someone who must constantly be on guard against Lyme disease.

49. **D** Mail merge information would most likely be found in the section under "Create a Mailing."

50. **B** This technical manual is divided into sections that list different possible business tasks.

SECTION II: TEST OF MATHEMATICS

1. **A** Richard's rate is 2 questions / 10 minutes. Be sure to compare the same units—minutes to minutes, or hours to hours.

   2 hours is equal to 120 minutes.

   Make an equation:

   $$\frac{2}{10} = \frac{x}{120}$$

   $$\frac{2}{10} * 120 = x$$

   $$24 = x$$

2. **B** Add the values: $4\frac{3}{4}$, $5\frac{1}{3}$, 3, $7\frac{2}{3}$, and $5\frac{1}{4}$.

   The integer parts of these numbers (4, 5, 3, 7, and 5) add up to 24.

   The fractional parts of these numbers $\left(\frac{3}{4}, \frac{1}{3}, \frac{2}{3}, \text{ and } \frac{1}{4}\right)$ add up to 2.

   (Notice that $\frac{1}{3} + \frac{2}{3} = 1$, and $\frac{3}{4} + \frac{1}{4} = 1$.) The total is 26 miles.

   The question asks for the average, so now divide by 5 (the number of values in the list.)

   $$\frac{26}{5} = 5.2, \text{ or } 5\frac{1}{5}.$$

3. **B** Since there are variables in the answers, you should Plug In to solve this question. In this case, since n and x are related to each other, it's best to plug in for one variable and evaluate for the value of the other.

   It's easiest to plug in for x. The question asks for the average of x, 12, and 15, so choose a number that makes this easy. Try 9: $x = 9$

   The average of 9, 12, and 15 is (9 + 12 + 15)/3, or 12. So, $n = 12$.

   Go to the answer choices. The question asks for the value of x, so plug in 12 for n. 9 is the target.

   A. $4 + 9 = 13$ eliminate. ✗

   B. $3(3) = 9$ keep. ✔

   C. $36 + 9 = 45$ eliminate. ✗

   D. $3(21) = 36$ eliminate. ✗

   E. $12 - 9 = 3$ eliminate. ✗

4. **E** We know that the vending machine contained 42 items, and was left with 11 items. We can subtract to find that 31 items were sold during recess.

5. **D** In order to calculate the value of the items sold during recess, we need to know the cost of each item, plus the number of items sold. Choice (A) gives us the cost of each item. By using the information in (B) and (C), we can find out how many of each type were sold during recess. What about the number of packs of gum remaining in the machine? We know that there are eleven items left, so we can find this number by subtracting the totals given in (B) and (C).

6. **A** To solve this problem, translate the question into a mathematical equation:

"The sale price is approximately what percent of the original price?" can be translated as

$$175 = \left(\frac{x}{100}\right) * 250$$

Then, solve.

$$\frac{175}{250} = \frac{x}{100}$$

$$\frac{175}{250} * 100 = x$$

$$.7 * 100 = x$$

$$70 = x$$

7. **D** You can use a proportion to solve this problem.

$$\frac{\$4.25}{\$100} = \frac{\$63.75}{x}$$

$$\frac{4.25}{(100 * 63.75)} = \frac{1}{x}$$

$$\frac{4.25}{6375} = \frac{1}{x}$$

$$\frac{6375}{4.25} = x$$

$$1500 = x$$

8. **B** When comparing numbers, remember to Ballpark, and compare answers two at a time. $\frac{3}{14}$ and $\frac{3}{16}$ have the same numerator, so compare the denominators. $\frac{3}{14}$ is the larger of these two, since it has a smaller denominator. Eliminate (E), since it is not the largest value. $\frac{3}{14}$ is close to $\frac{3}{15}$, which means that it is close to $\frac{1}{5}$, or 0.2. This is larger than both .02 and .063, so eliminate (A) and (D). $8\frac{3}{4}$ percent is close to 9 percent, which is equal to .09. This is smaller than $\frac{3}{14}$, so eliminate (C).

9. **B** There are 36 total possible combinations to spin (1 & 1, 1 & 2, 1 & 3, and so on). Of these, there are six possible combinations that would total 7: (1 & 6), (2 & 5), (3 & 4), (4 & 3), (5 & 2), (6 & 1).

$$\frac{6}{36} = \frac{1}{6}.$$

Note: since 1 & 6 is different from 6 & 1 (for instance), they need to be counted separately.

10. **D** From the problem, we have descriptions of dolls with brown hair and dolls with black hair. Thus, not all dolls have black hair.

11. **C** The first step is to calculate the total number of inches of ribbon Pam needs. Multiply 31 by 22 to get 682 total inches. Then, we need to convert this number to feet. The key conversion is that there are 12 inches to 1 foot. If we divide 682 by 12, the result is 56, remainder 10. If you got (E), be careful. Choice (E) is labeled as 682 feet, not 682 inches.

12. **E** To calculate the perimeter of the rectangle, add the lengths of all sides. Remember that rectangles have two pairs of congruent sides.

$4l + 4l + 7w + 7w$
$= 8l + 14w.$

13. **D** Julie must grade 134 tests, which we can estimate at 130 tests. It takes 6.5 hours to grade 130 tests ($\frac{130}{20}$), so Julie will finish a short time after 3:30 P.M. Be sure to approximate during the problem. The phrase "best estimate" is your key to approximate.

14. **D** The equation can be written as follows: $8x - 3 = 37$. Translate the statement. "3 less" becomes -3; "8 times a number" becomes $8x$; "is 37" becomes $= 37$. Further, if you have trouble setting up the equation, you can backsolve. Plug the answer choices into the question to see which answer choice will give you the correct value.

15. **B** Backsolving is the easiest way to solve this problem. Starting with (C), multiply $\frac{1}{4}$ by 4. The result is 1, which is too high. Eliminate (C) and try a smaller number. Try (B). Multiply $\frac{1}{4}$ by 2, and the result is $\frac{1}{2}$. Choice (B) works.

16. **D** Calculate 65% of 5020, which equals 3263. That means that 3,263 employees work in the sales department. Since the question asks how many employees do NOT work in the sales department, eliminate (B). To finish the problem, subtract 3,263 from the total.

$5020 - 3263 = 1757.$

You can also recognize that, if 65% of employees work in the sales department, that means that 35% do not work in the sales department (100% − 65% = 35%).

$5020 * .35 = 1757$

17.　C　Together, the three have $42.00 (11 + 15 + 16). The total amount of money they need is $63.00 ($21.00 × 3). Together, they need $21.00, which works out to $7.00 per person.

18.　A　Order of operations dictates that parenthesis and multiplication be performed first. This means that 6 + (26 × 2) is the same as 6 + 52. Since that is NOT equivalent to the expression in the question (6 × 52), select (A). Eliminate (B), (C), (D), and (E), since they are equivalent to (6 × 52). One method that can be used is prime factorization. 6 × 52 = (2 × 3) × (2 × 2 × 13) = 2 × 3 × 2 × 2 × 13. Choice (B) is equivalent to 6 x 52, since the associative property shows: 2 × 3 × 2 × 2 × 13 = (2 × 3 × 2) × (2 × 13) = 12 × 26. Choice (D) is equivalent, since 2 × 3 × 2 × 2 × 13 = (2 × 3 × 2 × 2) × 13 = 24 × 13. Choicie (C) is equivalent. Using the correct order of operations, parenthesis must be performed first. (2 + 4) × (40 + 12) = 6 × 52. Choice (E) is equivalent, since (2 × 3) × (13 × 4) = 6 × 52. Note that it is not necessary to actually calculate the values of these expressions; only to know whether or not they are equivalent.

19.　A　The difference between approximately 1,000,000 and 900,000 is 100,000. Approximate to save time and needless calculation.

20.　B　Translate the problem into an equation.

"Jessica's monthly rent is $50 more than $\frac{1}{2}$ of Michael's monthly rent."

$640 = $50 + $\frac{1}{2}r$

21.　E　We are told that 9% of the population is made up of 13–16 year olds. To find the number of 17–19 year olds, we need to add the percentages for all the other age groups, and subtract the total from 100%. This number is 11%, making the percent of teenagers equal to 20%.

22.　D　First, we need to calculate the percentage of people between this group. The total is 25% + 22% + 13%, or 60%. 60% of 125,000 is equal to 75,000.

23.　B　Before rounding, add the two numbers together. The sum of 3.468 and 7.397 is 10.865. To round to the nearest tenth, look at the digit in the hundredths place, in this case 6. Since the number is 5 or greater, round up. The correctly rounded number becomes 10.9.

24.　D　It may be easiest to first figure out how many eggs the cafe needs for 4 dozen omelets. 4 dozen omelets is 48 omelets (4 * 12). Each omelet uses three eggs, for a total of 144 eggs. The purchase cost of these eggs is $2 per dozen, so, for 12 dozen eggs, they pay $24 total (144 eggs = 12 dozen). The sale price of 48 omelets is $192 total. (48 * $4). The profit is $192 – $24, or $168.

25.　C　First, eliminate any answer choice that does not increase. Towns B and E do not see an increase. Next, calculate the percent increase using the percent change formula. Town C has the largest increase, with a percent increase of 100%. Note that the largest change in population doesn't automatically indicate that largest percent increase. Town A increases by 50,000 people, but that is only a 25% increase.

26. **A** To find the percent increase, we first need to find the total state population for each year. The total in 1996 is 600,000, and 685,000 in 1997. Our percent change fraction is $\frac{85,000}{600,000}$. Only (A) is close. (Approximate—a third of 600,000 would be 200,000; a fourth of 600,000 is 150,000; we know that (C) and (B) are too large.)

27. **D** First, we need to calculate the current amount of money that Howard earns per week. By multiplying 12 by $6.00/hr, we find that Howard earns $72.00 per week. To get to $114.00 per week, Howard wants to increase his weekly pay by $42.00. Divide this total by his rate of $6.00 per hour, and we get the answer—7 more hours.

28. **C** Add the two fractional amounts together. In order to get the same denominator for each fraction, change to $\frac{1}{4}$ to $\frac{2}{8}$. Then, sum the numbers. The result is $39\frac{5}{8}$ pounds.

29. **E** This is a ratio question, so we should use the ratio box to write down all the given information. Unlike most ratio questions, here we are given information about three things (roses, tulips, and carnations). No problem—we just need to add another column to the ratio box. A completed ratio box will look like this:

	Rose	Tulips	Carn.	Whole
Ratio (parts)	3	2	1	6
Multiply By	12	12	12	12
Actual Number	36	24	12	72

Be careful to select the total number of roses, which is what the question is asking for.

30. **B** Choice (A) is too small. It is smaller than .00268. Choice (B) fits between the two values. Choices (C), (D), and (E) are all larger than .0339.

31. **E** If Bob rode his bicycle, we know that the distance between Bob's home and Kathleen's apartment must be between 4 miles and 15 miles. Only (E) meets this requirement.

32. **C** The information given tells us how Bob will get to a given destination, depending on the number of miles it is away from his home. If we know that a destination is 20 miles away, we know that Bob will take the bus. Without additional information, we don't have any way of calculating the number of miles Bob traveled on his bicycle, or on foot. We also can't calculate the speed at which Bob travels.

33. **B** Rearrange the equation to get:

$28 = 4x$

$7 = x$

34. **A** We know Tommy's rate in miles per hour. First, find the total number of hours it will take Tommy to ride 360 miles. We can solve this using a proportion:

$$\frac{12 \text{ miles}}{1 \text{ hour}} = \frac{360 \text{ miles}}{x \text{ hours}}$$

After cross-multiplying, we find that $12x = 360$. $x = 30$ hours. However, we want the answer in days, not hours. Let's convert hours to days. There are 24 hours in one day, so we have:

$$\frac{30 \text{ hours}}{1 \text{ day}} \times \frac{1 \text{ day}}{24 \text{ hours}} = \frac{5}{4} \text{ or } 1.25 \text{ days}$$

35. **D** If you have any questions about this problem, choose any number. If you select the number 10, and multiply it by $\frac{1}{2}$, the result is 5. What number do you divide 10 by to get 5? 2. Remember, the fraction bar is a shorthand way to express division. $\frac{1}{2}$ means 1 divided by 2.

36. **C** The best approach for this problem would be Plugging In the Answers. Since the question asks for the largest possible number of quarters, start by plugging in the largest number. If Marge has 247 quarters, that would mean that she has $61.75 (247 * .25 = 61.75). This number is too large, since the question states that Marge has $24.70. Eliminate (A). 118 quarters would total $29.50. This number is also too large. Eliminate (B). 98 quarters would total $24.50. This is just under Marge's total amount of $24.70. She would have 20 cents left over, which could be pennies, nickels, or dimes. Select (C). One other approach for this question would be to recognize that the total amount in quarters should be $24.50, since that is the largest number (up to $24.70) which is evenly divisible by quarters. If she has $24.50 in quarters, that means she has 98 quarters (24.50 / .25 = 98).

37. **E** If we simplify the equation, we find that $3z = 10$. Rather than solve for z, simply multiply the entire equation by 3. That gives us $9z = 30$. You can save time and calculations by looking for $9z$ only—don't worry about the value of z.

38. **B** Plug in (-5) for x:

$(3 * (-5) + 2) * ((-5) + 5)$
$= ((-15) + 2) * (0)$
$= (-13) * (0)$
$= 0$

39. **C** To round to the nearest thousand, take a look at the hundreds place. In this example, the hundreds digit is a 4, meaning that we should not round up the number. The correctly rounded number is 623,000.

40. **D** First, subtract the surgeries she performs on Monday. This leaves Lara with 20 surgeries to perform, and 4 days left. Divide 20 by 4 to get the correct answer of 5 surgeries per day.

41. **C** You can use a proportion to set up this problem.

$$\frac{60}{6} = \frac{x}{5}$$

$$\frac{300}{6} = x$$

$$50 = x$$

You can also estimate that 5 miles is almost as long as 6 miles, so the time should be a little less than 1 hour. Eliminate (D) and (E), as they are too large.

42. **E** The total amount of coins at the beginning is 116. Once Steve removes a quarter from the jar, there are 115 coins. The probability of choosing a nickel is $\frac{51}{115}$, and the probability of choosing a dime is $\frac{36}{115}$. Since the question asks for the probability of a nickel OR a dime, add the two probabilities together.

$$\left(\frac{51}{115}\right) + \left(\frac{36}{115}\right) = \left(\frac{51}{115}\right).$$

You can eliminate (B) once you realize that it is a trap answer based on a misreading of the question (note the denominator 116).

43. **C** The highest temperature shown in the table is 22º, and the lowest is -11º. To find the difference, subtract the smaller number from the larger number: 22 - (-11), or 22 + 11.

44. **A** Mitch must spend a total of $1,576.00 each month, leaving him with $424.00 in spending money. If we divide this total by 4, there is $106.00 available per week.

45. **D** Plug in for *x*. *x* must be a value between −1 and 0, so try (−0.5). $(−0.5)^2 = .025$, so both (I) and (II) are true in this case. $(−0.5)^3 = (−0.125)$, which makes (III) false. (Note that the values are negative.) Since this is a "must be" problem, that means that (III) CANNOT be included in the correct answer. Eliminate (C) and (E). You should plug in one or two more times, worrying only about (I) and (II) now, but you'll find that for every value of *x* between −1 and 0, these two statements are always true. Choice (D) is correct.

46. **B** Show C runs for 20 minutes, meaning that Show A runs for a total of 40 minutes. 40 minutes after 9:30 is 10:10.

47. **E** The longest show is Show D, which runs for 45 minutes. If Show E ends at 2:30, it must start at least 45 minutes earlier, or before 1:45. Only (E) works.

48. **B** This question is best solved by Backsolving. First, we can eliminate (C), (D), and (E). If there are more boys in the class, then the class will have less than 50 percent girls. These three answer choices are too high. To backsolve, start with one of our remaining answer choices. If we select (B), we're saying that there are 29 girls in the class. This would mean that there are 23 more boys, for a total of 52 boys. 29 girls and 52 boys give us the desired total of 81 students in the class.

49. **D** (D) is the contrapositive of the statement (If not B, then not A). Choice (A) is incorrect—the problem has nothing to do with checkers. (B) is false—students outside of Julie's class can enjoy chess. Choice (C) is false—the statement says that everyone in the class likes chess. Choice (E) is false for the same reasons as (B).

50. **D** To solve this problem, plug in 95° for F, and don't forget to Ballpark. $\left(\dfrac{9}{5}\right)$ is almost equal to 2, and 32° is close to 30°.

$$F \approx 2C + 30$$
$$95 \approx 2C + 30$$
$$65 \approx 2C$$
$$32.5 \approx C$$

You could also Plug In the Answers, by plugging in for C in the formula. Starting with choice (C),

$$F \approx 2*70 + 30$$
$$F \approx 140 + 30$$

Choice (C) is too large. Try (B) next:

$$F \approx 2*35 + 30$$
$$F \approx 70 + 30$$

This is very close to 95°.

SECTION III: TEST OF WRITING

Topic 1

A local public school system is considering a plan to convert Jefferson High into an all-male school, and Franklin High into an all-female school. Students in the district would be required to attend a same-sex school. Many in the school system think that all-male and all-female high schools would benefit students, and provide a more educational atmosphere. To what extent do you agree or disagree with the supporters? Support your opinion with specific reasons.

Sample Essay #1: Overall Score = 4 (Pass)

Dividing high school students into same-sex schools is certainly not a new concept and has been attempted in many countries with varying degrees of success. The concept assumes that separating the sexes will help improve the students' ability to learn by reducing the distractions provided by the opposite sex. After all, the model assumes, if students aren't thinking about making eyes at the girl or boy at the adjoining desk, they're more likely to have their attention on the teacher. But is this necessarily true? And might splitting up the students into separate-sex schools create more problems than are solved by doing so? After careful thought, I oppose the conversion of Jefferson and Franklin High Schools into same-sex schools, both for the logistical problems of the conversion, and the social implications that such a move would create.

First, I'm assuming that the current school system is the more traditional co-educational setup, where males and females attend the same classes. If we are to split them up by gender, does this mean we'll have to bus them to their new school? If we implement this plan we may inadvertently add time and stress to their daily commute to school, which is not necessarily conducive to learning.

Second, we have to ask if the programs, facilities, and the teachers are similar enough in each school to justify separating the students. We certainly wouldn't want to put one of the genders in a less desirable learning environment than the other. For example, do both schools have the same budgets for sports? Are the classrooms, computer facilities, and playgrounds the same? Are the teachers equally competent, and competent enough, in fact, to teach in the new gender-divided model? Call me cynical, but I'm also concerned that the women's programs in particular will suffer if the female students are moved to a separate school.

Third, by separating the students by sex, we are depriving them of the opportunity to learn valuable social skills necessary for success in later years at college and in the workplace. High school in this country has always been a place where young people learn to work with members of the opposite sex, sharing common learning experiences and participating in group activities. These experiences, properly observed and monitored by the high school staff, provide a foundation for the same skills they will have to utilize in college and in life.

In the final analysis, I think the benefits are far outweighed by the deficits. The "distractions" of the opposite sex attending the same school are less disruptive than those caused by wrenching them away from their friends, and moving at least half of each population to a new setting. And most importantly, I think that separating the students by gender will deprive them of the chance to develop the social skills they will need in the future. After all, the world is filled with both men and women, and the interaction between the sexes in the workplace has never been more prevalent that right here and right now.

Sample Essay #2: Overall Score = 3 (Marginal Pass)

Eight to ten years before I entered my high school, it was a unisex school. However at the time the school couldn't survive so it had to merge with its sister school. Today, I could see why the people would think unisex schools would create a more academic environment for students. I would agree with the supporters of same-sex schools. The academic benefits seem to outweigh the negatives.

There are so many pressures on students today to "fit in." If you don't have the "cool" clothes you are an outcast and often considered unpopular. By having same-sex schools, girls won't have pressure to impress boys. I remember stressing more about whether boys thought I was "cool" than about my algebra homework. Peer pressure will always exist in schools, even with a same-sex school. However, I don't think the pressure will be nearly as great. Students, especially girls, would benefit from relaxed social pressures in a same-sex school. Instead of focusing on what they look like and who is wearing what, some girls can focus more on school.

Some people may argue that having unisex schools would hurt students. The concern may arise that the lack of interaction with the other sex may cause problems later. However, through my experience with friends who attended same sex schools, this was not a problem. The unisex schools often had dances where both sexes would attend (or sporting events that both sexes would support). I don't think this would be a problem if events were organized that would include both sexes. Also, school is for learning and social events after school would only enhance a focus on academics during the school hours.

Although many may disagree that same-sex schools would help student academics, I think it would help. Having same-sex schools takes away many pressures students encounter in co-ed schools. By taking these pressures away, students then can focus more on their academics.

Sample Essay #3: Overall Score = 2 (Marginal Fail)

I am thinking that considering converting the Jefferson High School into an all-male school and Franklin High School to an all-female school is a very bad idea. I am unsure what benefits would be here. Maybe people think boys and girls shouldn't be together because they would distract from each other. This may be true but this is not a reason to keep them in different schools. Boys will still distract boys and girls will also be distracting girls and so what is the point? It seems better to have boys and girls all together.

First, if the school district makes Jefferson into an all-male school, and Franklin into an all-female school, getting to the schools might take a really long time. Instead of just going to the school you are closest to, some students will have to travel to the farther school. That could be costly for students in more time lost, and they might have to be bussed. Then schools have to spend more money on bussing and drivers, instead of other costs. Some boys and some girls will spend more time traveling to and from school then they should.

Also, how can the boys learn about girls if they never see them? Of course, it is that we don't want them seeing too much of the girls, but in class where is there harm? And the same thing for the girls. The girls should be seeing the boys also and know them every day. This makes students very happy, and happy students learn much better.

Therefore, I think the educational atmosphere can be achieved in a school where the boys and girls are all together. They can take classes together and learn together and play sports and everything and I do not see the problem where there is a lesser education as a result. The boys and girls are also in fact used to seeing each other every day. What will happen when they always don't? This could be bad for their development into adult persons. Adults do not go to different jobs just because they are male and female. Thus, I believe that one should leave things as they will be and let boys and girls go to class together.

Sample Essay #4: Overall Score = 1 (Fail)

I'm not really sure if the school district should convert Franklin and Jefferson into same-sex schools. I guess it depends on what kind of student you are. If you are comfortable in an environment with both males and females, then you probably don't want same-sex schools. But if you have trouble and feel pressure dealing with members of the opposite sex, a same-sex school may help you focus more on your studies.

I remember that when I was in high school I really wanted to ask out this girl in my math class. It sounds kind of dumb but all I thought about in class was her, you know, one of those silly crushes. But that's all I thought about, and I didn't do well in math class at all. Maybe it was because I never really liked math, but I think that to some extent my bad grade was because I wasn't focusing on the teacher but instead on her. So, maybe I would have done better if she wasn't in that class, and there were only guys there. On the other hand, a friend of mine had a girlfriend that went to another school, and when things weren't going well for him, he still thought about it in classes and stuff. So it might not be as bad if it were a guy only school, but I'm not saying that everything would be perfect with the schools that way.

So, as I have shown there are some advantages and disadvantages to the idea by the school board. Ultimately, it should go to a vote, and allow the people in the district to decide. I'm not sure what I would vote, cause each side has some points. I don't really care if the schools stay the same or change.

Topic 2

All of us have at some point in our lives had someone whom we've admired, someone we've looked up to. Write about your hero. Identify who the person is, and why he or she is your hero. What qualities does he or she possess that you admire? What have you learned from your hero that has influenced who you are today?

Sample Essay #1: Overall Score = 4 (Pass)

In northwest Fresno, California, there are still a few remaining acres of old-growth fig trees. These gnarled old trees, looking dusty even after a healthy spring rain, march along in rows as straight and even as the strings on a guitar. There were hundreds of acres of fig trees at one time, but homes and businesses gradually have replaced them until there are just a few fields left. What most people don't know is that for each and every one of these trees, someone had to dynamite a hole in the hardpan that lies under all of the alluvial soil that makes up the bedrock of the San Joaquin Valley. That someone was my grandfather, and he's my hero.

He'd go out each day and meticulously dig down where the new tree would go, measure his fuse, crimp the blasting cap (often with his teeth), and set off the charge. Oftentimes, when blasting canals for irrigation, he'd have to place his charge in an old innertube filled with dirt, light the fuse, seal the tube and swim with the dynamite to the location of the blast, dive down and place the charge, then swim away to safety. That I'm here to tell the story testifies to his expertise.

I had the opportunity to see him use this skill once when I was just seven years old. My parents had purchased a new home, and in the days before professional landscapers, were planning to put in the yard themselves. My grandfather, without asking (and being a firm believer in trees) came out to our new house one Saturday morning with some dynamite and a selection of flowering trees to plant.

I watched him carefully measure out the fuses and then test a length to determine how fast they burned. I asked him if he was doing that so he'd have time to run away. Then, as he was threading the blasting cap through the dynamite, he told me something I'll never forget. He said, "You never run away from dynamite, Brett. You might slip and fall and get hurt when the charge goes off. No, you make sure you plan carefully, measure everything twice, then walk away." And that's just what he did. He lit the fuse, looked down to make sure it was burning true, turned around and strolled back to the corner of the house where Dad and I had taken cover. Just as he stepped around the corner, there was a "whump" (not too big, you understand, just enough to do the job), and the tree was ready to plant.

When he headed up the Fresno Unified School District in the 1950s, he had a different kind of planting to do. The district had no money and no classrooms. He got some old Quonset huts from an abandoned army base and set up classrooms in fields that belonged to rancher friends of his, many times in fig orchards if you can believe it. The parents would take the kids out to wherever the classes were held. The county, while being sympathetic, would turn a blind eye for a while, but then would come out and condemn the structures. My grandfather would apologize, take them down and move then to another location. He performed this sleight of hand until the bond issues finally passed and the district had enough money to build actual classrooms.

What did I learn from this man? My grandfather taught me that hard work, intelligently planned and for a good cause is its own reward. He taught me to plan carefully, measure exactly, and to persevere in the face of adversity. And, the man after whom they named the Carroll H. Baird School, taught me to never run away from a sputtering fuse, but to walk.

Sample Essay #2: Overall Score = 3 (Marginal Pass)

A hero in my mind is someone to look up to and admire. Some people's heroes are movie stars or athletes. My hero, however, is my mom. She possesses qualities that not many people have. My mom is truly an amazing person, and I hope someday, I will be as good a mother, friend, co-worker, and wife as she is.

I have been lucky to have such a wonderful mom. Growing up, she always was there to cart my brother and I to various sports games or dance lessons. She never complained, but was always at the sidelines, cheering us on. Not only did she take us places, she made sure every night we had a warm meal on the table.

However, it wasn't until recently when I learned what a strong and positive person my mom was. During a recent year, my mom suffered many family tragedies, losing her husband and both her parents. This would cause most people to go into a deep depression, but not my mom. Instead, she lent my brother and me her shoulder to cry on when we needed it and taught us that "all things happen for a reason."

My mom's outstanding qualities don't stop there. She went to work full time so we could have insurance benefits, and continued with a second business at night in order to contribute to our college tuition. My mom has become "mom" to many of my friends because she treats them like they too are her kids. There's usually no debate when a bunch of my friends are trying to figure out where to stay when we are traveling in the area. "Let's go stay at Ann's house," they say, "because her mom is the coolest!" It's pretty rare to find an adult that all of us enjoy so much.

I'm proud to say that my mom is my friend. Our daily interactions together have helped me realize just how special she is. She may not have a great jump shot, or be a leading actress or model, but she is the most important person in my life. She is my hero because I hope to be as strong and loving as she has been. I try to model myself after her. I admire her composure, her compassion, and her friendship. She is an inspiration to us all.

Sample Essay #3: Overall Score = 2 (Marginal Fail)

At 4:00 A.M. my friend gets a page. As he struggles to find his glasses, he knows that he only has thirty seconds to get ready. Five minutes later, he is in the intensive care unit helping to save the life of a newborn child. My hero is my friend Chris (actually, I should call him Dr. Chris). What he does is so amazing!

I can't believe that he is only twenty-five and already a doctor. That is something everyone could look up to. Not like Doogie Howser or something dumb like that, but in a real way. I admire how hard he has studied and practiced to become a doctor. His hours are incredibly long, but his drive is even greater. I hope to one day have the dedication to my teaching profession that he has in his medical career. These are the skills that he possesses that I admire so much—drive, dedication, and a never-give-up attitude. When I'm struggling, I think of what he goes through, and that motivates me to work harder.

Chris chose to specialize in cancer treatment. That seems so difficult for me. I'm not sure if I could handle dealing with cancer patients. It seems so dark. I mean, it must be really hard to try to help people that might not have a good chance of living. But Chris has chosen to do that. I guess someone needs to do the difficult jobs, and I'm glad that people like Chris are willing to do them.

If Chris wasn't my hero, I'd probably have to choose my favorite baseball player. But I chose Chris. I'm lucky to have him as a friend.

Sample Essay #4: Overall Score = 1 (Fail)

I have from time to time admired a person but I have always been disappointed. It seems to me that us Americans spend too much time and energy in unwarranted hero worship which could be spent in better ways. I have had my hopes built up by admiring sports figures, statesmen, and politicians, but the admirable qualities I thought I saw always turned out to be majorly flawed. In fact, I think spending too much time admiring the qualities of other people can lead to other problems.

In the past I have admired the honesty of politicians, only to be disappointed when they finally get to office, then don't do what they said. They may be crooks or thieves. Sports figures have disappointed me when I find out they use drugs to make there performance better than it should be, or cheat at the game there supposed to be playing. Sometimes a historical figure seems to be admirable, but they eventually aren't—they usually have faults only that come out later.

So I think hero worship is a bad idea. Better instead would be to admire yourself and only judge your actions against you. If one can't admire yourself, you might as well give up and that's why I no longer try to find admirable qualities in other people. The only thing I ever learned from a "hero" is not to learn from them.

Chapter 12
Practice Test 2

SECTION I: TEST OF READING

Directions: Each statement or passage in this test is followed by a question or questions based on its content. After reading a statement or passage, choose the best answer to each question from among the five choices given. Answer all questions following a statement or passage on the basis of what is stated or implied in that statement or passage. Be sure to mark all of your answers in the Reading Section of your answer document.

Note: Some passages contain numbered sentences, blank lines, or underlined words that are to be used for your reference in answering the questions that follow those passages.

Read the passage below. Then answer the three questions that follow.

One of the most daring deep-space missions NASA has ever planned is about to be launched. Deep Space 1, or DS1, will be unique for two reasons—its ion propulsion engine, and its self-navigation system. If DS1 goes well, it will become the model for a new generation of spacecraft.

DS1 is unique in the way in which it will get from place to place. DS1 will be pushed through space by an engine that works by ionizing electrons. Electrons will be fired into xenon gas, stripping the xenon elements of an electron and giving the atoms an electric charge—ionizing them. The ions are then accelerated through an electric field and emitted from thrusters at up to 65,000 m.p.h. This constant push will add 15–20 miles per hour daily to the spacecraft's speed. That will add up. Thanks to this process, the spacecraft requires about one-tenth the weight of fuel used in a conventional aircraft.

Possibly more innovative is the navigation system. The "brain" of the system will scan stars and asteroids to map its location, allowing it to know precisely where it is, and make any necessary adjustments. What would these innovations mean to an automobile? Well, imagine your car finding its own way from San Diego to New York, to a specific shopping mall, at only 300 miles per gallon!

1. Which one of the following statements would the author most likely agree with regarding NASA's opinion of the DS1 spacecraft?

   A. NASA believes that the DS1 will eventually lead to cars that can drive themselves.

   B. NASA believes that the DS1 spacecraft, if successful on its mission, will become the model for future space travel technology.

   C. NASA will use DS1 until ion propulsion technology is too costly.

   D. NASA believes that DS1 technology will be the leading pioneer in artificial intelligence.

   E. NASA hopes that DS1 technology can be used for passenger trips to the moon.

2. The author puts the word "brain" in quotations in the third paragraph in order to:

   A. imply that NASA has created a new type of intelligent being.

   B. show how similar the navigation system is to a human brain.

   C. indicate that the navigation system will make decisions, similar to decisions a human would make.

   D. show that the system is incapable of any decision making without human influence.

   E. state a belief that new aliens may be found by the DS1 spacecraft.

3. Which of the following techniques does the author use to help the reader better understand the DS1 system?

   A.   a technical breakdown of ion propulsion technology

   B.   a chart

   C.   a hypothetical story that describes the spacecraft

   D.   a metaphor that relates DS1 technology to a machine we know how to use

   E.   a parable

Read the passage below. Then answer the question that follows.

    Millions of students taking out college loans just received more financial aid. Earlier this year, Congress passed legislation, retroactive to July 1, that lowered the interest rate on new, federally guaranteed student loans to 7.46% from the previous rate of 8.25%. Further, the legislation states that those with more than $30,000 in debt may soon have an extra fifteen years to repay outstanding loans.

4.   The passage answers all questions below EXCEPT:

    A.   What is the new interest rate for federal student loans?

    B.   Who is eligible to receive additional time to repay college debts?

    C.   When does the new loan program begin?

    D.   How much will a student who is $30,000 in debt save as a result of the new laws?

    E.   What was the old interest rate for federal student loans?

Read the passage below. Then answer the three questions that follow.

I'm not much of a tennis player. Sure, I can go out and hack like any weekend warrior, but I don't need to be worried about new advances in equipment, or having the best technology. Yet, that's exactly what I have. Last week, I went out and purchased a new, oversized-head, titanium-based racquet. I may not be a good player, but boy, do I look good.

Apparently, I'm not alone. New racquet technologies have led to a number of advances in the past few years, and sales have exploded. New racquets feature larger heads, longer necks, and lighter body weight. All of this comes at a cost. New racquets range from $175 to $300. Of course, a player of my caliber probably doesn't need to purchase such a racquet, but then again, isn't it cool to tell a fellow competitor you are playing with PX2 technology (whatever that is!)?

My local tennis pro, someone who could actually use this technology, claims that the new racquets will help all players. The larger racquet size allows greater court coverage, and more power and stability. Lighter weight racquets are easier to move around; however, that comes with the risk of less control of the ball coming off the racquet. In the end, though, I didn't make my decision based on lighter weight versus string control versus a larger racquet head. I made my decision based on the racquet that sounded the most intimidating!

5. The author uses the phrase "weekend warrior" to describe himself as:

A. a top-flight athlete.

B. a recreational player.

C. a temperamental competitor.

D. a tennis professional.

E. a racquet manufacturer.

6. The author's main point of the passage is:

A Advances in technology have harmed the tradition of tennis.

B. Oversized racquets provide more reach for players.

C. Only professional athletes should be concerned about new advances in racquet technology.

D. Looking good is more important than playing well.

E. Although some players may not need new tennis racquets, they may enjoy having the best equipment.

7. An appropriate title for this passage is:

A. The History of Tennis Racquets

B. New Tennis Technologies: I Don't Need Them, but I Like Them

C. Impact of Oversized Racquets on Tennis Serves

D. Technology in Sports

E. One Man's Tennis Journey

Read the passage below. Then answer the five questions that follow.

Forced to hunt for new prey, killer whales are devastating sea otter territory off the Alaskan coast, disrupting the food chain and setting off an ecological cascade. The whales have created damage with such alarming efficiency that a vast ecosystem now seems to be at risk of collapse.

The problem began when fish stocks started to decline in the Bering Sea, probably as a result of commercial fishing, or changes in the ocean currents and temperatures. Because of this lack of food, seals and sea lions are thinning out, losing some of their insulating blubber. Killer whales, therefore, aren't getting the same diet from seals and sea lions as they used to, forcing them to feed on sea otters. The otter populations have collapsed, allowing their prey, sea urchins, to multiply out of control. Sea urchins have now begun to devour the kelp forests on the ocean floor at an alarming rate. The kelp forests are crucial to a number of habitats.

8. Otter populations have declined off the Alaskan coast primarily because:

   A. Sea urchins are multiplying at record rates.

   B. The kelp forests are being destroyed.

   C. Whales have been forced to search for additional food in their diets.

   D. Commercial fishing is killing otters.

   E. Global warming is making the otter population sick.

9. This passage would most likely appear in:

   A. a newspaper article.

   B. the journal of marine biology.

   C. an editorial.

   D. a biology textbook.

   E. a doctoral thesis.

10. Which of the following best outlines the structure of the passage?

    A. A statement is made, then supported through an example.

    B. A theory is stated, and the steps leading up to that theory are then explained.

    C. A question is raised, then answered.

    D. An experiment is stated, followed by the conclusion of the experiment.

    E. An argument is stated, then refuted.

11. Which of the following is the best definition for the author's use of "cascade"?

    A. a waterfall

    B. an arrangement

    C. a chain of events

    D. a fabric

    E. a tool

12. The main point of the passage is:

   A.   Sea lions and seals are losing weight.

   B.   Global warming is hurting the sea otter population.

   C.   The ecosystem is changing.

   D.   The ocean floor is being eaten up at an alarming rate.

   E.   The otter population in northern Alaska is suffering as a result of new attacks by killer whales.

Read the passage below. Then answer the question that follows.

It simply isn't fair that big banks continue to charge user fees for customers using "foreign" ATMs. Now, in addition to being charged for using a machine that does not belong to your bank, you must pay an additional fee to the institution that owns the machine. _____
_____. At least those institutions understand how much I dislike all these extra charges.

13. Which of the following sentences, inserted into the line above, would best complete the meaning of the passage?

   A. While small banks can't offer as many services, they do offer checking without ATM fees.

   B. Sometimes, calling a customer service manager will help you eliminate the charges.

   C. Congress has considered making these user transactions illegal.

   D. Banks just make me so angry.

   E. If we all boycott banks that include these charges, they will be forced to change their practices.

Read the passage below. Then answer the four questions that follow.

1) Tom Purcell, twenty-nine, leaves his job on Wednesday nights at 6 P.M. to go back to school. 2) Even with a bachelor's degree in biology, and a master's degree in computer science, Tom still felt he needed to go back to school to further his career. 3) His company agreed, and will be paying the $2,000 per semester tuition.

4) Tom's story is not unique. 5) More and more, Americans are returning to school for quick, practical courses that allow them to keep up with the competition, and rapid changes in technology and business. 6) The rush to these type of "quickie" courses does not mean that graduate degrees are no longer popular. 7) Instead, these courses are used to supplement any employee's education. 8) There is no longer a natural end to when one should complete his or her education. 9) Further, these new courses allow working individuals to learn and work at the same time, eliminating the difficult decision of whether or not to go back to school full time.

10) The "classroom" is changing as well. 11) More and more, companies are customizing courses for their employees in conjunction with major universities. 12) Classes are held at the workplace, and the curriculum is determined jointly by both leading professors from the university and company administrators. 13) Together, a curriculum is created that provides new information relevant to the workplace. 14) Clearly, adult education has never been better.

14. Which of the following sentences represents an opinion of the author rather than a fact?

    A. 3

    B. 11

    C. 12

    D. 13

    E. 14

15. Which of the following provides the best outline for the passage?

    A. A topic is introduced, then supported by examples.

    B. An example is given, followed by counter-arguments against the example.

    C. A specific story is told, followed by general explanations.

    D. A general story is told, followed by specific explanations.

    E. A theory is tested, then refuted, and another theory is created.

16. Which of the following statements would the author most likely support?

    A. Only professional scholars should develop course curricula.

    B. Continuing education in the workplace allows employees more flexibility than traditional postgraduate classes.

    C. Education ends after any postgraduate degrees are completed.

    D. Companies allow employees to take additional courses strictly to keep them at their current jobs longer.

    E. Adult education is on the decline.

17. The passage implies that many companies are supporting employees decisions to go back to school because:

    A. Companies feel continued education will benefit their employees.

    B. Companies fear losing employees to other companies that provide additional training.

    C. Companies need to use federal education grants before they expire.

    D. Companies feel this is the only way to stay on top of new technological advancements.

    E. Companies prefer to control the curricula of their employees' classes.

Read the index below. Then answer the two questions that follow.

Experiments	
Double-blind experiment	734
Experiment basics	753–765
Models	741–750
Observation experiments	784–785
Screening experiments	751–752
Two-factor experiment	768–780
2K experiment	781–783

18. On what pages would you find information about the ways to study and calculate experiments?

    A. 734

    B. 753–765

    C. 784–785

    D. 751–752

    E. 781–783

19. Which of the following best describes the primary organizational pattern used in the section of the book dealing with experiments?

    A. alphabetical

    B. chronological

    C. from easiest to hardest

    D. by type of experiment

    E. by invention

Read the passage below. Then answer the three questions that follow.

Stung by broken industry promises, farmers are livid at massive crop failure and crop damage using "genetically superior" seeds. In the American southeast, growers who used genetically manipulated cotton seeds suffered some of the worst crop failure ever. Farmers' organizations around the world are linking up to stop genetically engineered seeds from being introduced.

20. Which of the following, if true, would weaken the farmers' claim that genetic seeds are to blame for their poor crop production?

   A. The seeds were only tried for one season, which had poor weather conditions.

   B. The growers of the American northwest experienced the same type of problems with genetic seeds.

   C. Cotton seeds are regarded as the best type of genetic seed.

   D. Growers in the Southwest were pleased with genetic seeds in tomato and corn production.

   E. Genetically engineered seeds are endorsed by the government.

21. From the passage, it can be assumed that:

   A. Currently, the greatest concern for farmers in the American southeast is the problem with genetically engineered seeds.

   B. The previous belief was that genetically engineered seeds would be successful in crop production.

   C. Farmers have strong lobbying influences at the national level.

   D. Genetically engineered seeds are the future of cotton farming.

   E. Genetically engineered seeds are currently in use throughout all of the United States.

22. The author's use of the words "linking up" is best defined as:

   A. attaching.

   B. collaborating.

   C. molding.

   D. building.

   E. connecting.

Read the passage below. Then answer the four questions that follow.

Geneticist Edward Fugger and his colleagues at Genetics and IVF Institute have created a recent breakthrough that will allow parents to choose the sex of their future child. The process involves using a method to stain sperm with fluorescent dye. Female producing sperm, which carry more genetic material than male producing sperm, will glow more brightly. A machine can be used to automatically sort brighter sperm from dimmer ones. So far, the procedure has worked. Of 14 pregnancies involving couples who wanted girls, 13 produced females.

This novel approach to baby making does pose a number of ethical questions. While few argue against gender selection in order to avoid sex-linked genetic diseases, many people are concerned about using this technology more casually. Some families may choose to have a child to balance out families, or simply because some parents have gender preferences. Could such choices eventually lead to an imbalanced sex ratio?

_____.

23. Which of the following best summarizes the overall meaning of the passage?

   A. IVF has created a successful new fertility drug.

   B. An imbalanced sex ratio may be a result of allowing parents to choose the sex of their children.

   C. It now may be possible to avoid creating children with known sex-linked genetic defects.

   D. New methods in science may allow for parents to choose the sex of their children, which could lead to many ethical concerns.

   E. Fluorescent dye helps to identify different types of sperm.

24. Which of the following best outlines the structure of the passage?

   A. I.   Statement

        II.   Facts

        III. Quotations

   B. I.   Theory

        II.   Examples

   C. I.   Research

        II.   Implications

   D. I.   Question

        II.   Answer

   E. I.   Quote

        II.   Thesis

        III. Examples

25. Which of the following provides the best definition for the author's use of the word "breakthrough"?

A. insight

B. division

C. crack

D. law

E. promotion

26. Which of the following sentences, when inserted into the blank above, would best complete the meaning of the passage?

A. The best solution is to let the government set a policy.

B. Regardless, this technology should become available to the common household in the very near future.

C. Not in my opinion, because a perfect family has one boy and one girl.

D. Before this technology becomes common, we need to take a long look at the possible societal and moral implications of selecting a child's sex.

E. I guess we'll have to wait and see.

Read the passage below. Then answer the five questions that follow.

"Top-100" lists have been popular for years, and I assume that they will continue to be for decades. For some reason, everyone seems to be making a list—everything from the top movies, to the top rock albums, to the top cartoon shows.

What most people don't realize is that these lists really tend to be nothing more than publicity stunts. The local bookstore lists its "Top-100" books? Wow, what a great way to boost sales of 100 books within the store! The president of that bookstore acknowledges that fact, expressing the list as "a way to bring attention to some of the country's most important books." Further, who are these so-called "experts" that create these lists? I'm concerned about people viewing these lists as facts, not subjective opinions from a group of scholars. _____ _____.

Nonetheless, we play along, and I must concede that at times it can be quite fun, if not sophomoric. As I'm writing this, I can overhear two colleagues debating about their favorite movies. We all have our lists, and its fun to compare and contrast (of course, mine are truly the best). It's even more fun to point out what is wrong with other, more "professional" lists.

27. What would be an appropriate title for the passage?

   A.   Top-100 Lists—Fun For Us All

   B.   What's Our Obsession with Rankings?

   C.   Top-100 Lists—Academic Merit, or Shameless Promotion?

   D.   New Promotional Methods in Bookstores

   E.   Why I Love Rankings

28. The author's tone can be best described as:

   A.   somewhat angry.

   B.   incredibly elated.

   C.   seriously concerned.

   D.   playfully sarcastic.

   E.   deeply despairing.

29. Which of the following, if inserted into the blank, would best complete the meaning of the second paragraph?

   A.   There are no correct answers to these lists, just the opinions of those lucky enough to have a vote.

   B.   Scholars would have come up with a very different list of the "Top-100" books.

   C.   Scholars are better informed than you or me to determine what books or movies belong on these lists.

   D.   Your favorite book is probably different than my favorite book.

   E.   Those who do not agree with the lists probably received a different education than the authors of the lists.

30. Which of the following statements below would the author most likely support?

A. A vote should determine which people get to participate in the creation of these lists.

B. Stores should continue to promote these lists as a way to generate additional income.

C. Top-100 lists should no longer be created.

D. One positive thing about Top-100 lists is that they often generate debates among friends and workers.

E. A nonprofit organization should be created to generate more Top-100 lists.

31. The author feels the primary reason companies create "Top-100" lists is to:

A. invite debate to challenge previously held beliefs about what is good and what is not.

B. reward the scholars who spend time and energy reviewing books and movies.

C. provide a way to increase interest in a field, thereby increasing sales in that field.

D. create a list that will be reviewed later in history.

E. encourage employees to come up with their own lists.

Look at the graph below. Then answer the question that follows.

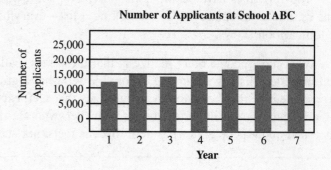

32. Which of the following can be concluded from the chart above?

A. the number of spaces available at School ABC

B. an approximate number of applicants to ABC from Year 1 to Year 7

C. the percentage of males applying to ABC

D. the percentage of females applying to ABC

E. which year "Year 7" represents

Read the passage below. Then answer the three questions that follow.

Judith Harris has written a new controversial book called *The Nurture Assumption*. Although it has been out for only one month, it has already been provoking passionate debate among scientists and therapists because it argues that parents make only a single, lasting contribution to their children's future—their genes. Judith argues that peer groups, not parents, determine the sort of people children will become. Her conclusions are based on her analysis of scientific research, especially with twins. Identical twins raised in the same home are no more alike than those raised apart. And two children adopted by the same parents turn out no more alike than a duo raised separately.

Harris' implications are profound. Does this mean that a parent's love and affection doesn't matter? Harris, a grandmother and writer of psychology textbooks, without any academic affiliations or a Ph.D., claims that "good parents sometimes have bad kids." Child development experts tend to disagree. It looks as if *The Nurture Assumption* will be the focus of great debate in psychology.

33. In which publication would this passage most likely appear?

   A. a book review publication

   B. a psychology journal

   C. a child development textbook

   D. an editorial page

   E. a parenting book

34. Which one of the following statements would Judith Harris most likely support?

   A. It is okay to ignore your children, because your actions will not affect them.

   B. In order to be an expert in child development theory, one must have a Ph.D. and post-doctorate research.

   C. Peer influence is the primary determinate of how a child will develop.

   D. Parents who spend more time with their children are more likely to raise better kids.

   E. Development during the first two years of a child's life plays a crucial role in determining their future success.

35. Which of the following best describes the main point of the passage?

   A. Parents do not have an influence on their children's behavior.

   B. Judith Harris' book is selling well.

   C. Judith Harris' book contains new theories about parental influence on children that will likely spark much debate in child psychology.

   D. Judith Harris is not affiliated with an academic institution.

   E. Twins are the best indicators of measuring the influence parents have on children.

Read the passage below. Then answer the question that follows.

Many pregnant women avoid eating fish due to mercury levels found in many common freshwater and saltwater fish. Doctors recently concluded a study of 720 pregnant women who ate saltwater fish as often as 12 times per week, which found no evidence of harm to mothers or their children up to age five.

36. Which of the following best describes the results of the study described in the passage above?

    A. Consuming up to 12 servings of fish per week is safe for pregnant mothers.

    B. Freshwater fish contain more mercury than saltwater fish.

    C. Pregnant women who consume saltwater fish have not shown any problems associated with mercury intake during pregnancy, nor have their children.

    D. Children who consume saltwater fish are in danger of mercury poisoning.

    E. Children are in danger of contracting certain diseases later in life if their mothers ate saltwater fish while pregnant.

Read the passage below. Then answer the three questions that follow.

In California, countless radio and television ads that oppose Proposition 200 are appearing. From the way the campaign sounds, it seems as if many small local groups are opposed to Proposition 200. Yet a closer look reveals a disturbing trend in political advertising. Large utility companies, who figure to suffer the most if Prop. 200 passes, have carefully crafted a misleading message designed to sap the Prop. 200 effort. The opponents of the measure, the ads proclaim, are small, grassroots consumer and environmental groups—the little guys who really care about utility regulation and its impacts on our community. What the ads don't tell you is that many of the groups and individuals that claim to be against Prop. 200 are actually on the payroll of these large utility companies. More careful research needs to be done to find out exactly who is and who is not funding these initiatives. If "Citizens against Prop. 200" is just a front for the big utility companies who are afraid the proposition will pass, the public will continue to be misled.

37. Which of the following best describes the main point of the passage?

A. Prop. 200 should not be approved.

B. Utility deregulation is a complex initiative.

C. Advertising plays a key role in determining the outcome of state propositions.

D. "Citizens against Prop. 200" include big businesses.

E. Advertisements and groups opposing Prop. 200 have misled the public by implying that a grassroots effort is the force behind Prop. 200 opposition.

38. Which of the following assumptions can be made about the author's position toward Prop. 200?

A. The author is in support of the proposition.

B. The author is opposed to the proposition.

C. The author supports utility deregulation.

D. The advertising practices of those opposed to Prop. 200 are of greater concern than the wording of the bill.

E. The author will vote for Prop. 200 to show his anger toward the advertisements against Prop. 200.

39. The author uses the word "sap" in the passage above to mean:

A. weaken.

B. strengthen.

C. lengthen.

D. underline.

E. postpone.

Read the passage below. Then answer the four questions that follow.

A toy magazine recently promoted "Reference Boy" as the new interactive toy of the year. Like many other blockbuster hits of the last five years, Reference Boy's rise to fame provides evidence that children don't decide what is popular for the holidays. That decision is predetermined by toy executives looking for the next "must-have" product. Buying a popular toy has become a status symbol for parents, sometimes resulting in chaotic shopping conditions. Last year, demand for the popular Young Mike Action Figure was so great that parents resorted to nothing short of guerilla tactics to secure the popular toy for their son or daughter. Limited supplies pushed the market value of the toy as much as twenty times over the list price.

It appears the hype for these toys will come to a quick end. Today, you can walk into any store and purchase dozens of Young Mike Action Figures, at retail cost. Those parents who previously paid up to $400 for one Young Mike last holiday season would be lucky to resell it today for $10.

As the hype for the "cool" toys continues, toy makers are using it to their advantage, and profit. The Reference Boy release didn't hit store shelves quietly—after an appearance on a network morning show, and an afternoon talk show, the rush began. Toy company executives are planning product releases similar in glitz and glamour to movie or album releases. If the trend continues, toy executives may see record profits this holiday season. Toy executives hope the economy will stay strong.

40. Which of the following best describes the overall summary of the passage?

   A. Popular toys are more the result of parental and company influence than children's opinions about the toys.

   B. Product releases are the new trend in toy promotion.

   C. Toys may sharply decrease in value, even after a record year of profits and high demand.

   D. If a toy is mentioned on a network sales will increase immediately.

   E. Reference Boy is the hot new toy for this holiday season.

41. According to the passage, why are toy executives planning large-scale product releases?

   A. Sales are always greatest at a large product release party.

   B. Large-scale exposure of certain toys has recently meant an immediate explosion in sales.

   C. Toys should be able to compete financially against music and books.

   D. Executives want to promote the toys show, for a very limited period of time.

   E. Executives hope these product releases will keep demand for a product high for several years.

42. Which of the following sentences is least relevant in the third paragraph?

    A.   sentence 1

    B.   sentence 2

    C.   sentence 3

    D.   sentence 4

    E.   sentence 5

43. Which of the following statements would the author most likely support?

    A.   The toy market cannot sustain itself at its recent rate of growth.

    B.   Children must be asked which toys they enjoy before parents determine which toys are "cool."

    C.   Lately, "cool" toys seem to affect parents as much as, or more than, children.

    D.   Reference Boy will not be popular next fall.

    E.   For many years, the toy industry has quietly promoted its products, and for long term growth, it should not deviate from that formula.

Read the table of contents below. Then answer the two questions that follow.

Getting Around San Francisco:	
Bus:	67
Car and motorcycle:	68
Taxi:	72
Bicycle:	74
Ferry:	78
Walking:	80
Organized tours:	81

44. On what page would you look to find information on how to get from the airport to a hotel by cab?

    A.   67

    B.   68

    C.   72

    D.   74

    E.   78

45. Which of the following best describes the way in which this table of contents is organized?

    A.   alphabetically

    B.   by cost

    C.   by time

    D.   by category

    E.   by age

Read the passage below. Then answer the three questions that follow.

It's hard to learn to play catch. In the beginning, you use your arms to cradle the ball against your chest; then you use both hands; then one. Soon, you're an expert. You're running down fly balls with ease, and firing throws across your body. I'm not sure if you ever become an expert on parenting. _____ _____.

A game of catch is an essential gesture of parenthood, too, I believe, when families are working well. Everyone tosses to be understood. The best part of the game is the silence. I enjoy playing catch with my son. Just like catch, our relationship is one that moves back and forth. I take what I can get from my son, and he takes what he can get (or get away with) from me. We make compromises and adjustments when we are able to, but for the most part things come and go, back and forth, just like a ball when we're sharing a nice day of playing catch.

46. Which of the following sentences, if inserted into the blank above, would best complete the meaning of the first paragraph?

    A. Parenting can never be perfected.

    B. Like playing catch, parenting is hard to learn.

    C. Just as I have become more comfortable playing catch, I have become more comfortable being a father.

    D. Few ballplayers are both great athletes and great fathers.

    E. My son is great at playing catch.

47. Which literary technique does the author use to describe his relationship with his son?

    A. alliteration

    B. a metaphor

    C. a parable

    D. a myth

    E. a fable

48. The author's tone is best described as:

    A. reflective.

    B. remorseful.

    C. forgiving.

    D. proud.

    E. temperamental.

Read the passage below. Then answer the two questions that follow.

Most teachers receive tenure status and lifetime job protection after three years on the job, after which terminating a teacher becomes a very difficult and long process. Teachers faced with termination have a long time before any serious action can be taken—principals seeking to dismiss them must usually file several written reports, wait a year for improvement, file additional poor evaluations, appear at a hearing, and maybe even show up in court to defend the firing. During this process, the teacher still gets paid. This entire process results in few terminations—just 44 of 100,000 tenured teachers were dismissed between 1991 and 1997 in the state of Illinois. Many states are moving to streamline their firing procedures. Next year, Florida will cut the time a teacher has to show improvement before a dismissal hearing to 90 days. Firing procedures are unnecessary for an overwhelming majority of the fine men and women teaching our children. However, _____ _____.

49. Which of the following best summarizes the main point of the passage?

A. Teachers deserve tenure due to their hard work for low salaries.

B. Florida is changing their policies regarding teacher dismissal.

C. There is a debate among teachers about being tenured after only three years.

D. Most current teacher termination procedures involve many steps, and extend for months, even years.

E. Teachers' unions are concerned about wrongful terminations of teachers who have done nothing wrong.

50. Which of the following phrases, if inserted into the blank above, would best complete the meaning of the passage?

A. Teachers should be given every benefit of the doubt before termination.

B. Firing procedures need to allow more time for appeals.

C. If teachers aren't fired, there should be a law that protects them from having to go through termination procedures again.

D. A swift procedure will ensure equality for all.

E. When they are necessary, it is important that bottlenecks do not slow down the process.

SECTION II: TEST OF MATHEMATICS

Directions: Each of the questions in this test is followed by five suggested answers. Select the best answer in each case. Be sure to mark all of your answers in the Mathematics Section of your answer document.

1. What is the difference between 2.5 and .167?

    A.   .83

    B.   2

    C.   2.333

    D.   2.667

    E   4.17

2. Nancy and May played volleyball for 63 hours in June, and for 89 hours in July. How many more hours did they play in July than in June?

    A.   6 hours

    B.   16 hours

    C.   26 hours

    D.   63 hours

    E.   89 hours

3. What number could be added to the following set of data so that the median and mode of the set are equal?

42, 36, 59, 23, 61, 30, 75

A. 42

B. 36

C. 33

D. 23

E. 10

Read the information below and then answer the question that follows.

Christopher is preparing a nursery that requires a variety of potting soil. He purchases 27 3/4 pounds of Desert soil and 8 5/6 pounds of Garden soil.

4. What is the total amount of soil purchased?

A. $39 \frac{5}{12}$ pounds

B. $36 \frac{7}{12}$ pounds

C. $35 \frac{7}{12}$ pounds

D. $35 \frac{5}{12}$ pounds

E. $33 \frac{7}{12}$ pounds

5. In his sociology class, Adam took three tests. He scored a 78 on his first test, and a 90 on his second test. If Adam had an average of 81 in his class, what did Adam score on his third test?

    A. 75

    B. 81

    C. 83

    D. 90

    E. 243

6. Frank is going to buy turkey sandwiches for his employees. A sandwich costs $3.25, and each topping or condiment costs an extra $.25. Each order of cheese costs an extra $.50. Here is the list of what Frank will buy:

    2 sandwiches without cheese, with 2 condiments each
    2 sandwiches with cheese, with 1 condiment each

    Assuming no tax, what is the total cost of the sandwiches?

    A. $14.75

    B. $15.00

    C. $15.50

    D. $16.00

    E. $16.50

7. What is the best estimate of 50 + 49 + 48 + 47 + 46 + 45 + 44 + 43 + 42 + 41 + 40?

   A. 550

   B. 500

   C. 450

   D. 400

   E. 300

Monica drives to several different students' homes every day for tutoring. During the first full week in September, her daily mileage ranges from a low of 36 miles to a high of 102 miles.

---

8. From the preceding information, which of the following must be true regarding Monica's average daily mileage for the week?

   A. Her average for all 7 days is between 36 and 102 miles.

   B. Her average for all 7 days is 69 miles.

   C. Her average for all 7 days is greater than 69 miles.

   D. Her average for all 7 days is lower than 69 miles.

   E. Her average for all 7 days is any number between 0 and 100 miles.

9. Multiplying a number by $\frac{3}{4}$ is the same as dividing that number by

   A. $\frac{9}{16}$

   B. $\frac{3}{4}$

   C. 1

   D. $\frac{4}{3}$

   E. 4

Use the chart and information given below to answer the question that follows.

```
┌─────────────────────────────────────────────┐
│          InterTech Employee Roster            │
│                                               │
│   Department              Total               │
│   Engineering              64                 │
│   Marketing               123                 │
│   Product Design           56                 │
│                                               │
└─────────────────────────────────────────────┘
```

As an employee is preparing the employment roster above, she notices that her own department, Human Resources, has not been included in the report. She also knows that there are a total of 282 employees in these four departments.

10. Based on the chart above and the given information, what is the accurate number of Human Resources employees at InterTech?

   A. 19

   B. 27

   C. 39

   D. 87

   E. 282

11. At a school supplies store, the price of a blackboard is reduced from $70.00 to $56.00. By what percent is the price of the blackboard decreased?

   A. 10%

   B. 14%

   C. 20%

   D. 56%

   E. 86%

12. At his office, Adam did a survey on what his employees wanted for lunch, sandwiches or pizza. Adam received 34 more votes for pizza than sandwiches. If Adam received a total of 76 votes, how many votes did he receive for sandwiches?

   A.   21 votes

   B.   40 votes

   C.   42 votes

   D.   84 votes

   E.   110 votes

13. The price of a dress is $120.00. If during a sale the price is marked down 15%, what is the new price of the dress?

   A. $18.00

   B. $90.00

   C. $102.00

   D. $105.00

   E. $135.00

14. What is the value of 654,322 rounded to the nearest thousand?

    A. 654,000

    B. 654,300

    C. 654,400

    D. 655,000

    E. 655,300

15. Mike and Julie collect pictures. They want to place all of their pictures into photo albums. If Mike and Julie own 412 pictures, and each album holds a maximum of 34 pictures, what is the minimum number of photo albums Mike and Julie must purchase so that every picture is contained in a photo album?

    A. 11 albums

    B. 12 albums

    C. 13 albums

    D. 20 albums

    E. 34 albums

Questions 16 and 17. Use the information below to answer the questions that follow.

Chris, Fiona, and Rich are at a baseball game.

They ate a total of 7 hot dogs, 3 bags of peanuts, and 4 soft drinks.

Rich ate more hot dogs than Chris.

Fiona ate 1 bag of peanuts and 1 hot dog.

Hot dogs cost $.75 more than peanuts, but less than soft drinks.

---

16. Which of the following facts can be determined from the information given above?

    A. who ate the most hot dogs

    B. how many bags of peanuts Rich ate

    C. the total cost of all the food

    D. the cost of a hot dog

    E. the number of soft drinks Chris drank

17. If peanuts cost $.50, what is one possible total for the cost of the peanuts, hot dogs, and soft drinks eaten by Rich, Chris, and Fiona?

    A. $10.25

    B. $11.75

    C. $13.25

    D. $15.25

    E. $16.50

18. In a recent store promotion, customers received three game stamps for every purchase of a large drink. If Rick has collected sixty game stamps, how many large drinks has he purchased?

    A. 3

    B. 18

    C. 20

    D. 26

    E. 57

19. Joe needs to add the fractions $\frac{1}{2}$, $\frac{3}{4}$, and $\frac{2}{5}$. Which of the following methods should Joe use to add these fractions most efficiently?

    A. Use the "subtract from one" technique.

    B. Multiply the denominators.

    C. Use a common denominator of 10.

    D. Use a common denominator of 40.

    E. Use a common denominator of 20.

20. What is the best estimate of the following expression:

    $$\frac{(282.4) \times (11.85) \times (9.2)}{(3.11) \times (70.35) \times (8.827)}$$

    A. 3.5

    B. 9.2

    C. 15.8

    D. 20.3

    E. 70.35

Goods Sold at Company Y

21. In order for the total amount of goods sold to equal 150,000, how many goods were sold by Tom?

   A. 30,000

   B. 35,000

   C. 40,000

   D. 45,000

   E. 47,000

22. $10y - 36 + 4y - 6 + y = 3$. What is the value of y?

   A. 3

   B. 4

   C. 6

   D. 10

   E. 36

23. The value $\frac{3}{8}$ falls between which of the following pairs of percents?

   A. 15% and 20%

   B. 25% and 30%

   C. 35% and 40%

   D. 45% and 50%

   E. 55% and 60%

24. If the value of x is between $-.345$ and $.008$, which of the following could be the value of x?

   A. -1.1

   B. $-.45$

   C. $-.08$

   D. $.08$

   E. $.345$

25. Rick, Marty, and Ben all own baseball cards. There are a total of 3,500 cards between them. If Marty owns 70% of the baseball cards, how many cards does Marty have?

   A. 1,050 cards

   B. 1,225 cards

   C. 2,450 cards

   D. 2,800 cards

   E. 3,430 cards

26. Oliver is building a fence around his yard. When finished, the fence will be 170 feet long. For five days straight, Oliver builds 25 feet of the fence each day. After these five days, how much is left for Oliver to build?

    A.   25 feet

    B.   45 feet

    C.   50 feet

    D.   65 feet

    E.   70 feet

27.   James wants to send 300 thank-you cards. He can write 12 per day. If he begins February 1, when would he expect to be finished?

    A.   February 12

    B.   February 13

    C.   February 25

    D.   February 26

    E.   March 12

Use the following chart to help answer Question 28.

Student	Questions Answered Correctly	Percentile Score	Stanine Score
Kristen	32	52%	
Jen		44%	
Debbie		82%	
Amy	37		6

28. Place the order of students' scores from lowest to highest:

    A.   Amy, Kristen, Debbie, Jen

    B.   Kristen, Debbie, Amy, Jen

    C.   Jen, Kristen, Amy, Debbie

    D.   Debbie, Kristen, Amy, Jen

    E.   Debbie, Amy, Jen, Kristen

29. Arash walked 485 yards from class to the cafeteria. How many feet did Arash walk?

    A.   40 feet

    B.   161 feet

    C.   1,455 feet

    D.   2,100 feet

    E.   5,820 feet

30. During Johnna's freshman year of college, she attended class for 3 hours each day. If there are 165 days of class, how many hours of class did Johnna attend?

    A. 325 hours

    B. 348 hours

    C. 425 hours

    D. 468 hours

    E. 495 hours

31. At a high school, 2 out of every 5 students go to Butterick College. If there are 240 students, how many are expected to go to Butterick College?

    A. 24 students

    B. 96 students

    C. 120 students

    D. 144 students

    E. 180 students

Use the table given below to answer the question that follows.

SupplyMart Price List	
Ream of paper	$ 2.00
Box of crayons	$ 3.45
Dry erase marker	$ .65

32. A teacher purchased the following: 2 dozen reams of paper, 17 boxes of crayons, and 33 dry erase markers. Which answer represents this purchase?

    A.   24($2.00) + 17($.65) + 33($3.45)

    B.   2($2.00) + 17($.65) + 33($3.45)

    C.   (24 + 17 + 33) + ($2.00 + $.65 + $3.45)

    D.   (2 × 12) + $2.00 + 17($3.45) + 33($.65)

    E.   24($2.00) + 33($.65) + 17($3.45)

33. What percent of 20 is 5?

    A.   1%

    B.   5%

    C.   25%

    D.   40%

    E.   75%

34. A designer dress is discounted 15% to $425. Which of the following equations could be used to determine its original price, p?

    A. $.85p = \$425$

    B. $.85p + .15p = \$425$

    C. $p = \$425 + .15$

    D. $.15p = \$425$

    E. $p = \$425 - .15$

35. In 1996, the total number of CDs sold at Brandt's record store was 250,000. In 1997, that number rose to 300,000. What was the percent increase in the number of CDs Brandt's record store sold?

    A.   17%

    B.   20%

    C.   50%

    D.   75%

    E.   105%

36. Which of the following numbers is smallest?

    A.   .25

    B.   .0088

    C. $\dfrac{1}{8}$

    D.   .0067

    E.   .111

37. The school board is proposing a 5% increase in the number of students per classroom. Currently, there are 20 students per class. How many students would there be per class with the proposed increase?

    A. 21

    B. 22

    C. 23

    D. 24

    E. 25

Use the figure below to answer the question that follows.

38. Which answer best represents the shaded part of the box shown above?

    A. $\dfrac{3}{4}$

    B. $\dfrac{2}{3}$

    C. $\dfrac{2}{5}$

    D. $\dfrac{1}{3}$

    E. $\dfrac{1}{4}$

39. There are 120 books in Ms. Wilson's classroom library. If $\frac{1}{3}$ of the books are nonfiction, and $\frac{3}{8}$ of the nonfiction books are about animals, how many nonfiction books in the library are about animals?

    A. 45

    B. 40

    C. 25

    D. 15

    E. 5

40. $\frac{3}{4} = \frac{9}{x}$. What is the value of x?

    A. 3

    B. 4

    C. 9

    D. 12

    E. 36

41. In her biology class, Brooke took seven tests. On her first six tests, Brooke received test scores of 90, 88, 87, 92, 85, and 92. If her total on seven tests was 612, what did she score on her seventh test?

   A. 78

   B. 85

   C. 88

   D. 90

   E. 92

Use the graph below to answer the two questions that follow.

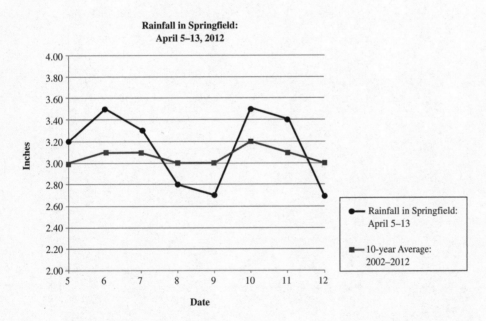

**Rainfall in Springfield:
April 5–13, 2012**

42. Of the eight days shown, on approximately what percent of the days did the rainfall exceed the 10-year average rainfall?

   A. 12%

   B. 25%

   C. 38%

   D. 63%

   E. 75%

43. Between which two dates shown did the greatest decrease in rainfall occur?

   A.   April 5-6

   B.   April 6-7

   C.   April 7-8

   D.   April 9-10

   E.   April 11-12

44. How many boxes are needed to hold 52 cupcakes if each box holds
    12 cupcakes?

   A. $3\frac{1}{3}$

   B.   4

   C. $4\frac{1}{3}$

   D.   5

   E. $5\frac{1}{3}$

45. On a recent test, Steve got 60% of the questions correct. Stephanie got 70% of the questions correct. If there were 150 questions on the exam, how many more questions did Stephanie answer correctly than Steve?

    A   1 question

    B.   10 questions

    C.   15 questions

    D.   25 questions

    E.   90 questions

46. Mike has a bucket containing 13,086 marbles. He buys half that number of marbles, and adds them to his bucket, approximately how many marbles does he now have in his bucket?

    A.   6,500 marbles

    B.   13,000 marbles

    C.   20,000 marbles

    D.   26,000 marbles

    E.   39,000 marbles

47. Fiona is playing with a complete deck of 52 cards. If she draws one card at random, what is the probability that she will select a heart?

A. $\frac{1}{4}$

B. $\frac{1}{2}$

C. $\frac{1}{8}$

D $\frac{1}{13}$

E $\frac{1}{20}$

48. −7 is greater than which of the following numbers?

A. −10

B. −4

C. 0

D. 1

E. 8

49. A rectangular yard, measuring 50 feet long by 40 feet wide, contains a rectangular swimming pool. If the yard is 10 feet wider than the swimming pool on each side, what is the perimeter of the swimming pool?

   A.   100 feet

   B.   120 feet

   C.   140 feet

   D.   160 feet

   E.   180 feet

50. Consider this statement:

   If Mitch directs the movie, then he will also appear in it.

   Which of the following statements must be true?

   A.   Mitch does not appear in the movie; therefore, he did not direct it.

   B.   Mitch did not direct the movie; therefore, he does not appear in it.

   C.   Mitch appears in the movie; therefore, he directed it.

   D.   Mitch appears in the movie; therefore, he did not direct it.

   E.   Mitch did not direct the movie; therefore, he appears in it.

SECTION III: TEST OF WRITING

Directions: The Writing Section consists of two essay topics. Be sure to write about the assigned topics. Essays on topics of your own choice will not be acceptable. Your written responses should be your original work, written in your own words, and should not be copied or paraphrased from some other work. Since both topics are weighed equally in scoring, you should plan to spend about the same amount of time on each topic.

The essay topics in this test are designed to give you an opportunity to demonstrate your ability to write effectively. Spend some time considering each topic and organizing your thoughts before you begin writing. For each essay, be sure to address all parts of the topic; to support generalizations with specific examples; and to use multiple paragraphs.

You may use any blank space provided in this test booklet to make notes or to prepare a rough draft for each essay. However, your score will be based solely on the versions of your essays written in the space provided in your answer document. Please write as neatly and legibly as possible. To ensure that you have enough space for your entire essay, please do NOT skip lines; do NOT write in excessively large letters; and do NOT leave wide margins.

Topic 1

The amount of money available from the state budget for school district X has not increased in the last three years, despite the increasing number of students and rising administrative costs. As a result, members of the school board have formed partnerships with local businesses. Some of these partnerships involve free books, maps, and textbooks from a particular company. Others involve food from local fast-food establishments. Supporters of these partnerships argue that local businesses are helping out the community, and deserve recognition for their contributions. Critics argue that the school board should not form such partnerships, because schools will become tainted with "corporate advertising" throughout the school. Should schools allow corporate partners to help provide funding and materials? If so, should there be any restrictions on what can and cannot be donated?

Support your opinion with specific reasons.

Topic 2

What is the best class you have taken? Did you enjoy the class because of the teacher or because of the subject matter? Write about your favorite experience as a student. What has this classroom experience taught you that you will be able to use when you become a teacher?

Chapter 13
Practice Test 2:
Answers and
Explanations

ANSWER KEY

	Reading				Mathematics	
1.	B	26.	D	1.	C	26.	B
2.	C	27.	C	2.	C	27.	C
3.	D	28.	D	3.	A	28.	C
4.	D	29.	A	4.	B	29.	C
5.	B	30.	D	5.	A	30.	E
6.	E	31.	C	6.	C	31.	B
7.	B	32.	B	7.	B	32.	E
8.	C	33.	A	8.	A	33.	C
9.	A	34.	C	9.	D	34.	A
10.	B	35.	C	10.	C	35.	B
11.	C	36.	C	11.	C	36.	D
12.	E	37.	E	12.	A	37.	A
13.	A	38.	D	13.	C	38.	E
14.	E	39.	A	14.	A	39.	D
15.	C	40.	A	15.	C	40.	D
16.	B	41.	B	16.	A	41.	A
17.	A	42.	E	17.	E	42.	D
18.	B	43.	C	18.	C	43.	E
19.	D	44.	C	19.	E	44.	D
20.	A	45.	D	20.	C	45.	C
21.	B	46.	C	21.	D	46.	C
22.	B	47.	B	22.	A	47.	A
23.	D	48.	A	23.	C	48.	A
24.	C	49.	D	24.	C	49.	A
25.	A	50.	E	25.	C	50.	A

SECTION I: TEST OF READING

1. **B**   The information is contained in the last sentence of the first paragraph in the passage.

2. **C**   Often, an author will use a word in quotations to imply a meaning similar to the literal meaning of the word. Choice (B) is out of scope. Choice (D) is wrong, and (A) and (E) are not stated anywhere in the passage.

3. **D**   The use of the automobile example is designed to show the impressive features of the DS1 system.

4. **D**   Although the number $30,000 is contained in the passage, we cannot tell exactly how much money someone in debt will save. All we know is that they may be eligible for extended payment options.

5. **B**   If you are unfamiliar with the phrase, information in the passage implies that he is not an experienced tennis player. The first sentence of the passage ("I'm not much of a tennis player") helps to eliminate (A) and (D).

6. **E**   The author takes a lighthearted tone in this passage, and is the first to acknowledge that he does not need the new racquets. However, he enjoys learning about and using the top of the line racquets.

7. **B**   Choices (D) and (A) are out of scope. Choice (C) is too specific. Choice (E) does not provide an appropriate title for the passage.

8. **C**   The chain of events is described in the second paragraph. The primary reason the otter population is declining is due to killer whales' need for additional food, since sea lions and seals have been losing weight.

9. **A**   The information is not too complex, therefore (B) and (E) should be eliminated. Very little opinion, if any, is stated in the passage, so eliminate (C). Since the information is described as recent, it would most likely appear in a newspaper article.

10. **B**   The passage starts with the claim that the otter population is in great danger. That theory is supported by explaining how the otter population is being destroyed at an alarming rate.

11. **C**   While (A) is the most popular definition, the author uses the word here to indicate a tragic series of events. This series of events is then described in the next paragraph.

12. **E**   Statements (A) and (D) are true, but not central to the overall theme of the message. Choice (C) is too general to convey the meaning of the passage.

13. **A**   One clue is the first few words of the next sentence—"at least those institutions." We know that the blank sentence must talk about some types of institutions other than big banks.

14. **E**   The statement, "adult education has never been better" represents the feelings of the author, and would be difficult to prove. All other statements are facts.

15. **C** The passage starts with the story of Tom Purcell. From there, we learn about the growing trends in adult education.

16. **B** In the passage, the author describes the advantages of taking classes while still collecting an income and at the convenient location of the workplace.

17. **A** We could try to speculate why many companies are providing educational assistance to their employees, but we cannot prove any of the explanations. Choices (B), (D), and (E) all seem like good reasons, but we can't prove them. We can infer, however, that companies believe these programs are beneficial. Companies are reimbursing employees and setting up their own programs, both of which indicate a belief that there is value in these programs.

18. **B** The category of "experiment basics" is where one could find general information on how to perform experiments. Most of the other categories list specific types of experiments.

19. **D** Most of the subheadings under the category of experiments list different types of experiments and remember that the question stem asks for the *primary* organizational pattern used, so Choice (D) is correct even though "Experiment Basics" is not a type of experiment. All of the other items in the list are types of experiments, to the primary organizational pattern is indeed types of experiments, Choice (D). We have no way of evaluating answer choices (C) and (E).

20. **A** The farmers claim that the reason for their poor crop production is due to the seeds. In order to weaken that claim, another reason needs to be provided to explain the poor crop production. Poor weather does provide a reason.

21. **B** The passage starts by describing farmers upset over "broken promises" and failed results. At some point, farmers must have been told about the benefits of genetically engineered seeds.

22. **B** The goal of the farmers is to gain support from as many other farmers as possible to fight against genetic seeds. The farmers seek to collaborate with as many other groups as possible.

23. **D** When asked for the main idea, remember to skim the passage using the 2-T-2 technique.

24. **C** We can eliminate (D) and (E) because the passage does not start with either a question or a quote. Choice (A) can be eliminated because the passage does not end with a quotation.

25. **A** The scientists have found a new method that has yet to be discovered by anyone else. This key piece of insight is the focus of the article.

26. **D** The main point of the paragraph is that there are ethical considerations with this new technology. It would be out of place for the author to suddenly state his own views, as in (C) and (E), or end the issue immediately, as in (A) and (B).

27. **C** The author is concerned about Top-100 lists being viewed as factual truths, instead of just promotional items designed to spark debate.

28. **D** The author uses sarcasm to make his point. The best example of this is the third sentence of the second paragraph.

29. **A** Choices (B), (C), and (E) contradict the author's overall message. Choice (A) correctly completes the author's claim to the overall meaning of the passage.

30. **D** The author admits that it is enjoyable to debate what items should and should not be on Top-100 lists.

31. **C** This can be found in the second paragraph of the passage.

32. **B** We can add up the total number of applicants for each of the years labeled 1 through 7.

33. **A** The passage is very vague and general, therefore we can eliminate choices (B), (C), and (E). The passage does not state any strong opinions, making a book review the most likely publication.

34. **C** A statement very similar to this can be found in the first sentence of the second paragraph.

35. **C** If you selected (A), you selected the main point of Judith Harris' book, NOT the main point of the passage.

36. **C** The study found no harm to mothers or their children who consumed saltwater fish during pregnancy.

37. **E** The focus of the passage is the misrepresentation of names and advertisements of groups against Prop. 200.

38. **D** We cannot assume that the author will vote against the issue. The author has made no statements about why he is against the issue, only that he is against the advertising practices.

39. **A** To gain a better understanding of the vocabulary in context, read the remainder of the sentence, which uses the word "misleading" to help define "sap."

40. **A** The passage describes how toys are becoming new status symbols for parents, and what toy companies are doing to profit from this trend.

41. **B** The passage mentions how toy sales took off after exposure on a network show. Toy executives are using these product release events with this effect in mind.

42. **E** The final paragraph describes how national exposure can lead to large sales. Speculation on the economy is not relevant to the overall meaning of the paragraph.

43. **C** The passage describes the impact new toys have on parents.

44. **C** Information on how to travel by taxi can be found on page 72.

45. **D** The different ways to travel around San Francisco are broken down into different modes of transportation—walking, biking, cars, and so forth.

46. **C** The goal of the final sentence in the first paragraph is to link the idea of playing catch with the role of being a parent. Choices (B) and (D) mention both topics, but (C) provides a better connection between the two areas.

47. **B** The game of catch is a metaphor for his relationship with his son.

48. **A** The author reflects on what it feels like to play a game of catch, and what it feels like to raise his son.

49. **D** The passage describes the lengthy procedures used to terminate a teacher who is not in good standing.

50. **E** Choices (A) and (B) go against the general point of the passage. Choice (D) is out of scope. Choice (E) best fits the desire to speed up termination procedures that currently take a very long time.

SECTION II: TEST OF MATHEMATICS

1. **C** When subtracting decimals, be sure to align the decimals vertically, as shown below:

$$\begin{array}{r} 2.500 \\ -\ \ .167 \\ \hline =2.333 \end{array}$$

2. **C** To find the answer, subtract the two values.

3. **A** To find the median, first put the list in numerical order.

   23, 30, 36, 42, 59, 61, 75

   The middle number is 42. This is the median. The question asks, which number can be added in order to make the median the same as the mode. Currently, there is no mode, since each number is unique. However, if we add another 42 to this list, then the mode would be 42, and the median would also be 42.

4. **B** To solve this problem, add the two values together, and don't forget to Ballpark. Starting with the integer parts, add 27 + 8 = 35. Eliminate (E), since it is too small. The two fractional parts $\left(\frac{3}{4}\right)$ and $\left(\frac{5}{6}\right)$ are each close to 1, so their sum is close to 2. That brings the total close to 37, which means that (A) is too large, and you can probably feel comfortable choosing (B) from the remaining choices. To add the fractions, use common denominators:

   $$\left(\frac{3}{4}\right) + \left(\frac{5}{6}\right) = \left(\frac{9}{12}\right) + \left(\frac{10}{12}\right) = \left(\frac{19}{12}\right).$$

   This is equal to $1\frac{7}{12}$. That means the total is $35 + 1 + \frac{7}{12}$, or $36\frac{7}{12}$.

5.   **A**   Start by filling in the information given into the average circle. The number of things is three (3 tests), and the average is 81. Multiply to find the total of 243. 243 is the sum of the three tests. If we subtract the first two exams (78 and 90) from 243, we are left with 75, his score on the third test. Choice (E) is a partial answer. It gives us the total for all three tests.

6.   **C**   4 sandwiches equal $13.00. There are 6 condiments that cost a total of $1.50, and two orders of cheese, which cost $1.00 total. The total sum of Frank's order is therefore $15.50.

7.   **B**   Rather than take the time to add each individual value, estimate, and use Ballparking. There are eleven numbers. If all eleven were equal to 50, the sum would be 550. Eliminate (A). If all eleven were equal to 40, the sum would be 440. Eliminate (D) and (E). The middle value is around 45. 45×11 is approximately 500, which is the correct answer.

8.   **A**   The average of a set of numbers must always be between the lowest and highest numbers, so (A) must be true. To understand why (B), (C), and (D) can be eliminated, it may be helpful to think about how the **sum** affects the average. Using the average pie, we know that the

sum = (average) * (number of values).

If the average is equal to 69, that just means that the sum is equal to (69*7), or 483. If you make an equation as follows:

(36 + __ + __ + __ + __ + __ + 102) = 483

Then there are practically unlimited combinations of numbers that you may choose in order to make the sum equal to 483. (For example, 36 + 69 + 69 + 69 + 69 + 69 + 102.) In other words, it is possible.

However, it's just as easy to choose numbers that total LESS than 483, or GREATER than 483. The sum cannot be determined, so you should eliminate (B), (C), and (D). Choice (E) should be eliminated, because it is not specific enough and does not include all possible values; therefore, it is not the best answer compared to (A).

9.   **D**   Division is the opposite, or the reciprocal of multiplication. The reciprocal of $\frac{3}{4}$ is $\frac{4}{3}$. You could also select a number to see how this works. $12 \times \frac{3}{4}$ is 9. 12 divided by $\frac{4}{3}$ also gives us 9.

10.   **C**   The total number of employees is 282. Subtract 282 − (64 + 123 + 56).

282 − 243 = 39

11.   **C**   This is a percent decrease question. Use the formula for percent change = difference ÷ original.

The difference between the two amounts is $14.00, and the original amount is $70.00. That reduces to $\frac{1}{5}$, which is 20%.

12. **A** Estimate to find the correct answer. First, if there were more pizza votes than sandwich votes, the number of sandwich votes needs to be less than half the total number of votes. Only (A) is less than half of the total number of votes.

13. **C** First, you should be able to eliminate some answer choices. If the dress is on sale, the new price will be lower than the original price of $120.00. Thus, (E) cannot be correct. Choice (A) is extremely small—the price has only been discounted by 15%. To find 15% of $120.00, multiply .15 × 120.00. The result is $18.00. Subtract $18.00 from the original price to get the new total of $102.00.

14. **A** In rounding to the nearest thousand, look at the hundreds place. In this case, since the hundreds place has a value less than 5, do not round up. The correct answer is 654,000.

15. **C** Divide the number of pictures by the number of pictures per album. 412 divided by 34 comes out to be more than 12 (it won't divide evenly—there will be a remainder). Thus, we need 13 albums in order to hold all the photographs.

16. **A** We know that they ate a total of 7 hot dogs. Fiona ate one hot dog, and Rich ate more than Chris. While we don't know exactly how many hot dogs Rich ate (he may have had 6, 5, or 4), we know that Rich had the most.

17. **E** If peanuts cost $.50, the total cost of peanuts is $1.50. From the information given above, we know that hot dogs cost $.75 more, or $1.25. The total cost of hot dogs is $1.25 × 7, or $8.75. Soft drinks must cost more than $1.25. The total of peanuts and hot dogs is $10.25. Four soft drinks must cost more than $5.00 ($1.25 × 4). So, the total must be more than $15.25. Only (E) works.

18. **C** This is a proportion question. First, identify the relationship we are given: 3 game stamps: 1 large drink. We set this equal to the one we want to know: 60 game stamps: ? large drinks. The equation looks like:

$$\frac{3 \text{ game stamps}}{1 \text{ large drink}} = \frac{60 \text{ game stamps}}{x \text{ large drinks}}$$

If we cross multiply, we get $3x = 60$; $x = 20$.

19. **E** When adding fractions, it's most efficient to find the lowest common denominator. This is the lowest number that can be divided by each of the existing fractions. Look at choices (C), (D), and (E), since they each mention using a common denominator. 10 would not work as a common denominator, since 10 is not divisible by 4 (the denominator for $\frac{3}{4}$). Eliminate (C). 40 would work as a common denominator, since it is divisible by 2, 4, and 5. However, since this is not the lowest possible common denominator, this is not the most efficient way to add these fractions. Eliminate

(D). 20 would work as a common denominator, since it is divisible by 2, 4, and 5. This is the lowest possible common denominator for these fractions. Choose (E). Eliminate (A), since subtracting from one will not result in the sum of the fractions. Eliminate (B), since multiplying the denominators will not result in the sum of the fractions.

20. **C** Rewrite the problem to be:

$$\frac{280 \quad 12 \quad 9}{3 \quad 70 \quad 9}$$

You can simplify and reduce this further, to come out to approximately 16.

21. **D** If we add up the number of goods sold by all the other people, we get 105,000. To get to 150,000, we need to have Tom sell 45,000 goods.

22. **A** Simplify the equation to get:

$15y - 42 = 3$

$15y \qquad = 45$

$y \qquad = 3$

23. **C** Don't forget to Ballpark. $\frac{3}{8}$ is halfway between $\frac{2}{8}$ and $\frac{4}{8}$. $\frac{2}{8}$ is equal to $\frac{1}{4}$, which is 25%. $\frac{4}{8}$ is equal to $\frac{1}{2}$, which is 50%. Eliminate (A) and (E), since they are outside the range of these two values. The value of $\frac{3}{8}$ is 37.5%, which is halfway between 25% and 50%. The answer that has the correct range is (C).

24. **C** Choices (A) and (B) are smaller than −.345 (they are to the left of −.345 on the number line). Choices (D) and (E) are greater than .008.

25. **C** First, we can approximate the number of cards that Marty owns. If he has 70% of the total, then we know he'll have more than half. Choices (A) and (B) are too small, and can be eliminated. To get the exact total, multiply .7 × 3,500.

26. **B** Multiply to find out how much of the fence Oliver has built. 5 × 25 = 125 feet. Subtract this from the total of 170, and we get 45 feet remaining.

27. **C** First, figure out how many days it will take James to write all of the cards. $\frac{300}{12} = 25$, so it will take 25 days. Include February 1, since the problem states that he "begins" on that day. That means that James works on cards on the days 1-25. He should finish on February 25.

28. **C** From the first column, we know that Kristen scored less than Amy. This allows us to eliminate (A) and (E). From the second column, we know that Jen scored lower than two other students. Eliminate (B) and (D). The correct answer (C) is the only one remaining.

29. **C** There are three feet in one yard. Multiply 485 by 3 to get the correct total.

30. **E** Multiply the number of hours per day times the total number of days. $165 \times 3 = 495$.

31. **B** This is a proportion question. We are given the relationship 2 students go to Butterick College: 5 total students. If we set this equal to our unknown relationship, we have the equation:

$$\frac{2 \text{ students to Butterick}}{5 \text{ total students}} = \frac{x \text{ students to Butterick}}{240 \text{ total students}}$$

If we cross multiply, we get $5x = 480$. $x = 96$.

32. **E** To calculate the cost of 2 dozen reams of paper, multiply $24 \times \$2.00$. The cost of 17 boxes of crayons is $17 \times \$3.45$. The cost of 33 dry erase markers is $33 \times \$.65$. The answer that reflects this correctly is choice (E).

33. **C** To correctly translate this question, remember that "what percent" means "$\left(\dfrac{x}{100}\right)$," "of" means multiply, and "is" means "=."

$$\left(\frac{x}{100}\right) * 20 = 5$$

Then solve for x.

$$\frac{x}{100} = \frac{5}{20}$$

$$x = \frac{500}{20}$$

$$x = 25$$

34. **A** The amount of the discount is 15%, and the discounted price is $425. If the original price is 100% of p, then the discounted price is 85% of p (100% − 15% = 85%). In other words, 85% of p gives us the discounted price of $425.

35. **B** This is a percent increase problem. Use the formula for percent change = difference ÷ original. The difference between the two amounts is 50,000, and the original amount is 250,000. That reduces to $\dfrac{1}{5}$, which is 20%.

36. **D** First, turn (C) into a decimal. $\dfrac{1}{8}$ is equal to .125. Now we can compare across all answer choices. In the tenths column, only (B) and (D) have a zero—eliminate all others. In the thousandths column, (D) has a 6 while (B) has an 8. (D) is smaller.

37. **A** 5% of 20 is equal to 1. If we add 1 more student to the total of 20, we get the new total of 21.

38. **E** There are 36 squares total. 9 squares are shaded. The fraction of shaded squares is $\frac{9}{36}$, or $\frac{1}{4}$.

39. **D** The question is asking for $\frac{1}{3}$ of $\frac{3}{8}$ of 120. For fractions and percents, remember that "of" means multiply. Calculate $\left(\frac{1}{3}\right) * \left(\frac{3}{8}\right) * 120$. It may be easy to start with $\left(\frac{1}{3}\right) * 120$, which is 40. Then multiply $40 * \left(\frac{3}{8}\right)$, which equals 15.

40. **D** Cross multiply to get $3x = 36$. Divide by 3 to get $x = 12$.

41. **A** First, we need to find the total number of points Brooke scored on her first six tests. Adding these together gives us a total of 534. If the total of all seven tests is 612, we can subtract to find the score on the seventh test. $612 - 534$ is 78.

42. **D** The gray line shows the 10-year average rainfall for the indicated dates. The black line shows the rainfall for the eight dates indicated in April 2012. There are FIVE points on the black line that are higher than the gray line. $\frac{5}{8} = .625$, which is approximately 63%.

43. **E** The question asks for the greatest DECREASE. Compare each answer.

    April 5-6 shows an increase. Eliminate (A).

    April 6-7 shows a decrease of about 0.2.

    April 7-8 shows a decrease of about 0.5.

    April 9-10 shows an increase. Eliminate (C).

    April 11-12 shows a decrease of about 0.7. Since this is the greatest decrease, select (E).

44. **D** If you divide $\frac{52}{12}$ directly, you'll get $4\frac{1}{3}$. However, the question asks how many boxes are needed. Since we can't have $4\frac{1}{3}$ boxes, we must use 5 boxes.

45. **C** Take each statement step by step, and write down the information you find. First, Steve answered 60% of the questions correct. 60% of 150 questions is $90(\frac{60}{100} \times 150)$. Next, find the number of questions Stephanie answered correctly. She answered 105 questions correctly $(\frac{70}{100} \times 150)$. The difference between Stephanie's total and Steve's total is $15(105 - 90)$ questions.

46. **C** Mike has approximately 13,000 marbles. If he adds half of that amount, he adds approximately 6,500 marbles (13,000 × .5). The sum of 13,000 and 6,500 is 19,500 marbles. Choice (C) is the closest answer.

47. **A** There are four types of cards in a deck—hearts, clubs, diamonds, and spades. There are four possible outcomes, and we want one of them. Thus, the probability is $\frac{1}{4}$.

48. **A** If you plot the points on a number line, only (A) is to the left of –7 on the number line. For negative numbers, the number closest to zero on the number line is the greater number.

49. **A** If the yard is 10 feet wider on each side, then the swimming pool is 30 feet by 20 feet. The perimeter is 30 + 20 + 30 + 20, which equals 100.

50. **A** Statement (A) is a contrapositive of the If-Then statement that is presented in the problem. If we denote the If-Then statement as If A, Then B, the contrapositive is If Not B, then Not A. It is the only logical inference we can make from the information given. If Mitch does not appear in the movie, we know that he did not direct the movie.

SECTION III: TEST OF WRITING

Topic 1

The amount of money available from the state budget for school district X has not increased in the last three years, despite the increasing number of students and rising administrative costs. As a result, members of the school board have formed partnerships with local businesses. Some of these partnerships involve free books, maps, and textbooks from a particular company. Others involve food from local fast-food establishments. Supporters of these partnerships argue that local businesses are helping out the community, and deserve recognition for their contributions. Critics argue that the school board should not form such partnerships, because schools will become tainted with "corporate advertising" throughout the school. Should schools allow corporate partners to help provide funding and materials? If so, should there be any restrictions on what can and cannot be donated? Support your opinion with specific reasons.

Sample Essay #1: Overall Score = 4 (Pass)

The issue of allowing corporate advertising in public schools is a controversial one. Some argue that private money will become a vital part of helping to fund our schools, especially during difficult economic periods. Others believe that corporate partnerships can negatively commercialize a school by bringing corporate logos into the school environment. After careful thought, I believe the school board should allow funding and donations from corporate partners, but with specific regulations that minimize the possibility of a school becoming a corporate billboard.

If the school board is struggling in its effort to provide all of its desired programs and materials to students, it should look for outside help. New textbooks and computers are important to help students learn the most relevant information. Children need exposure to the latest technology in order to be ready for the outside world. Private money can help make those budget dreams a reality. If done well, schools can form powerful alliances with the community. Schools can draw from the knowledge and expertise of various businesses, and learn how to bring that information to their students. Schools can benefit with extra dollars to spend on items that would otherwise be unavailable. Ultimately, the concern of the school board needs to be the quality of education its students are receiving. If the budget does not allow for the board to completely provide for its students, it should look for outside help.

Of course, there are some possible dangers associated with corporate partnerships. If not done properly, corporate products can quickly commercialize a school. Corporate logos could start to appear on everything from textbooks to a student's lunch. As adults, we can recognize when a business is advertising to us. We can make decisions about what products we do and do not want to use. However, children, especially those in elementary school, probably can't recognize subtle advertising. We should not allow corporations an opportunity to form brand loyalties at a very early age with our children.

In order to prevent the commercialization of our schools, the district must set tough guidelines when receiving gifts from corporate sponsors. If private corporations are donating goods instead of money, their logos should be removed from the goods. We don't want our children in an environment that tries to force product loyalty at an early age (imagine the horror of reading "This textbook brought to you buy Slushy, the drink for the next generation," on the cover of a mathematics book). Children already receive enough advertising, mainly through television. To be fair, corporations deserve recognition for their donations. After all, they should expect to "do well by doing good." I would recommend that the school board put together a list of all corporate donors, and send that list to all parents. That way, parents can see which companies are supporting their children, and repay those companies by supporting their businesses. There should be space for corporate advertising in parent newsletters or bulletins. Schools may even want to create plagues recognizing the efforts of private businesses. Corporations deserve exposure for these good deeds, and there are ways to provide that exposure without posting billboards all over campus.

Unfortunately, budget crunches and an increasing number of students have left the school district with less money per student. Sadly, this comes at a time when operating costs are higher, and technology changes are rapid. Corporate donations can help fill in the gap, and so we should allow them, for the good of our children. If done properly, the school board can give proper recognition to its corporate partners without tainting the classroom environment. It is important that we keep the classroom a place for learning, not a place for advertising.

Sample Essay #2: Overall Score = 3 (Marginal Pass)

The school board will be making a big mistake if it allows local businesses to provide money and materials to support the school. There are too many possible dangers associated with using outside private businesses, and monitoring the partnerships would take school board members away from their real jobs—helping the students.

Probably the greatest concern of business sponsorship is the free and unfiltered advertising that would accompany the donation of materials. I've heard of one school that has a lunch every Thursday from the fast-food restaurant "Taco Hut." The employees of the restaurant come down in their uniforms and serve lunch to students all day. The items are exactly the same as those served at their fast-food establishments. I've even heard that the workers will give out mascots of Taco Hut Joe to students. As you can see, it makes a ton of sense for the people at Taco Hut to do this. They lose some money each week by giving out free lunches, but they will receive that back in bunches if they create a new generation of children who like to go to Taco Hut. Parents should have more influence on what they introduce their children to.

While corporate logos and advertisements seem the most obvious, a more subtle concern would be that corporations would donate material that is unobjective or biased, therefore tainting the objectivity of material taught in the classrooms. For example, a local computer company might donate a bunch of materials and manuals on the history of computers. These could be used in a computer class. But what if they portray their company in too favorable a view? What if the information they include is biased so that their company appears to be much better than it actually is? We all know that textbooks, no matter who they are written by, have certain biases. However, a textbook from a private company could be very skewed from the truth.

I'd prefer school board members to figure out how to revise their budget or raise more money within the school than to look to outside companies for assistance. There are too many potential dangers in working with outside corporations. While corporate money may seem to help solve a number of problems, it could unfortunately create a whole new set of problems.

Sample Essay #3: Overall Score = 2 (Marginal Fail)

I disagree that the school board should look to local businesses to provide additional funding for their school. It would be much better if the school board looked to parents and the government for additional funding. These two groups are a more reliable way of getting money.

Local funding by businesses may not last. You could get corporate funding one year, and then all of a sudden it may be gone the next year. For the school board, that would be very difficult to plan for. If a company gave $5,000 one year, and then none the next, it would provide a difficult challenge for the board to decide how to create a budget (not knowing how much money they have is tough). Businesses would probably give when the economy is good, but that's ironic cause when the economy is good the school board would probably have enough money already. So it's when the economy isn't good that schools will need to find additional money.

If the school board wants to make a lasting change on the budget problem, it needs to make its case to the local or statewide government. It should compile a list of what is missing from its school and request it. It should ask that someone high up in the school administration come visit the school and reevaluate its budget formula for the school. Maybe the way in which money is distributed is out of date, and someone can change that. Or maybe someone will see that things aren't getting done and go back and change some rules to help the school.

Finally, parents can help the school to raise money. Bake sales, raffles, etc. are all ways to raise money for the school. Also, if parents donate money directly, they probably won't have any requests for it unlike corporations. Parents are the most concerned about the schools being good for their students, so they are the most likely to give.

Therefore, the school board should look to parents and the state school administration to raise money instead of local businesses, for the reasons I've listed above.

Sample Essay #4: Overall Score = 1 (Fail)

If the school board needs money, it should get it any way it can. And if local businesses are willing to give back to the community and the school, who are we to stop them?

Money is tight these days at schools. Look at the date on some of the textbooks at a local scholl and you'll see that some materials have not been updated in a really long time. More money could change that. I would prefer to have students have all new books and computers than watching a school district struggling on its own.

A little advertising for the businesses seems like a fair exchange for lots of money from the company. As the old saying goes "There's no such thing as a free lunch".

Topic 2

What is the best class you have taken? Did you enjoy the class because of the teacher or because of the subject matter? Write about your favorite experience as a student. What has this classroom experience taught you that you will be able to use when you become a teacher?

Sample Essay #1: Overall Score = 4 (Pass)

When I reflect on my high school experience, I can vividly remember almost everything that happened during my fourth period Latin class; everything, that is, except the subject material. Mr. Cser turned a difficult and boring topic into an exciting event. My friends and I actually looked forward to his class prior to lunch. Mr. Cser's enthusiasm, concern for his students, and passion toward his profession, have influenced my decision to become a teacher and provide platforms that I aspire to reach.

Mr. Cser possesses a wonderful charm and enthusiasm, which turned a dull language class into an excited classroom. Attending his class was like attending a rock concert. Mr. Cser would lecture while feverishly walking back and forth across the room, raising his voice at the hint of something interesting. He provided humor and support within his class, putting all students in a good mood before the end of the period. When the bell ended the class at around 12:15 P.M., students left with a smile on their face, ready to discuss the previous 45 minutes of class. Discussions of his class would occupy most of the lunchroom talk for most of that year.

Latin was certainly not my favorite subject. In fact, I found it to be the most challenging subject I studied in high school. In general, I excelled in English and History classes, and therefore poured most of my energy into those areas. For two years, I had received mediocre grades in Latin. When I had Mr. Cser for my third year of Latin, though, things began to change. Mr. Cser possessed a rare ability to inspire me to study the language. Once you witnessed the passion that he brought to the subject, it was hard to dislike the material. Sure, it was still difficult, but I began to take an interest in the topic thanks to Mr. Cser. I felt that he had given the class so much of his dedication and energy that

I needed to give back the same effort. That year, I spent more time on Latin than any other topic, and my improved grade reflected that effort.

At times, our Latin class would not focus on the language at all. If Mr. Cser could tell that students were too exhausted to study another round of conjugating verbs, he would avoid the topic entirely and have one of his "life chats." Somehow, he was able to turn these discussions into very thoughtful and relevant debates, unlike most teachers, who treated such discussions like a bad public service announcement. These discussions did not occur often—maybe only five or six times that year. But each day, I left the room with a lot to think about. He challenged us to always do the right thing, to take accountability for our actions, and to be fair. In many ways, he had the ability to be a parent and a role model.

I've known for quite some time that my career goal was to become a teacher. Mr. Cser would rank quite highly on my short list of people who have helped influence my decision to pursue teaching. Mr. Cser has taught me that one of my responsibilities as a teacher is to excite students about the subject material. I now know that subject matter alone does not determine a student's interest in a class. The effort and concern shown by a teacher can have a dramatic influence on how students view a class. If I can bring the same passion and energy to my science classes as Mr. Cser brought to his Latin classes, I believe that many seventh graders will have newfound excitement about the world of science. I'm not sure I can recreate the atmosphere of Room 12's "Cser Palace," but I know I can make Science Lab 4 a fun place to learn.

Sample Essay #2: Overall Score = 3 (Marginal Pass)

How do you choose which of your classes is the best? Is it as simple as the one you get the best grade? Or is something that provides you with more meaning and experience long after the class is over? Is it the quality of the teacher, or the quality of the material that is studied? I'm sure that people can come up with reasons to justify a number of ways to rate which class is the best. For me, my "Teamwork and Leadership Seminar" my senior year of college was my best class, not for the material or the instructor, but for the interactions with my classmates.

The teamwork and leadership seminar was a two unit class that several of us took during our senior year of college. It was recommended to students who wanted to gain some experience tackling problems in a group environment. The students that enrolled in the class did so for many different reasons. Some were going into consulting jobs, and wanted some group work experience before entering the business world. Others, like my boyfriend and me, were going to be teachers. And some just took the class because they said it sounded easy! Well, it wasn't. The course was designed to present situations with a number of problems, and the groups were to come up with action plans to resolve the problems. Some of these problems were failing businesses, others were disputes between political parties, and others were environmental problems. Each problem was complex, without easy answers.

Once we received a topic, the group would have approximately one week before it needed to present the case and action plans to the instructor. I learned a lot about teamwork in this class. It was amazing how difficult it was to actually get the group organized and on the "same page". Some of the students were definite leaders—wanting to organize the group, and use their solution to the problem. Others like myself were much more reserved—happy to contribute, but reluctant to organize what everyone else would be doing. This group dynamic was great exposure to the real working environment. I can often compare various people in my leadership class to current people I work and teach with.

It was disappointing though when I once asked our instructor for some help. I received a response that was something like "go figure it out yourself", without any encouragement or guidance. If there is anything I've learned from this classroom experience, it would unfortunately be what <u>not</u> to do in a classroom. I know he had taught the class for many years, and that he wanted students to really work on their own, but he seemed to carry no concern for the students either. I'll be sure not to do that when I get my own classroom.

Sample Essay #3: Overall Score = 2 (Marginal Fail)

All of us have had a class or two that we find very memorable. Mine would have to be Biology with Mrs. Stumpf. I still remember it today, even though I took the class my freshman year of high school. I really enjoyed the class because of the way in which she organized her classes.

We did a different thing in Biology each day. On Monday, we would get a basic lecture from Mrs. Stumpf. The lectures were always pretty dull, but they were only once a week so I managed to survive them. Tuesday's were a discussion day, which was more open to student-teacher interaction. We would discuss a relevant topic to the chapter of material that we were studying. Wednesday was homework and problem sets. We would review the answers to the home work problems that were asigned on Monday. Then, on Thursday we would be in the lab, doing an experiment. We would always have a lab partner to do the experiments with. Finally, the week ended on a down note, cause there were quizzes every Friday. These quizzes and a final test were the only thing that determined your grade, so they were very important.

I'm not sure if I really liked Biology all that much, but at least it was interesting. You knew that you only did the same thing once per week, which was good. The Biology class was the final class of the day, so I was already pretty restless. Luckily, Mrs. Stumpf mixed up the material.

Sample Essay #4: Overall Score = 1 (Fail)

It would definitely have to be Chemistry 6A. And it would definitely not be because of the teacher. That guy was not a good lecturer at all. But I would still choose Chemistry 6A because I like Chemistry and because I got a good grade in the class.

This was the first class of three Chemistry classes that I needed to take in order to pass out of my general education science requirements. I liked the class because I had most of the material already in high school, so it wasn't all that challenging. But I still had to perform really well on the final. I went in to the final test with a score of around 88, and I had to get the average up to a 91 in order to get an A. So, I studied a ton for that test, even the stuff I already knew, just in case I forgot some of the details or something. Well, when I got my grades over the internet, I was pleased to see that my work paid off, and I got an A in Chemistry. Unfortunately, that wasn't the case when I later took Chemistry 6B.

ABOUT THE AUTHOR

Rick Sliter has worked with The Princeton Review since 1993. Rick previously served as the Director of the San Diego office, and as the Executive Director of The Princeton Review in Palo Alto, CA. Nationally, Rick has served on research and development teams to produce course materials for the SAT, some of the SAT subject test exams, and the GMAT. In addition to this book, Rick has written test preparation books for California high school exams in Algebra and Geometry. Rick holds a BA in Quantitative Economics from the University of California, San Diego, and an MBA from The Anderson School at UCLA. When not immersed in the world of test preparation, Rick can be found playing a number of sports, or watching them on television.

Completely darken bubbles with a No. 2 pencil. If you make a mistake, be sure to erase mark completely. Erase all stray marks.

1.

YOUR NAME: _____
(Print)
Last   First   M.I.

SIGNATURE: _____   DATE: __/__/__

HOME ADDRESS: _____
(Print)
Number and Street

_____
City   State   Zip Code

PHONE NO.: _____
(Print)

IMPORTANT: Please fill in these boxes exactly as shown on the back cover of your test book.

2. TEST FORM

6. DATE OF BIRTH

Month		Day		Year	
○ JAN					
○ FEB	⓪	⓪	⓪	⓪	
○ MAR	①	①	①	①	
○ APR	②	②	②	②	
○ MAY	③	③	③	③	
○ JUN		④	④	④	
○ JUL		⑤	⑤	⑤	
○ AUG		⑥	⑥	⑥	
○ SEP		⑦	⑦	⑦	
○ OCT		⑧	⑧	⑧	
○ NOV		⑨	⑨	⑨	
○ DEC					

3. TEST CODE

4. REGISTRATION NUMBER

7. SEX
○ MALE
○ FEMALE

The Princeton Review®

5. YOUR NAME

First 4 letters of last name | FIRST INIT | MID INIT

(A) through (Z) bubble columns

Test ①
Start with number 1 for each new section.
If a section has fewer questions than answer spaces, leave the extra answer spaces blank.

Section I—Reading

1. (A) (B) (C) (D) (E)
2. (A) (B) (C) (D) (E)
3. (A) (B) (C) (D) (E)
4. (A) (B) (C) (D) (E)
5. (A) (B) (C) (D) (E)
6. (A) (B) (C) (D) (E)
7. (A) (B) (C) (D) (E)
8. (A) (B) (C) (D) (E)
9. (A) (B) (C) (D) (E)
10. (A) (B) (C) (D) (E)
11. (A) (B) (C) (D) (E)
12. (A) (B) (C) (D) (E)
13. (A) (B) (C) (D) (E)
14. (A) (B) (C) (D) (E)
15. (A) (B) (C) (D) (E)
16. (A) (B) (C) (D) (E)
17. (A) (B) (C) (D) (E)
18. (A) (B) (C) (D) (E)
19. (A) (B) (C) (D) (E)
20. (A) (B) (C) (D) (E)
21. (A) (B) (C) (D) (E)
22. (A) (B) (C) (D) (E)
23. (A) (B) (C) (D) (E)
24. (A) (B) (C) (D) (E)
25. (A) (B) (C) (D) (E)
26. (A) (B) (C) (D) (E)
27. (A) (B) (C) (D) (E)
28. (A) (B) (C) (D) (E)
29. (A) (B) (C) (D) (E)
30. (A) (B) (C) (D) (E)
31. (A) (B) (C) (D) (E)
32. (A) (B) (C) (D) (E)
33. (A) (B) (C) (D) (E)
34. (A) (B) (C) (D) (E)
35. (A) (B) (C) (D) (E)
36. (A) (B) (C) (D) (E)
37. (A) (B) (C) (D) (E)
38. (A) (B) (C) (D) (E)
39. (A) (B) (C) (D) (E)
40. (A) (B) (C) (D) (E)
41. (A) (B) (C) (D) (E)
42. (A) (B) (C) (D) (E)
43. (A) (B) (C) (D) (E)
44. (A) (B) (C) (D) (E)
45. (A) (B) (C) (D) (E)
46. (A) (B) (C) (D) (E)
47. (A) (B) (C) (D) (E)
48. (A) (B) (C) (D) (E)
49. (A) (B) (C) (D) (E)
50. (A) (B) (C) (D) (E)

Section II—Mathematics

1. (A) (B) (C) (D) (E)
2. (A) (B) (C) (D) (E)
3. (A) (B) (C) (D) (E)
4. (A) (B) (C) (D) (E)
5. (A) (B) (C) (D) (E)
6. (A) (B) (C) (D) (E)
7. (A) (B) (C) (D) (E)
8. (A) (B) (C) (D) (E)
9. (A) (B) (C) (D) (E)
10. (A) (B) (C) (D) (E)
11. (A) (B) (C) (D) (E)
12. (A) (B) (C) (D) (E)
13. (A) (B) (C) (D) (E)
14. (A) (B) (C) (D) (E)
15. (A) (B) (C) (D) (E)
16. (A) (B) (C) (D) (E)
17. (A) (B) (C) (D) (E)
18. (A) (B) (C) (D) (E)
19. (A) (B) (C) (D) (E)
20. (A) (B) (C) (D) (E)
21. (A) (B) (C) (D) (E)
22. (A) (B) (C) (D) (E)
23. (A) (B) (C) (D) (E)
24. (A) (B) (C) (D) (E)
25. (A) (B) (C) (D) (E)
26. (A) (B) (C) (D) (E)
27. (A) (B) (C) (D) (E)
28. (A) (B) (C) (D) (E)
29. (A) (B) (C) (D) (E)
30. (A) (B) (C) (D) (E)
31. (A) (B) (C) (D) (E)
32. (A) (B) (C) (D) (E)
33. (A) (B) (C) (D) (E)
34. (A) (B) (C) (D) (E)
35. (A) (B) (C) (D) (E)
36. (A) (B) (C) (D) (E)
37. (A) (B) (C) (D) (E)
38. (A) (B) (C) (D) (E)
39. (A) (B) (C) (D) (E)
40. (A) (B) (C) (D) (E)
41. (A) (B) (C) (D) (E)
42. (A) (B) (C) (D) (E)
43. (A) (B) (C) (D) (E)
44. (A) (B) (C) (D) (E)
45. (A) (B) (C) (D) (E)
46. (A) (B) (C) (D) (E)
47. (A) (B) (C) (D) (E)
48. (A) (B) (C) (D) (E)
49. (A) (B) (C) (D) (E)
50. (A) (B) (C) (D) (E)

The Princeton Review

Completely darken bubbles with a No. 2 pencil. If you make a mistake, be sure to erase mark completely. Erase all stray marks.

1.

YOUR NAME: _____
(Print)   Last   First   M.I.

SIGNATURE: _____   DATE: ___ / ___ / ___

HOME ADDRESS: _____
(Print)   Number and Street

City   State   Zip Code

PHONE NO.: _____
(Print)

IMPORTANT: Please fill in these boxes exactly as shown on the back cover of your test book.

2. TEST FORM

3. TEST CODE

A	J	0	0
B	K	1	1
C	L	2	2
D	M	3	3
E	N	4	4
F	O	5	5
G	P	6	6
H	Q	7	7
I	R	8	8
		9	9

4. REGISTRATION NUMBER

0	0	0	0	0	0	0	0
1	1	1	1	1	1	1	1
2	2	2	2	2	2	2	2
3	3	3	3	3	3	3	3
4	4	4	4	4	4	4	4
5	5	5	5	5	5	5	5
6	6	6	6	6	6	6	6
7	7	7	7	7	7	7	7
8	8	8	8	8	8	8	8
9	9	9	9	9	9	9	9

5. YOUR NAME

First 4 letters of last name | FIRST INIT | MID INIT

A B C D E F G H I J K L M N O P Q R S T U V W X Y Z

6. DATE OF BIRTH

Month	Day	Year
JAN		
FEB	0 0	0 0
MAR	1 1	1 1
APR	2 2	2 2
MAY	3 3	3 3
JUN	4 4	4
JUL	5 5	5
AUG	6 6	6
SEP	7 7	7
OCT	8 8	8
NOV	9 9	9
DEC		

7. SEX
MALE
FEMALE

The Princeton Review

Test 2 Start with number 1 for each new section.
If a section has fewer questions than answer spaces, leave the extra answer spaces blank.

Section I—Reading

1. A B C D E
2. A B C D E
3. A B C D E
4. A B C D E
5. A B C D E
6. A B C D E
7. A B C D E
8. A B C D E
9. A B C D E
10. A B C D E
11. A B C D E
12. A B C D E
13. A B C D E
14. A B C D E
15. A B C D E
16. A B C D E
17. A B C D E
18. A B C D E
19. A B C D E
20. A B C D E
21. A B C D E
22. A B C D E
23. A B C D E
24. A B C D E
25. A B C D E
26. A B C D E
27. A B C D E
28. A B C D E
29. A B C D E
30. A B C D E
31. A B C D E
32. A B C D E
33. A B C D E
34. A B C D E
35. A B C D E
36. A B C D E
37. A B C D E
38. A B C D E
39. A B C D E
40. A B C D E
41. A B C D E
42. A B C D E
43. A B C D E
44. A B C D E
45. A B C D E
46. A B C D E
47. A B C D E
48. A B C D E
49. A B C D E
50. A B C D E

Section II—Mathematics

1. A B C D E
2. A B C D E
3. A B C D E
4. A B C D E
5. A B C D E
6. A B C D E
7. A B C D E
8. A B C D E
9. A B C D E
10. A B C D E
11. A B C D E
12. A B C D E
13. A B C D E
14. A B C D E
15. A B C D E
16. A B C D E
17. A B C D E
18. A B C D E
19. A B C D E
20. A B C D E
21. A B C D E
22. A B C D E
23. A B C D E
24. A B C D E
25. A B C D E
26. A B C D E
27. A B C D E
28. A B C D E
29. A B C D E
30. A B C D E
31. A B C D E
32. A B C D E
33. A B C D E
34. A B C D E
35. A B C D E
36. A B C D E
37. A B C D E
38. A B C D E
39. A B C D E
40. A B C D E
41. A B C D E
42. A B C D E
43. A B C D E
44. A B C D E
45. A B C D E
46. A B C D E
47. A B C D E
48. A B C D E
49. A B C D E
50. A B C D E

International Offices Listing

China (Beijing)
1501 Building A,
Disanji Creative Zone,
No.66 West Section of North 4th Ring Road Beijing
Tel: +86-10-62684481/2/3
Email: tprkor01@chol.com
Website: www.tprbeijing.com

China (Shanghai)
1010 Kaixuan Road
Building B, 5/F
Changning District, Shanghai, China 200052
Sara Beattie, Owner: Email: sbeattie@sarabeattie.com
Tel: +86-21-5108-2798
Fax: +86-21-6386-1039
Website: www.princetonreviewshanghai.com

Hong Kong
5th Floor, Yardley Commercial Building
1-6 Connaught Road West, Sheung Wan, Hong Kong
(MTR Exit C)
Sara Beattie, Owner: Email: sbeattie@sarabeattie.com
Tel: +852-2507-9380
Fax: +852-2827-4630
Website: www.princetonreviewhk.com

India (Mumbai)
Score Plus Academy
Office No.15, Fifth Floor
Manek Mahal 90
Veer Nariman Road
Next to Hotel Ambassador
Churchgate, Mumbai 400020
Maharashtra, India
Ritu Kalwani: Email: director@score-plus.com
Tel: + 91 22 22846801 / 39 / 41
Website: www.score-plus.com

India (New Delhi)
South Extension
K-16, Upper Ground Floor
South Extension Part–1,
New Delhi-110049
Aradhana Mahna: aradhana@manyagroup.com
Monisha Banerjee: monisha@manyagroup.com
Ruchi Tomar: ruchi.tomar@manyagroup.com
Rishi Josan: Rishi.josan@manyagroup.com
Vishal Goswamy: vishal.goswamy@manyagroup.com
Tel: +91-11-64501603/ 4, +91-11-65028379
Website: www.manyagroup.com

Lebanon
463 Bliss Street
AlFarra Building - 2nd floor
Ras Beirut
Beirut, Lebanon
Hassan Coudsi: Email: hassan.coudsi@review.com
Tel: +961-1-367-688
Website: www.princetonreviewlebanon.com

Korea
945-25 Young Shin Building
25 Daechi-Dong, Kangnam-gu
Seoul, Korea 135-280
Yong-Hoon Lee: Email: TPRKor01@chollian.net
In-Woo Kim: Email: iwkim@tpr.co.kr
Tel: + 82-2-554-7762
Fax: +82-2-453-9466
Website: www.tpr.co.kr

Kuwait
ScorePlus Learning Center
Salmiyah Block 3, Street 2 Building 14
Post Box: 559, Zip 1306, Safat, Kuwait
Email: infokuwait@score-plus.com
Tel: +965-25-75-48-02 / 8
Fax: +965-25-75-46-02
Website: www.scorepluseducation.com

Malaysia
Sara Beattie MDC Sdn Bhd
Suites 18E & 18F
18th Floor
Gurney Tower, Persiaran Gurney
Penang, Malaysia
Email: tprkl.my@sarabeattie.com
Sara Beattie, Owner: Email: sbeattie@sarabeattie.com
Tel: +604-2104 333
Fax: +604-2104 330
Website: www.princetonreviewKL.com

Mexico
TPR México
Guanajuato No. 242 Piso 1 Interior 1
Col. Roma Norte
México D.F., C.P.06700
registro@princetonreviewmexico.com
Tel: +52-55-5255-4495
+52-55-5255-4440
+52-55-5255-4442
Website: www.princetonreviewmexico.com

Qatar
Score Plus
Office No: 1A, Al Kuwari (Damas)
Building near Merweb Hotel, Al Saad
Post Box: 2408, Doha, Qatar
Email: infoqatar@score-plus.com
Tel: +974 44 36 8580, +974 526 5032
Fax: +974 44 13 1995
Website: www.scorepluseducation.com

Taiwan
The Princeton Review Taiwan
2F, 169 Zhong Xiao East Road, Section 4
Taipei, Taiwan 10690
Lisa Bartle (Owner): lbartle@princetonreview.com.tw
Tel: +886-2-2751-1293
Fax: +886-2-2776-3201
Website: www.PrincetonReview.com.tw

Thailand
The Princeton Review Thailand
Sathorn Nakorn Tower, 28th floor
100 North Sathorn Road
Bangkok, Thailand 10500
Thavida Bijayendrayodhin (Chairman)
Email: thavida@princetonreviewthailand.com
Mitsara Bijayendrayodhin (Managing Director)
Email: mitsara@princetonreviewthailand.com
Tel: +662-636-6770
Fax: +662-636-6776
Website: www.princetonreviewthailand.com

Turkey
Yeni Sülün Sokak No. 28
Levent, Istanbul, 34330, Turkey
Nuri Ozgur: nuri@tprturkey.com
Rona Ozgur: rona@tprturkey.com
Iren Ozgur: iren@tprturkey.com
Tel: +90-212-324-4747
Fax: +90-212-324-3347
Website: www.tprturkey.com

UAE
Emirates Score Plus
Office No: 506, Fifth Floor
Sultan Business Center
Near Lamcy Plaza, 21 Oud Metha Road
Post Box: 44098, Dubai
United Arab Emirates
Hukumat Kalwani: skoreplus@gmail.com
Ritu Kalwani: director@score-plus.com
Email: info@score-plus.com
Tel: +971-4-334-0004
Fax: +971-4-334-0222
Website: www.princetonreviewuae.com

Our International Partners

The Princeton Review also runs courses with a variety of partners in Africa, Asia, Europe, and South America.

Georgia
LEAF American-Georgian Education Center
www.leaf.ge

Mongolia
English Academy of Mongolia
www.nyescm.org

Nigeria
The Know Place
www.knowplace.com.ng

Panama
Academia Interamericana de Panama
http://aip.edu.pa/

Switzerland
Institut Le Rosey
http://www.rosey.ch/

All other inquiries, please email us at
internationalsupport@review.com